LAKṢAṆACANDRIKĀ

LAKṢAṆACANDRIKĀ

[A Commentary on the *Taittirīya-Prātiśākhya* by Mahādeva Rāmacandra Gadre]

Critically Edited with Introduction

by

NIRMALA RAVINDRA KULKARNI

BKP

BHARATIYA KALA PRAKASHAN

DELHI (INDIA)

First Published : 2004

ISBN : 81-8090-046-0

Published by : **C.P. Gautam**
BHARATIYA KALA PRAKASHAN
3421-A, IInd Floor, Narang Colony,
Tri Nagar, Delhi-110035.
Phone : 27393983, 30967505 (O)
27522129 (R)

Laser Typeset by : Twinkle Graphics, Delhi-110088.

Printed at : Salasar Imaging Systems, Delhi.

To

Prof. V.N. JHA

Director

Centre of Advanced Study in Sanskrit,
Pune.

Who has initiated me in the field of research.

PREFACE

Somewhere in 1988-89 a pair of mss caught my attention while I was casually going through the manuscript catalogue of the Vaidik Samshodhan Mandal, Pune. It was the Lakṣaṇacandrikā (LC), a commentary on the Taittirīya Prātiśākhya. This particular text was not recorded by the then authentic sources. I observed that it quotes many important yet lost Śikṣā texts. For this reason I planned to edit the text critically. I had worked on the Taittirīya Padapāṭha for my Ph.D. degree. Working on the Taittirīya Prātiśākhya was certainly a beneficial boost for me in understanding the ancient Indian tradition of phonetics and phonology as well as methods of preserving the sacred texts. The results of the same are presented here in a book form.

1. The first part is introductory and gives general information about the development of phonetics and phonology in ancient India. The contributions of the texts like the Śiksās and Prātiśākhyas are spelt out in comparison to the modern phonetics. Besides, the Taittirīya tradition of the Prātiśākhya and commentaries is briefed along with some notable features of the same. Peculiarities of the commentary Lakṣaṇacandrikā and its relation to the other texts are discussed in detail.

2. The second part presents the critically constituted text of the Lakṣaṇacandrikā. This particular edition is based on six mss. The text is appended with two appendices–sūtra-index, bhāṣya passages quoted by the LC–besides bibliography. I did not include notes and translation of the Taittirīya Prātiśākhya in this volume. These will be included in my forthcoming edition of the Vaidikābharaṇa, a commentary on the Taittirīya Pratiśākhya.

Many persons have helped me cordially to bring this particular commentary in a book form. At the very outset, I must pay my sincere thanks to the U.G.C. authorities for selecting me for the award of Research Scientist. Because of it I got an opportunity to work tension free in my favourite field of research, besides enjoining all necessary facilities.

I would like to pay my sincere thanks to my teacher, Prof. V.N. Jha, Director, C.A.S.S., for guiding me from time to time for my Ph.D. dissertation as well as for the present volume. I would be ever grateful to him for his valuable guidance and would like to repay his gururṇa by contributing in my own capacity in the field of research. I am also thankful to him for giving me an opportunity to study and to teach 'Ancient Indian Phonetics and Phonology' in the inter-disciplinary M.A. Course of Sanskrit Linguistics. It helped me in comparing the eastern concepts with those of the modern ones. Because of it I could understand the text of the Taittirīya Prātiśākhya in a better manner. Many of my basic doubts are removed by Dr. Sharma and by Dr. Patyal. I am very much thankful to both of them.

I would like to acknowledge the help extended by late Prof. M.P. Rege, the then President, Prajna Pathasala, Wai, for providing me the xerox copies of the manuscripts. I am also thankful to Dr. T.N. Dharmadhikari, the then Director, Vedic Samshodhan Mandal, Pune and to Shri M.K. Kulkarni, ex-librarian, Deccan College, for allowing me to handle the original mss and for providing the xerox copies of these. It is the cooperation of all the authorities of various libraries in Pune, which has transformed these manuscripts in a book.

I would be ever grateful to my teachers Prof. S.D. Joshi (former Director, C.A.S.S.) and Prof. S.D. Laddu (Curator, Bhandarkar Oriental Research Institute, Pune) and Dr. Goswami, ex-librarian, C.A.S.S. I am also thankful to all my friends and staff of C.A.S.S., who always encourage a lazy person like me.

Lastly, I extend my sincere thanks to my family members, especially my in-laws who encourage me by appreciating and helping me every now and then. I would be ever grateful to my father, Prof. D.A. Ambiye, as he has encouraged me in pursuit of Sanskrit studies in spite of many adverse situations.

At last, I must thank Mr. C.P. Gautam of Bharatiya Kala Prakashan for printing this book neatly and in time.

28th, May 2004
Pune

NIRMALA R. KULKARNI
Research Scientist
Centre of Advanced Study in Sanskrit
University of Pune.

CONTENTS

Introduction

1.0.0. The Oral Tradition : Analysis of language appeared in Indian thinking in the *saṁhitā* period itself, as the Rgvedic poets were busy analyzing the creative process of poetry. (cf. Ṛgveda 10.71) Later on because of the growth in the saṁhitā material and mainly because of changes in the phonemic system of the language, preservation of these saṁhitās became a pressing need. Besides, such literature was a sacred heritage and cultural asset to Aryans. Therefore, it was necessary to take all possible efforts to preserve these texts. It was achieved mainly by oral transmission of the texts from one generation to the other. Learning of the Vedas was made compulsory for a Brahmin that too only with oral instruction. The learning of the Vedas without oral instruction was condemned as *brahmasteya.*[1] The ancient Aryans were aware of the fact that a text may get corrupted even involuntarily. To overcome such natural limitation of human brain, they invented various modes of recitation. This was the immediate step taken towards the protection of the *saṁhitās*.

1.1.0. The Pāṭhas : The mode of recitation is called *pāṭha*. The *saṁhitāpatha* (*Sp*) is the original text recited continuously showing word-boundary features such as euphonic combination, compounding, prolongation etc. Understanding and preservation of that was made easy by another mode of recitation called the *padapāṭha* (*Pp*). A *Pp* removes the word-boundaries and morphemic features and presents the *Sp* without making any change in the word order.[2] Such an analysis enables a reciter not only in remembering each word of the text in its original form and order, but it also guides him in the reconstruction of the *Sp*. The third step towards such an exercise is the *kramapāṭ ha* in which a unit of two serial words is presented. Such a method shows the *saṁhitā* as well as the *pada* form of the word in the same text. These three types of texts never change the word order of the text. Over and above these texts, a chain of *pāṭhas* was invented using similar techniques. These are called *vikṛtipāṭhas*[3] as the word order is changed to some extent. The purpose of all such exercise was to strengthen the intact preservation of the Vedas. This is how the text was preserved intact by using various methods based on the oral transmission of the text.

1.2.0. The Dawn of Indian Phonetics : Formation and implementation of these methods was certainly a challenging task for the Vedic priests. It gave rise to the analysis of language on various levels, especially on phonetic level. Precursors of such analysis are found in the Saṁhitā- Brāhmaṇa period. The word '*akkhalīkṛtya pitaram na putraḥ*' (Ṛgveda 7.1.3) probably is the earliest reference to the oral tradition as well as to the prakṛtised form of the word *assara*. The Vājasaneyī Saṁhitā[4] uses the word *avasānya* for the last syllable of *pada*; which is very much important from the phonological point of view. The Brāhmaṇas use the terms *akṣara* (syllable), *varṇa* (phoneme), and *avasāna* and *varṇa- samāmnyāya* (alphabets) in the technical sense.[5] The Aitareya Brāhmaṇa[6] refers to a special type of pronounciation called *nyūṅkha* in which a syllable has to be uttered in sixteen varieties. Thus, leaving ample room for presumption that the oral tradition and phonetic analysis was in vogue. The Tāṇḍya-Mahā-Brāhmaṇa uses the word '*akṣareṣthāḥ*' *i.e.* consisting of syllables. The Āraṇyakas and the Upaniṣads have further developed these concepts with precise phonetic point of view. Here one cannot ignore the contributions of the Chāndoya Upaniṣad,[8] the Aitareya Āraṇyaka[9] and that of the Taittirīya Upaniṣad.[10] The Chāndogya Upaniṣad tries to map the differences among the vowels, consonants, and spirants.

1.2.1. The Contribution of the Aitareya Āitareya Āraṇyaka : The Aitareya Āraṇyaka (700 b.c.) records a significant number of linguistic discussions by the first generation of linguists such as Hrasva Māṇḍukeya, Sthavira Śākalya, Śūravīra Māṇḍukeya and Kauhaleya etc. These discussions though are garbed in the mystic explanations give an idea of the depth of the linguistic thinking. The text tries to find out the relation between two subsequent words[11] and thereby describes the nature of Saṁhitā as a unit to be uttered in duration of a single breath. This is the background for the Taittirīya Prātiśākhya rule '*atha saṁhitāyam ekaprāṇabhāve*' (TPr 5.1). It further explains the nature of the *saṁhitāpāṭha*, the *padapāṭha* and the *kramapāṭha* by using the oldest terminology *nirbhuja, pratṛṇṇa* and *ubhayam antareṇa* respectively.[12] Thereby, they arrived at the rules to form *Sp* on the basis of the *Pp*. It classifies the sounds into two main categories as vowels (*svara*) and consonants (*vyañjana*). It further groups them as *sparśa* (contact sounds), *ghoṣa* (voiced) *ūṣman* (spirants or hissing sounds). In addition to these for the first time Hrasva Māṇḍukeya recognizes the class of the *antaḥsthas i.e.,* of the semivowels.[13]

The main contribution of the text seems to be in identifying the similarity of human phonetic apparatus with that of the musical instrument. It calls the human phonetic apparatus as *daivī vīṇā* (divine lute) and says that the *manuṣī vīṇā i.e.,* lute invented by human beings is modelled on the divine one and further shows the similarity probably by taking into consideration three factors energy, oscillation and resonance as in any musical instrument the sound is produced because of these three factors. To quote the text verbatim,

अथ खल्वियं दैवी वीणा भवति, तदनुकृतिरसौ मानुषी वीणा। यथा अस्याः शिरः एवममुष्याः शिरः, यथा अस्याः उदरम् एवम् अमुष्याः अम्भणम्, यथा अस्यै जिह्वा एवम् अमुष्याः वादनम्, यथा अस्याः तन्त्रयः एवम् अमुष्याः अङ्गुलयः, यथा अस्याः स्वराः एवममुष्याः स्वराः यथा अस्याः स्पर्शाः एवममुष्याः स्पर्शाः। यथा ह्येवेयं शब्दवती तर्द्मवती एवमसौ शब्दवती तर्द्मवती, यथा त्वेवेयं लोमशेन चर्मणाऽपिहिता भवत्येवम् असौ लोमशेन चर्मणाऽपिहिता स यो हैतां दैवीं वीणां वेद श्रुतवदनो भवति, भूमिप्रास्य कीतिर्भवति। (3.5)

Thus, the Aitareya Āraṇyaka probably has paved path for the science of phonetics and phonology, which was further developed by the Taittirīya Upaniṣad by reserving a special chapter for phonetics, entitled as Śiksāvallī. It defines the scope of the term as *varṇaḥ, svaraḥ, mātra, balaṁ, sāma* and *santānaḥ.*[14] It means that a *śikṣā* gives instruction regarding phonemes, accents, and duration of pronunciation, manners of articulation, melody and continuous recitation.

1.3.0. The Lakṣaṇa Texts : Thus, sufficient efforts were made to describe how the sound is produced and how does it behave in the Sanskrit, particularly in the Vedic language. There was an ample room for discussion on phonetic and phonological issues as the Vedic texts were handed down by oral instructions. Such comments, which basically arose while teaching a student, generated various types of texts. These are called *lakṣaṇa* texts. In general we may say that observations on a particular aspect of a *saṁhitā* is called *lakṣaṇa* or as Whitney says *lakṣana* means a comment.[15] Thus, the passing remarks made on a particular phonetic or grammatical feature of the *saṁhitā* text is called *lakṣaṇa*. These comments were further developed into independent manuals dealing with some aspect of the Vedic text. Such texts discuss the features of the Vedic texts either theoretically or simply by enumeration. The Śikṣas and the Prātiśākhyas (*Pr*)-the manuals of phonetics and phonology respectively-analyze the Vedic texts theoretically and were known as the *lakṣaṇas* in the traditional circles. For the same reason our commentator names his text as *lakṣaṇacandrikā.* On the other hand, there are innumerable texts like *mātrālakṣaṇa*, *plutalakṣaṇa, anusvāra-lakṣaṇa* that incorporate the word *lakṣaṇa* in their title and enumerate a particular feature of a Vedic text. Thus, in general the *lakṣaṇa* is a wider group in which texts like Sikṣās, prs, the Baiths (codified lists of the Vedic words) and *varṇā nukramaṇis* are included.[16] Needless to say, this group is oriented towards the text-critical study of the Vedas. The succeeding paragraphs give capsule information to the two types of the *lakṣaṇa* texts (1) the śikṣas and (2) the prāti- śākhyas, since these are of our prime concern.

1.4.0. The Śikṣās : A śikṣā means a text which aims at teaching correct pronunciation of the Vedic language. Therefore, it is defined as '*sikṣayati varṇān iti*'. The *śikṣāvallī* of the Taittirīya Upaniṣad clearly describes the corpus of the *Śikṣā* text in general as *varṇah, svaraḥ, mātrā, balam, sāma, santānaḥ i.e.,* A *śikṣā* aims at describing a phoneme, articulatory process, melody and rules of euphonic combination. Acarya Śaṅkara[17] defines the term as *śiksyate' nayeti varṇādyuccāraṇalakṣaṇam*| Sāyana[18] in similar manner describes the term as वर्णाद्युच्चारणप्रकारो यत्र उपदिश्यते सा शिक्षा तस्मात् स्वरवर्णाद्यपराधपरिहाराय शिक्षाग्रन्थोऽपेक्षितः।

According to M. Ghosh[19] this particular *vedāṅga* is evolved in two phases.

1. The first phase was just teaching of proper utterance of the Vedic sounds to a *brahmacarin* by his *ācārya.*
2. In the second phase these teachings were reduced to a system. Those systematized treatises are called the *śikṣā* texts.

Modern research proves that the *śikṣā* manuals, which are with us today, are not the original *śikṣā* texts. These were composed for practical purposes and were circulated in a group of a particular branch of a Veda. Therefore, we find similarity in terminology of the *śikṣās* belonging to a particular Veda.[20] Over and above, these also describe many features of the then living languages.[21]

1.5.0. The Prātiśākhyas : These are the sister systems of the *śikṣās*. The main goal of the *śikṣās* is to describe the articulatory process of the uttered sounds. Even the *prs* aim at describing sounds, however, used in a particular Vedic branch. The literal meaning of the term *prātiśākhya* ('*prati śākham bhavam*') shows its relation to individual branch of the Veda. Uvaṭa, the well-known commentator of the *prs*, points out the difference between the two types of the texts. He says–

शिक्षाच्छन्दोव्याकरणैः सामान्येनोक्तलक्षणम्।
तदेव इह शाखायाम् इति शास्त्रप्रयोजनम्॥[22]

i.e., the general description presented by the śikṣās etc. is specified by the prs. Therefore, in dilemma the *prs* are said to be authoritative. To quote a famous verse from the Vyāsa Śikṣā :

शिक्षा च प्रातिशाख्यं च विरुद्ध्येते परस्परम्।
शिक्षेव दुर्बलीत्याहु: सिंहस्येव मृगी यथा।।[23]

Chronologically, the Prs precede the existing śikṣās. The śikṣās are considered of later origin on two grounds-1. Many śikṣās are in verse form. 2. Many texts include *kṣa*, *jña* in the *akṣarasamāmnāya.*[24]

1.5.1. The content of the Prātiśākhyas : A *pr* in general is designed to take care of the following topics :

1. Phonology of a particular branch of the Veda.
2. Euphonic combination of the *saṁhitās.*
3. Pragṛhyas, the vowels, which do not undergo euphonic combination.
4. The units preceding *avagrahas* in the *Pp*, which undergo morphophonetmic changes such as lengthening, retroflexion etc.
5. The accents.
6. The other ancillary texts like *krama* etc.

Even a cursory look at these topics may suggest that these texts are not designed simply to describe the difference between the *Sp* and the *Pp*. However, they follow a system. The system has a core principle 'preservation through reconstruction'. It works on the following three levels :

1. Oral transmission of the original text *i.e.,* of the *Sp* preserves the text word by word. Here, mnemonics helps the reciter to restore the original text.
2. On the second level, the formal analytical texts like *Pps, Kps,* and eight types of *vikṛtis* use three types of devices *daṇda*, *avagraha* and *itikaraṇa.* With the help of these three devices these texts analyze the *Sp* in such a way that ultimately the analysis would lead to a definite and

unhampered reconstructed text. Here, each type of *pāṭha* strengthens the earlier one and ultimately it strengthens the *Sp*. The recurrent expression of the *prs* क्रमः संहितापददार्ढ्यार्थ *i.e.* 'a *kramapatha* is for strengthening the *Pp* and the *Sp*' supports the above thought.

3. The *Lakṣaṇa* texts intentionally frame rules to achieve the *Sp* on the basis of the *Pp* and guide a *reciter* to imagine the scenario of the *Sp*. It is not mere a description of the Vedic texts. Unless they are motivated by the principle 'preservation through reconstruction' they would have not adopted the direction from the *Pp* to *Sp* for analysis. Let us examine just two rules of the TPr to explain our stand. The opening *sūtra* of the fifth *anuvāka* reads–अथ संहितायामेकप्राणभावे।

   The *sūtras* hereafter describe the *sandhi* scenario of the *Sp*. The immediate *sūtra* reads : यथायुक्ताद्विधिः सा प्रकृतिः

   लक्षणचन्द्रिका–यथायुक्तात् यथास्थितात् पदपाठत् कूटस्थाद विचालितो यो विधिः सा प्रकृतिसंहिता विज्ञेया।

   (That is to be known as the fundamental text that is non-deviated disposal from the eternal (*kūṭastha*) *Pp* that does not change the word order. (यथास्थित)

The rule directly says that the succeeding rules describe the *Sp* on the basis of the *Pp*.

All the succeeding rules show us how to get the *Sp* from the *Pp*. *e.g.*, तत्र पूर्वं पूर्वं प्रथमम्। (While constructing the *Sp*) the first word should be combined with the immediately succeeding one. *e.g.* the word *bhakṣā* should be combined with *a* to result into *bhaksa* and would further be combined with *ihi* resulting in *bhaksehi*. This sequence should never be combined as *bhaksa* + *ehi* (*a* + *ihi*) as it may lead to *bhasaihi;* because such a reading would distort the *Sp*. From such examples we can say that the rules of the *Prs* aim at reconstructing the *Sp* from the *Pp*. Thus, the main purpose of the *Pp* and other such texts is 'preservation through reconstruction.' Of course there are some *Prs*, which direct the reciter from the *Sp* to the *Pp e.g.*, the AvPr. We may explain such apparent discrepancy by taking resort to chronological analysis of these *prs*. *Prs* showing the older stage never frame rules to arrive at the *Pp;* whereas the *Prs* of the later origin direct the reciter towards the *Pp*. The AvPr belongs to the second group. The *TPr* shows both the stages. It is not a text composed by a single person at a single segment of time. The kernel of the text is older showing rules from the *Pp* to the *Sp*. The chronological table of the *Prs* provided by S. Varma supports our stand.[25]

Thus, we may say that a *pr* in general provides aid to reconstruct the *Sp* on the basis of the *Pp*.

1.5.2. The Prātiśākhya Literature

Sr.no	*Saṁhitā*	*Author*	*Title*
1.	Ṛgveda	Śaunaka	Ṛgveda Prātiśākha
2.	Atharvaveda	—	Śaunakīyā Caturādhyāyikā
3.	Sāmaveda	—	1. Sāmatantra 2. Ṛktantra 3. Puṣpasūtra
4.	Taittirīya	—	Taittirīya Prātiśākhya
5.	Vājasaneyī	—	Vājasaneyī or the Kātyayana Prātiśākhya
6.	Maitrāyanī	—	Maitrāyaṇī Prātiśākhya[26]

1.5.3. The Contributions : Modern phonetics describes the production of linguistic sounds in the following lines :

(*a*) The air stream mechanism

(*b*) Organs of speech

(*c*) Points of articulation

(*d*) Position of glottis and the sounds produced

(*e*) Positions of velum and the sounds produced

(*f*) Manners of articulation

(*g*) Definition and description of vowels

Following the same line of description I would like to put forth the description found in ancient Indian treatises. This may enable us to talk about some of the knotty points creeping in the interpretation of the ancient texts.

(*a*) **The Air Stream Mechanism :** The sounds are generally produced because of two types of air steam mechanism, (*a*) because of eggressive air stream mechanism *i.e.,* while breathing out (*b*) and because of the ingressive air stream mechanism while breathing in. Such sounds are called implosives. Ancient Indian texts are aware only of the aggressive air stream mechanism as they describe the process of sound production as क्रमादूर्ध्वपथे चरन्[27] (while going upward it produces sound)

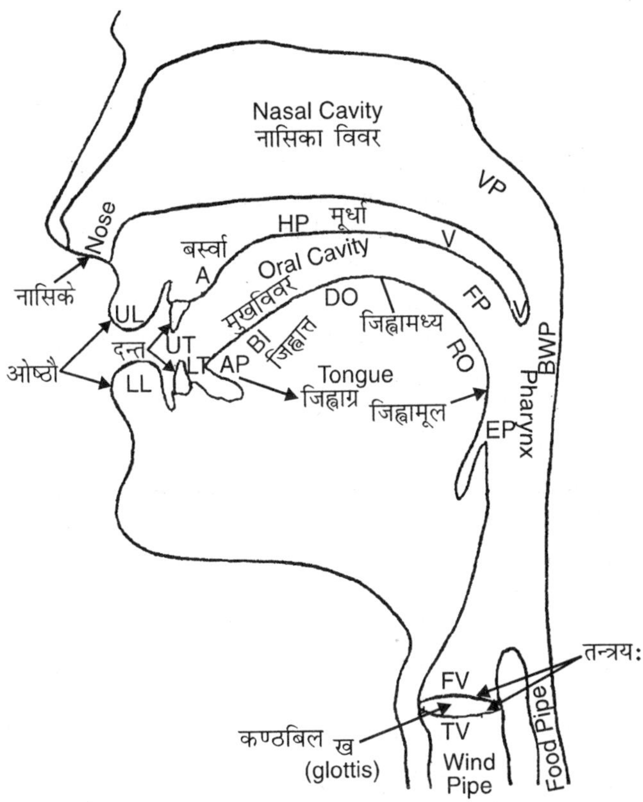

In Indian languages generally sounds produced by eggressive air stream mechanism are used. Exceptions are the two implosives of the Sindhi language. In the Vedic language the sounds produced by ingressive air stream mechanism are used. The corpus of Prs was the Vedic language. Hence, we do not find description of implosives.

(*b*) **Organs of Speech :** The diagram gives the names of the organs of speech as found in the *śiksa-pratisakhya* literature. Allen[28] doubted the knowledge of vocal chords. But this doubt can be sorted out with the help of the above quoted passage from the Aitareya Āraṇyaka, which uses the word '*tantrayaḥ*'. The glottis is referred to as *kha* or *kaṇṭhabila.* The *uras* (buccal cavity), *kaṇṭhaḥ* (throat) together forming the pharyngeal cavity, *mukha* (oral cavity) and *nāsike* (nasal cavity) and *śiras* (head) are called as resonators *prātiśrutkāni.*[29]

(*c*) **Points of Articulation :** This is the most important concept described by Indian phoneticians, esp. the Tpr. They speak in terms of place of articulation *i.e., sthāna* and the articulator (the *karaṇa*) further to suggest the idea of passive and active articulator respectively. They also differentiate between these in the context of vowels and consonants. *Sthāna* is defined as यत्र स्पर्शयति तत्स्थानम् in case of consonants or करण as यत्स्पर्शयति तत्करणम्। However, as यत्र उपसंहारः तत् स्थानम्, यदुपसंहरति तत्करणम्। In case of vowels as the vowels are not contact sounds. The term 'point of articulation' given by Pike is accepted recently in modern phonetics.

(*d*) **Positions of Glottis and the Sounds Produced :** Glottis is referred to as '*kha*' or '*kaṇṭhabila*'. It is the space between two vocal cords. Because of position of glottis certain additional qualities appear in sounds. These are termed as *anupradāna* in the *śikṣāprātiśākhya* literature. The TPr calls them as the *mūlaprakṛtayaḥ* (basic nature of a sound). Ancient phoneticians observe the following three states of glottis because of which the basic nature of the sound differs from the other :

1. Open glottis : Open glottis produces breath, it is the basic nature of *aghoṣa* sounds.

विवृते (कण्ठे) श्वासः (क्रियते)। तैप्रा. 2.5

Open

2. Closed glottis with vibration in vocal cords produces resonance; it is the basic feature of voiced (*ghosavat*) sounds.

   संवृते कण्ठे नादः क्रियते। (तैप्रा. 2.4)

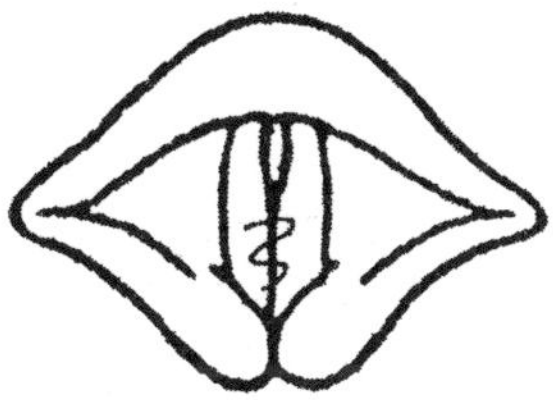

Voice

3. Glottis producing breathly Voice : When (1) the vocal folds are kept in a different position than in plain voice (2) there is vibration in the upper part of the vocal cords and (3) the air emits from the lower part. In such a condition more quantity of air comes out. The sounds produced in such a condition are called breathly voice in modern phonetics. Probably, the Tpr refers to the same state by saying *madhye hakāraḥ* (2.6) *i.e.,* it is a combination of *śvāsa* and *nāda*. Even the modern tradition of phonetics recognizes sounds such as *gha, jha* etc. as breathy voiced or voiced aspirated. These states of glottis by are included in the *bāhyaprayatna* later grammatical literature (External efforts are produced outside the oral cavity). मध्ये हकारः TPr. 2.6.

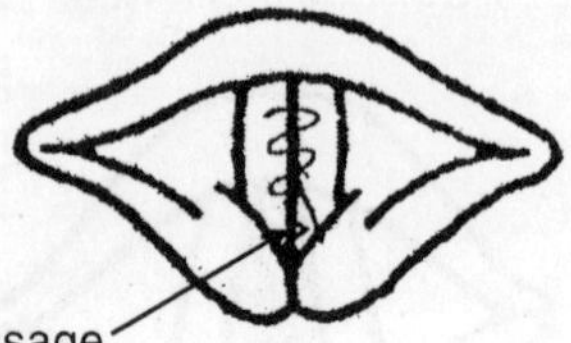

4. The fourth state of glottis is also referred to in the ancient texts, but in a different context. Modern phonetics refers to whisper state of glottis in which vocal cords are brought close, but are not vibrating, it cuts down the force of air stream and whisper sounds are produced. Right from the *Brāhmana* texts onwards we get the description of *upāṁśu* type of recitation. The TPr defines it as करणवत् अशब्दम् अमनःप्रयोगम् उपांशुतैप्रा. *i.e.,* Upāṁśu type of recitation is without audible sound, without application of mind, but with articulatory actions.

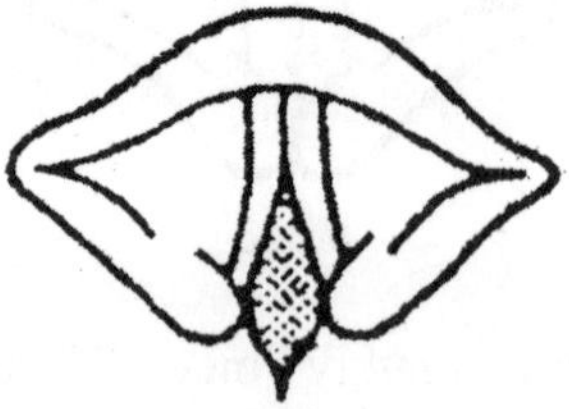

Whisper

5. Besides, it has also observed the murmur state of glottis, which is referred to as *dhvāna* in the text. I think this is the major theoretical contribution of the TPr.

(*e*) **Position of velum and sounds produced :** Because of velum three types of sounds are produced.

(*a*) Oral or *niranunāsika* or *ananunāsika* sounds are produced when velum closes the nasal cavity and air escapes through oral cavity.

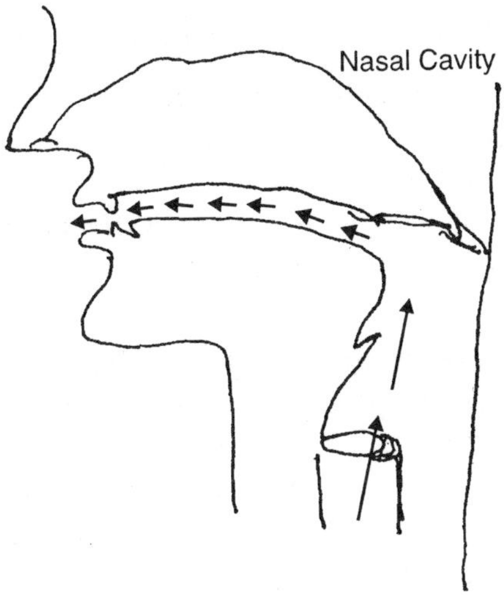

(*b*) Nasal or *anunāsika* sounds are produced when the volume closes the oral cavity and air escapes through nose.

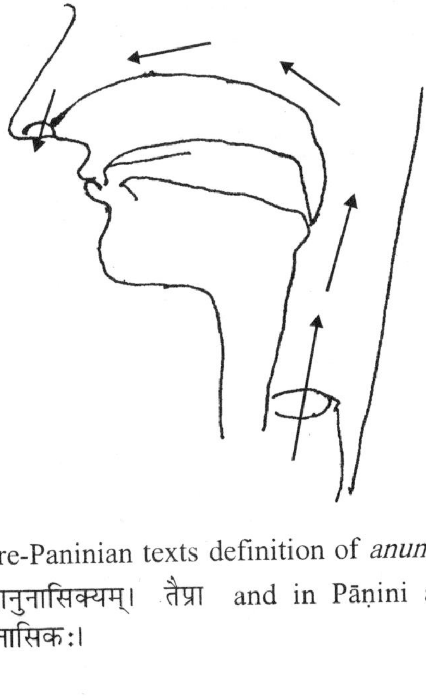

In the pre-Paninian texts definition of *anunāsika* is नासिका विवरणादानुनासिक्यम्। तैप्रा and in Pāṇini as मुखनासिकावचनोऽनुनासिकः।

Probably because the internal efforts take place in the oral cavity and the air is escaped only through the nasal cavity.

(*c*) The nasalized sounds are produced when both the cavities are open and air can escape through both the cavities. These are called *anusvāra, nāsikya, rakta* or *raṅga.* However, the description of these terms varies in certain texts. A thorough investigation in the background of the modern one is necessary.

(*f*) **Manners of articulation** are defined in modern phonetics in terms of type closure of the air or degrees of stricute of air or the relation of air and the articulators. Therefore we get terms like stops, plosives, affricates etc. In Indian phonetics *ābhyantara prayatnas* or internal efforts are defined in terms of contact between the *sthāna* and *karaṇa.* Therefore, the terminology is not parallel. Four degrees of contact are mentioned as स्पृष्ट, ईषत्स्पृष्ट, ईषद्विवृत and विवृत

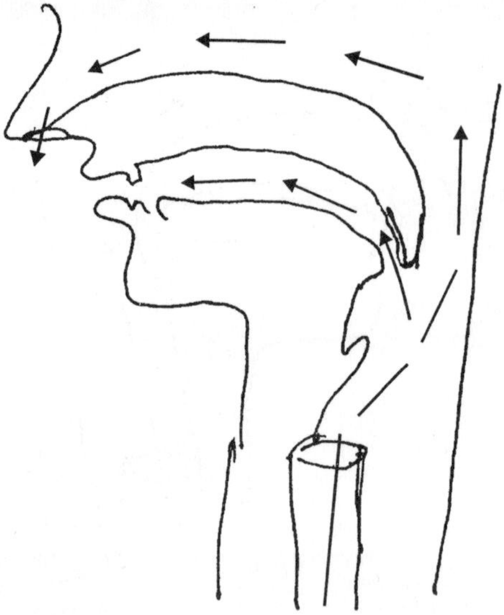

(*g*) **Definitions of vowels and consonants :** Vowels and consonants are defined in ancient tradition as follows :

1. यथा स्वरेण सर्वाणि व्यञ्जनानि व्याप्तानि एवं सर्वान् कामान् आप्नोति य एवं वेद। गोपथ ब्राह्मण।
2. स्वयं राजन्ते इति स्वराः अन्वक् भवति व्यञ्जनम्। महाभाष्य 1/2/23
3. यस्स्वयं राजते तं तु स्वरमाह पतञ्जलिः।
उपरिस्थायिना तेन व्यङ्ग्यम् व्यञ्जनमुच्यते।। तैप्रा (वैभ) 1.6
4. व्यञ्जनानि पुनः नटभार्यावित्। तद् यथा नटानां स्त्रियः रङ्गं गताः यो यः पृच्छाति कस्य यूयं कस्य यूयं इति तं तं तव इत्येवाहुः। एवं व्यञ्जनान्यपि यस्य अचः कार्यमुच्यते तं तं भजन्ते। पत. 6.7.2.

Traditional definitions of vowels and consonants differ from the modern ones for the following reasons :

1. Ancient phoneticians had in their front only the Sanskrit or the MIA languages. These languages belong to the IE family of languages. In these languages consonants cannot be produced independently. This characteristic was observed by ancient Indians as well as by the first generation of modern linguists.
2. But when the linguists discovered a new African language called Imbo; they observed that there are certain words without vowels. This fact disproves that consonants depend on vowels.
3. Therefore, a new definition based on the obstruction or modification of air stream was formulated. According to it 'a vowel is one that simply modifies the air stream and a consonant is produced because of the obstruction of air'.

In the description of vowels, however, the following factors are noted : lip rounding, part of the tongue, front, and central or back and openness of the oral cavity.

1.6.0. The Taittirīya Prātiśākhya : This particular text holds a prominent position in ancient Indian phonetic treatises as it presents a systematic disposal of various phonetic concepts. Allen W.S. (1953) and Varma S. (1961) had taken a fresh look in the chronology and contents of it and have praised it for its minute and advanced observations. The following could be considered as the pioneering contributions of the texts :

(*a*) Allen (1953) praises the graphic description of phonemes it arrives at. He frequently says that these descriptions go hand in hand with those given by modern phoneticians with the help of developed instruments. I may cite here some observations praised by him.

1. The TPr remarks–स्पर्शथानेषूष्माण: आनुपूर्व्येण। 2.44 करणमध्यं तु विवृतम्। (The fricatives are articulated in the same places as the corresponding stops; but the centre of the articulatory organs is open.) In this context Allen cites palatograms of modern Indian speakers, which are identical with the description of the TPr.

2. The description of *'y'* provided by the TPr is more accurate than that of the other *Prs.* It says–तालौ जिह्वामध्यान्ताभ्यां यकारे। 2.40

   In the pronunciation of '*y*', the edges and middle of the tongue touch the palate. Allen comments–"The accuracy of this particular statement would in fact be supported by palatographic evidence." We may also add the vowel '*e*' to the accurately described phonemes.

(*b*) The TPr categorically observes the difference in place of articulation and articulator in case of vowels and consonants. To quote–स्वराणां यत्रोपसंहार: तत्स्थानम्, य दुपसंहरति तत् करणम्। 2/31, 2.32

For consonants, where the articulator touches is the point of articulation of the place that touches is the articulator the organ.

Whereas in case of vowels the place of approximation is the place of articulation and that which articulates is the articulator.

(*c*) The description of articulation of the nasal and nasalized sounds is yet an unsolved problem of ancient Indian phonetics. Yet, one may say that the text provides a systematic account of prevailing views. It tries to distinguish between the *anunāsika,* anusv*āra and raṅga.*

(*d*) It also shows systematization in the description of concepts like *samānākṣara* and *pṛkta.* It uses three terms to describe the quantitative and qualitative status of a vowel. For the TPr, *samanākṣara* means a monophthog, *sandhyakṣara* means a diphthong and *pṛkta* is a vowel mixed with consonantal element. Such a treatment is strikingly in the contrast to the other *Prs.*

(*e*) It gives peculiar treatment to the *upasargas.* It does not count all prefixes enlisted in the other *prs* and those given by Panini. The Lakṣaṇacandrikā answers the problem "Why does the TPr count only ten prefixes?" It says the text counts only those *upasargas,* which are followed by *iti* in the *kramapāṭha.*

1.6.1. The Commentaries on the *Taittirīya Prātiśākhya* : The TPr is survived with eleven commentaries. Four among these have seen light of the day. Two of these are almost lost and the remaining ones are deposited in mss form in various libraries. All these are described in the following paragraph in a nutshell.

1. The Ātreyabhāṣya-a lost text
2. The Vārarucabhāṣya-a lost text
3. The Māhiṣeyabhāṣya or Padakramasadana by Māhiṣeya[30]
4. The Tribhāṣyaratna by Somayarya[31]
5. The Vaidikābharaṇa of Gārgya Gopala Yajvan[32]
6. The Śabdabrahmavilāsa of Vīra Rāghava Kavi (deposited GOML, Madras)[33]
7. The Varṇakramadarpaṇa by Bhairava (deposited in the GOML, Madras)[34]
8. The Taittirīya Prātiśākhya Vivaraṇa Vivaraṇa by Padmanā-bha (deposited Adyar Library, Madras)

9. The Vaidikabhūṣana or Bhūṣanaratna, anonymous (deposited in the Adyar Library, Madras)
10. The Mukura by P. Ganapatiśāstri[36]
11. The Lakṣaṇacandrikā by Mahādeva Rāmacandra Gadre.

Before the publication of Aithal 1991,[37] I could trace the name of the Lakṣaṇacandrikā while I was casually going through the catalogues of the Vaidik Samshodhan Mandal, Pune. Since it was not recorded in the then authentic sources, I felt it necessary to bring it to the notice of scholars by handing over a critical edition of it. As a stepping-stone towards such a work, I published a note describing the text.[38] Of course Aithal 1991 was extremely helpful to me in updating my bibliographical sources.

1.7.0. The Lakṣaṇacandrikā : General Observations

1. It is a peculiar feature of the LC that it does not accept the usual arrangement of the text accepted by other commentators. The other texts (except Padakramasadana) follows *adhyāya-sūtra* division. These commentaries divide the twenty-four *adhyāyas* directly into *sūtras.* The LC however, divides these *adhyayas* into two groups calling each of them as *adhyāya.* Each *adhyāya* consists of twelve *anuvākas.* Each *anuvāka* is further divided into *sūtras.* Thus, it follows *adhyāya-anuvāka-sūtra* division.

2. We may call the LC as an abbridged edition of the commentary Tribhāṣyaratna. It hardly makes any changes in the arguments of the TR. Rarely the examples are changed.

3. Normally, while discussing any technical term the application of that particular term is explained by quoting the rules wherein that term is actually used. The LC rarely quotes the rules from the *pr* to explain the application.

4. The LC extensively uses the technical terms introduced by Pāṇini in the line of the other commentaries.

5. As per the routine practice, the commentator quotes some sentences or verses from other texts either to support the

rules of the *pr* to shows some divergent opinions. It is peculiar to the LC that it quotes many verses from various *śikṣās*. *Śikṣā* studies at present pose various problems, especially that of textual criticism. Many *śikṣās* are not available even in the mss form. Texts like the LC provide us much material for the restoration of at least fragments of some *śikṣās*. It helps us in the reconstruction particularly of the Ātreya Śikṣā and that of the Māheśvara Śikṣā.

1.8.0 Critical Apparatus

There are six mss of the LC noticed sofar.

1. Ms A is deposited in the Vaidika Samshodhan Mandal. Pune (no 3813[39]] It is complete, ascribed on bluish paper (21.5x 8.5 cms) in a very good Devanāgarī characters, with less corruption. It contains 87 folios. Besides, few exceptions, it bears similarity with Ms D (described below).

The Beginning :

श्रीगणेशाय नमः। श्रीसरस्वत्यैनमः। श्रीगुरुभ्यो नमः।
विनायकं गुरुं भानुं ब्रह्माविष्णुमहेश्वरान्।
व्याख्यार्थे प्रातिशाख्यस्य भारतीं च नमाम्यहम्।

The Colophon :

मुक्ताभरणसंयुक्ता पूर्णचन्द्रनिभानना।
दिव्यमाल्यांबरधरा नीलेन्दीवरलोचना॥
आलोकोद्भासिवदना ताम्बूलग्रासिशोभिता।
शिवालिङ्गनसञ्जातपुलकोद्भासिविग्रहा॥
सच्चिदानन्दरूपाढया जगन्माता शिवाम्बिका।
अङ्कस्थयानयायुक्तात् प्रसादाच्च महेश्वरात्॥
गद्रे इत्युपनाम्ना च वेदविद्रामसूनुना।
महादेवेन विदुषा रचिता धीमतां मुदे॥
व्याख्येयं प्रातिशाख्यस्थ भाष्यशिक्षानुसारिणी।
अत्र न्यूनाधिकं किञ्चिज्जातं मन्दधिया क्वचित्।

तत्सर्वं शोधनीयं तु सर्वलक्षणदर्शिभिः।

इति श्रीगद्रे इत्युपनामकुरामचन्द्रात्मजमहादेवविरचितायां लक्षणचन्द्रि-कायां द्वितीयोऽध्यायः।

2. Ms B also is deposited in the VSM. (no. 3932]. It is incomplete and contains twenty eight folios. [21.5 X 8.5 cms.] It is scribed on paper in neat Devanāgarī characters. It presents quite authentic readings.

The Beginning :

श्रीगणेशाय नमः। श्रीऽमामहेश्वराभ्यां नमः।
अथ प्रातिशाख्यव्याख्याप्रारम्भः।

परब्रह्मशिवं शक्तिं ततश्चोमासदाशिवौ।
ईश्वरं पार्वतीं रुद्रं रुद्राणीं च जनार्दनम।
विरिञ्चिं च महासेनं हेरम्बं सूर्यभार्गवौ।
बृहस्पतिं च तत्पत्नीं तथान्यान् सकलान् गुरून्॥
नत्वा च प्रातिशाख्यस्य व्याख्या लक्षणचन्द्रिका।
महादेवाभिधेयेन यथामत्या विरच्यते॥

3. Ms C is deposited in the *Prājña pāṭhaśālā*, Wai [Maharashtra] No. 566. This ms is complete, scribed on paper admeasuring [21.5 × 8.5 cms] in very beautiful Devanāgarī characters. It shows almost no corrections and contains 78 folios.

   It is very important ms since it bears mark of autograph. The post colophonic remarks clearly state that the owner of it is the author himself. The scribe Mahadev Janardan Datye is his student. At two-three places we find additions made in different handwriting. We may guess that these are made by the author in his own handwriting. However, it would be a mere guess and not a confirmed truth. Ms E, B and F show relationship with this ms.

The Beginning :

श्रीगणेशाय नमः। श्रीउमामहेश्वराभ्यां नमः।
अथ प्रातिशाख्यव्याख्याप्रारम्भः।

परब्रह्म शिवं शक्तिं ततश्चोमासदाशिवौ।
ईश्वरं पार्वतीं रुद्रं रुद्राणीं च जनार्दनम्।
विरिञ्चिं च महासेनं हेरम्बं सूर्यभार्गवौ।
बृहस्पतिं व तत्पत्नींतथान्यान् सकलान् गुरून्।
नत्वा च प्रातिशाख्यस्य व्याख्या लक्षणचन्द्रिका
महादेवाभिधेयेन यथामत्या विरच्यते।

Colophon and Post-colophonic Remarks

मुक्ताभरण.................सर्वलक्षणस्पर्शिभिः।

इति गद्रेऽत्युपनामक-वेदार्थज्ञ-रामचन्द्रात्मज-महादेविरचितायांव लक्षणचन्द्रिकायां प्रातिशाख्यव्याख्यायां द्वितीयोऽध्यायः। श्रीउमा-महेश्वरार्पणमस्तु। शके 1799 ईश्वरनाम संवत्सरे चैत्रशुक्ल गुरुवासरे इदं पुस्तकं दात्ये इत्युपनामक जनार्दन भट्टात्मजमहादेवेन लिखितम्। गद्रे इत्युपनामक वेदार्थज्ञ-महादेव-भट्टस्येदं पुस्तकम्।

4. **Ms D** hails from Prājña Pātashala, Wai. no. 567.

It is complete and comprises eighty folios. It is scribed in good Devanāgarī characters. It shows similarity with MSA. At the end it quotes a number of verses describing *Lakṣaṇa* texts. Though it is much closer to MS A, occasionally it shows similarity with MS E, as if these two have a parent ms in common.

The Beginning :

श्रीगणेशाय नमः। श्री गुरुभ्यो नमः।

विनायकं गुरुं भानुं ब्रह्मविष्णुमहेश्वरान्।
व्याख्यार्थे प्रातिशाख्यस्य भारतीं च नमाम्यहम्।

Colophon :

इति प्रातिशाख्यव्याख्या समाप्ता।

5. **MS E** numbered 568 also hails from Prājña Pāthashala, Wai. It is incomplete, scribed in readable hand writing and contains 53 folios. It involves many corrections. It often

reads the readings similar to those of Ms A, but rubs out and corrects in the light of the readings of MS C. Thus, gets a lable of conflated ms. However, selected portions show similarity with MS D, which even MS C does not incorporate. Thus, leaves us to think of some common parent ms.

The Beginning :

विनायकं गुरुं भानुं.........नमाम्यहम्।

6. Ms F is also an incomplete ms deposited in the Deccan College, Pune, no. 983. It completes the first *Adhyaya* containing twelve *Anuvākas*, writes just three *sūtras* of the immediately succeeding *anuvāka* and ends. Though it shows much similarity with the Ms C, it incorporates many scribal errors.

The Beginning :

श्रीगणेशाय नमः। यथ प्रातिशाख्यव्याख्याप्रारम्भः।
परब्रह्म शिवं शक्तिं ततश्चोमासदाशिवौ।
...महादेवाभिधेयेन यथामत्या विरच्यते।।

The genealogical tree of these five mss could be drawn as below :

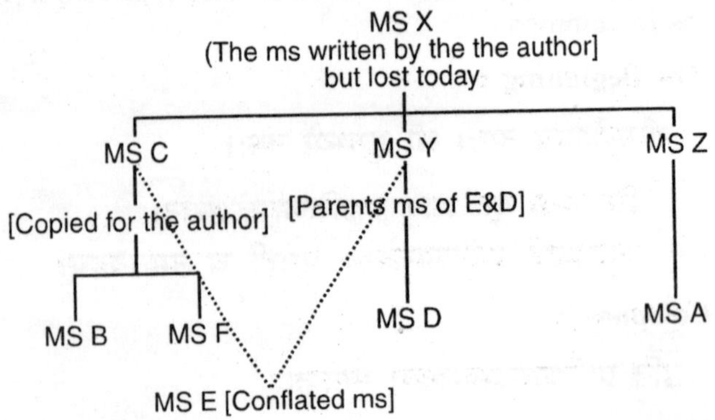

1.9.0. The Author

The problem of identification of the author does not arise

in case of this ms belonging to 19th cent., since the colophons of MSA and MSC give details of him. Not only these colophons, but even the opening verses of MS B and concluding verses of MS C echo the same information. To quote :

Ms B.

नत्वा च प्रातिशाख्यस्य व्याख्या लक्षणचन्द्रिका
महादेवाभिधेयेन यथामत्या विरच्यते।

MS C

गद्रे इत्युपनाम्ना च वेदविद्रामसूनुमा।
महादेवेन विदुषा रचिता धीमतां मुदे॥
व्याख्येयं प्रातिशाख्यस्य भाष्यशिक्षानुसारिणी।

Though we guess the complete name and identify him as a Vedic scholar from the text itself, for getting other information we have to take into consideration the following two books.

1. *Gadrekulavṛttānta* : This book tracing genealogy of Gadre families does mention Mahadev Ramachandra Gadre, but does not recognise him as the author of the LC. It gives more details about his father Ramachandra alies Rambhat Gadre. The book says that Rambhat Gadre was honoured by Smt. Anandbai Raste [widow of a Sardar of Peshavas] of Pune for his Vedic studies and she donated a piece of land at Wai, in 1808 A.D. Further the genealogical tables of Gadres given in the book speak of Mahadev Gadre as a son of the same Rambhat Gadre of Wai. The above quoted verses of the LC also recognise him as son of the Vedic scholar Rama (cf. वेदविद्रामसुनुना) The colophon of MS C clearly states that the author is the son of Ramachandra, welversed in the Veda. [वेदार्थज्ञरामचन्द्रामज].

Thus, the details given in *Gadre Kula Vṛttānta* are helpful in (*i*) getting information about the native place of the author. (*ii*) and in getting a relative date of the book *i.e.,* after 1808 A.D.

2. In getting some information about students of the author a manual on the Vedic scholars in Maharashtra helps us. This book speaks of the commentator though not through a special

note, but through some passing remarks. It says that Mahadev Ramchandra Gadre was a Vedic scholar, and was expert in reciting all the *vikṛtis* of the TS. He had composed a commentary on the TPr entitled *Lakṣaṇacandrikā* and was settled at Wai. He has taught the following students–

(*i*) Shri. Vishnu Ganesh Bhide [Birth 1843 A.D.]

(*ii*) Shri. Balambhatji Ramchandra Ranade [Birth 1893 A.D.]

(*iii*) Shri Mahadev Janardan Datye [Birth 1831 A.D.] He is the same disciple who has copied Ms C of the author. [cf. the colophon of MsC:] The MS C is dated *sake* 1799 *i.e.* 1877 A.D. this date also goes hand in hand with the relative date arrived at with the help of the above two books.

1.10.0. The LC and the Śikṣā literature

As it is observed with most of the commentaries that the commentators quote some passages from similar texts either to support the opinion expressed in the text or to show some divergent views. The LC does not claim to be an exception to this. It quotes extensively from various *śikṣās*. These quotations are not helpful only in explaining the context, but also in getting the extent and subject matter, of the *Śikṣā* literature. Present *Śikṣā* studies show that this particular branch of the *Vedāṅga* poses different types of problems, especially that of textual criticism. Many *śikṣās* are not available even in the ms form. Texts like the LC play role of anthologies and provide us some material for the restoration of at least fragments of some *śikṣās*. It helps us particularly in the reconstruction of the *Ātreya śikṣ ā* (Ās) and the *Māheśvara śikṣā* (MS). The following paragraphs take cognisance of quotations from these *śikṣās*.

I.11.1. The LC and the Āś

The Āś is an unpublished text deposited in ms form in the following libraries. Before publication of Aithal 1991, the Hamburg ms was not noticed by me.[40] It is the only complete ms. The rest bear the common name Āś, however, the subject matter of these differs from one another.[41] Thus, there is a room to relate these ms to a single source and could be said as the parts of one single ms. [may be of the Hamburg ms.] The LC refers to the Āś and quotes around twenty verses from it. Certainly it is an additional aid when the complete ms is either lost or not at hand. Here, I have made an attempt to attest these rules with the available mss. The rules could be fairly classified as follows in accordance with the subject-matter.

(*i*) doubling of phonemes

(*ii*) elision of phonemes

(*iii*) views on *vikṛtis* esp. on *jaṭā* and *krama*.

(*iv*) *svarabhakti*

(*v*) augmentation.

Let us discuss these topics one by one.

I.11.2 (*i*) Doubling of phonemes [*dvittva*]

1. स्वरपूर्वव्यञ्जनं द्विवर्णं व्यञ्जनपरम्।
लचं 'ह्रस्वपूर्वादनुस्वारयोगात् द्वीआन्तगौ नङौ'
इत्यात्रेयवचनात् ह्रस्वपूर्वयोः पदान्तयोः नङयोर्द्वित्वं स्यात्।

The *pr* rule deals with conditional doubling of a consonant. If a consonant is preceded by a vowel and followed by a consonant, it is reduplicated. The example cited by the commentator is उ ऊ प्रथस्व [TS 1.1.8]. Here, '*p*' of *pra* is doubled because it is preceded by u vowel and followed by the consonant *r*.

This condition of the TPr is further specified by the Āś and it is certainly complimentary on the part of the LC to cite passages from a text which discuss the issue with more details. The Āś says the nasal stops *n* and *ṅ* are doubled if occurred at the end of a word and are preceded by *anusvāra* which follows a short vowel. Thus, the environment of doubling of n and ṅ according the Āś is short vowel + *anusvāra* + n/ṅ.

However, do we find any word fitting in this condition *i.e.*, an *anusvāra* followed by *n*/*ṅ* and preceded by a short vowel in the same word. Probably the rule needs reconsideration.

(*ii*) सवर्णः सवर्गीयपरः॥ तैप्रा 1423

Doubling does not take place if a consonant is followed by a homogeneous consonant. Here, the LC quotes the following verse from the Āś.

ङानुनासिकपूर्वस्तु ककारो मध्य आगमः।
गकारश्च तकारे च धकारे च यथाक्रमम्॥

इत्यात्रेयवचनाज्जातयोरागमयोः ककारगकारयोः पूर्वस्य द्वित्वं न। 'पाङ्क्तः' (१.५.२), 'युङ्ग्ध्वम्' [३.४.८]

If the nasal stop *ṅ* is followed by *'t'* and *'dh',* the phonemes *'k'* and *'g'* are inserted respectively. Here, however, according to Ātreya tough *'ṅ'* is followed by *'k'* and *'g',* which belong to the same class, is not reduplicated.

Here again the general conditions stated by the TPr are laid down by the Āś more specifically.

(*iii*) पदान्तश्च व्यञ्जनपरः प्राकृतः। तैप्रा 14.28

This rule is governed by the *sūtra 'atha na'* [TPr 14-14] and therefore, negates doubling. The phoneme which occurs at the end of a *pada* if followed by any consonant does not undergo any change.

Here, the LC helps us by quoting several verses from the Āś to mark the exceptions.

(*a*) रेफात्पूर्वो नकारो यः पदान्तो यत्र दृश्यते।
विशेषं तत्र जानीयाद्दित्वमित्यभिधीयते।
तान् + रक्षध्वम्
तान्न् + रक्षध्वम्

i.e. n + r = nn + r

Here *n* is doubled even if it occurs at the end of a *pada* and followed by consonant, because the following consonant is *r.*

(*b*)[43] नकारान्तं पदं पूर्वं यवहेषु परेषु च।
नकारयवहामध्ये तत्र वर्णमसंयुतम्।

'अन्वारोहान् + विद्वान् + यजते'

n + y/v/h = n + y/v/h

If a *pada* ending in *n* is followed by *y*, *v*, or *h* another phoneme is not inserted in between *i.e.,* doubling does not take place.

(*c*) ङ नौ यत्र पदान्ते तु यवहेषु परेषु च।
द्वित्वं नैवाभिगच्छेतां ङ नौ व्यवृपरौ विना[44]
जनान् यातयति, एतान् होमान्, सहस्वान् वाजी,
पराङ्, वा, प्रत्यङ् होतारम्,

The phonemes *ṅ* and *n* if preceded by *y/v* and *h* are never doubled, except when preceded by *a* and *vṛ*. This phenomenon is also expressed by नान्तो यादि परेषु च। Ms C omits it, where as Ms A quotes it in the beginning of the passage.

(*d*) ह्रस्वपूर्वो नकारो यः पदान्तो वपरो यदि।
विशेषं तत्र जानीयाद्द्वित्वमित्यभिधीयते॥
वृत्रहन्वाजिनम्

If a final *'n'* preceded by a short vowel if preceeds *v*, it is doubled.

Short vowel + *n* + *v* = (short vowel + *n n*) + *v*. This rule is an exception to the TPr rule.

(*e*) नकारान्तं पदं पूर्वं वकाराद्रपरं यदि।
संयुतं तत्र जानीयाद्द्वित्वमित्यभिधीयते।

The phoneme *'n'* is doubled if occurs at the end of a word and followed by *v* combined with *'r'*.

यस्मिन्नवृत्रम्

short vowel + *n* + *v* = short vowel + *nn* + *v*.

(*f*) संयुतौ नवकारौ चेत् पदान्तो यत्र दृश्यते।
विशेषं तत्र जानीयाद्द्वित्वमित्यभिधीयते।

N is doubled if combined with *v* followed by *y*.

धिष्णियान्व्याघारयति

n + v + y

nn + v + y

Out of the four Mss of the Āś, the Trivendrum ms deals with the external and internal *sandhis*. However, the above quoted rules have no place in it. Hopefully, the Hamburg Ms might have included these.

I.11.3 Elision

(*i*) तुनुपूर्वो उदात्तयोर्वकारः। तैप्रा ५.१३

लचं-उदात्तयोस्तुन्वोः सतोरिति विभज्य। तुपूर्वो नुपूर्वो वा वलोपस्स्यादव्ययस्थश्चेत्। 'चादीनामेव वो लोप' इत्यात्रेयवचनाच्चादौ व श्चेति' व्यासवचनादव्ययस्थत्वम्। सत्वै [2.6.6] इन्वै [1.6.7]

The TPr rule describes elision of *v* if preceded by *t* or *n*. According to the LC, Ātreya and Vyāsa further specify that the phoneme *v* must belong to a particle. Even this rule also is not attested in any ms.

(*ii*) उत्पूर्वस्सकारो व्यञ्जनपरः। तैप्रा 5.14

लचं-'स्थास्तम्भोरेव लोपस्सनिमित्तेन यथा भवेत्' इत्यात्रेवचनम्।

In the TS, we find that in any form of स्था or स्तंभ, 's' is elided, if it preceeds *ut. e.g.* We get forms उत्थानम् or उत्तब्धयै। Moreover, these forms are restored in the *Pp* as उत्स्थानम् or उत्स्तब्ध्यै. Thus, in the *Saṁhitā*, *s* of *sthā* and *stambha* is elided. Though this rule is not attested in any of these mss, it is in agreement with any *śikṣa* of the TS. Moreover, P also has paid attention to this phenomenon and has duly recorded it in P 8.4.61 उदः स्थास्तंभोः पूर्वस्य।

(*iii*) एष स स्य इति च। तैप्रा 5.15

लचं-'एष स स्य हल्यूर्ध्वे च विसर्गो लुप्यते तथा'

इत्यात्रेयवचनाद्विसर्ग एव नान्यः। 'एष ते' [ ] स ते [ ] स्य वाजी

The purport of this rule is as follows : The words एषः and सः, and स्यः elision of visarga are followed by a consonant takes place. The LC support such elision *i.e.* only of the *visarga* by quoting a rule from the Āś. Fortunately, this rule is corroborated in the Trivendrum ms. It displays it in a corrupt form as :

यशस्तस्य उद्धे च विसर्गो अलुप्यत्रदध।

Here, the LC helps us in presenting a correct text as given above. Thus, a prime principle of textual criticism *viz.* "Prefer the harder reading to a simple one" could be applied here. Needless to say, the reading of the LC is the harder one.

(*iv*) न श्येती मिथुनी। तैप्रा 10.18[45]

लचं-एतयोरन्यस्य यत्वं न। 'दयेती अकुरुत' [५.५.८] मिथुनी अभवत् [५.३.६] यमिवर्ण उकारश्च वकारं भजति स्वयम्।

मिथुन्यत्र भवेदेव ह्यनार्षे तु स्वरे परे॥

इत्यात्रेयवचनात् च विलोमे यत्वं भवत्येव। अथ मिथुनी मिथुन्यथाथ मिथुनी।

The normal euphonic combination will be *yaṇ sandhi.* However, the *Sp* in the above cases does not show such *sandhi.* Ātreya further specifies that if the *anārṣa* vowel follows [*i.e.* in the *kramapāṭhā*] such *sandhi* duely takes place. *i.e.* the exception is found only in the *Sp* and not in the *vikṛtis* wherein the euphonic combination takes place when the word-order is changed. Such *sandhi* is called *viloma sandhi,*

(*v*) न सꣳसामिति रापरः॥ तैप्रा २३.४[46]

लचं-'मो लोपः'। क्विपि राजिन' इत्यात्रेयवचनात्। संसामित्येतयोर्मो न लुप्यते क्विबन्त राजति स्थ

रापरश्चेत्। सम्राजे। 'क्विपि राजि' इति नियमात् लोप एव।

Sometimes the prefix सम् or (साम् in secondary derivative) is added to the word राज and we get सम्राट्/साम्राज्य Here, we do not get *anusvāra* substituted in place lf म्. This phenomenon is discussed in the rule quoted above. Even here the LC, quotes a divergent opinion of Ātreya. According Ātreya 'm' is elided and is substituted by *anusvāra.* However, the LC fails to clarify the context intended by the Āś which is the *kramapāṭha* and other *vikṛtis.* The example in support of Ātreya is राज्ञे सं सं राज्ञे।

I.11.4. Views on *vikṛtis*

1. इतिपरोऽपि। तैप्रा 8.12

This rule occurs in the context of *jaṭā*, one of the *vikṛtis.* The LC refers to Ātreya twice while explaining this particular rule.

स्वरवर्णादभेदस्य यत्पदद्वितयस्य च।[47]

जटाविचक्षणैरुक्तं क्रमोच्चारणमत्र तु। इत्यात्रेयवचनात्।

By quoting Ātreya's argument the LC has supplied supporting information for the TPr rule. Ātreya says that under certain conditions *jaṭāpāṭha* resembles *kramapāṭha.*

अत्र विशेषमाहतुर्व्यासात्रेयौ–

संहितावत्क्रमो ज्ञेयो जाटा च विकृतादिषु।

पदद्वयनिमित्तं यदेकाभावेपि यत्र तु।

संहितावत्क्रमो ज्ञेयस्तद्वज्ज्ञेया जटा बुधैः॥

This description is shared by Vyāsa and Ātreya, both. The last two lines, which belong to the *Ātreya śikṣā* are attested in the VVRI ms.

I.11.5. *Svarabhakti*

1. रेफोष्मसंयोगे रेफस्स्वरभक्तिः॥ तैप्रा २७.७५

लचं-ऊष्मोत्तरस्य रेफस्य स्वरभक्तिर्बुधैस्स्मृता।

लकारस्य तदूर्ध्वे च स्वरभक्तित्वमुच्यते।[48] इत्यात्रेयः।

Among many verses quoted by the LC from various *śikṣ* *ās*, the verses from the Āś explaining *svarabhakti* run as above.

According to Ātreya, if *repha* is followed by an *ūṣman*, there is scope for *svarabhakti*. The *repha* gets *svarabhakti*. *e.g.* *Barhiṣā* will be uttered a *barehiṣā*. Similarly if an hissing sound is followed by l, l is uttered with additional 'e' *e.g.* *śatavalsa* is uttered as *śatavaleśa*. Thus, the Āś specifies the element to be lengthened.

1.18.6. Augmentation

(*i*) उपसर्ग, पाथ एष, अत्याति, धाम, परग, भूतगूर्तेषु छखिभुजेषु च। तैप्रा १४.८

लचं-"छखिभुजा इयुः पूर्वं धामापात्युपसर्गतः।
भूते च पाथ एषोति परमाघूर्ध्वतस्स्थिते।
इत्यात्रेयवचनाच्च।
अपेत्येतस्मात्परस्याति। छन्दाँस्यप अपच्छन्दाँसि।

According to the TPr, cha, khi and bhuja if preceded by either a prefix or the words पाथ एष, अति, आति, धाम, परम, भूते, the first consonant of the respective class is augmented here. *i.e.* c, k, and p are inserted respectively.

Ātreya extends the list by one word [This is not included in the *upasargas* by the TPr cf. TPr 1.15]. We do not know whether the Āś omits आति and replaces it by अप, or he cites आति in the immediately preceding line, which is not quoted by any of these Mss.

It seems that the additional occurrence of अप is possible only in the *viloma sandhis* taking place in the *vikṛtis*. The Āś, many a time, refers to *anārṣa pāṭhas*, therefore, has recorded the word, which causes insersion of c, k, & p.

(*ii*) ततस्त्वनुस्वारः। तैप्रा २५.३

लचं-अनुस्वारलक्षणमाह आत्रेयः। अध्याये तैत्तिरीयाणाम्

अनुस्वारो यदा भवेत्। तस्याद्यर्धो गकारस्या-
त्तच्छेषमनुनासिकम्।

The pronunciation of अनुस्वार presupposes so many theories. The TS has a peculiar style of pronouncing *anusvāra* which is called as "along with the sound (गुं) (गुंकारयुक्त). The *anusvāra,* which is not *parasavarṇa* is pronounced with the sound ग् and in the printed text sometimes it is represented by this *ṅ* sign. This particular pronunciation is preserved by some modern IA languages, *e.g.* Bengali. The Āś describes this peculiarity of the TS.

1.11.7. Observations

(*i*) From the above discussion it is clear that the LC helps us in identifying the subject-mater of the Āś.

(*ii*) Since at least two references are attested in the mss, there is a chance that other references also are from the Āś and this assumption may help in corroboration of these references in the Hamburg Mss of the Āś, which is the only complete ms.

(*iii*) The hypothesis proclaimed in one of my articles was–

"The Āś is either quoted or mentioned in various literature as one of the important *śikṣās.* When it is projected as an important *śikṣā*, anybody would expect it to opine on various subjects. Though a single ms does not give us a full-fledged picture of a *śikṣā*, these four mss (or more if available by fluck) together may be able to present a better picture."[46] This hypothesis was confirmed after the publication of Aithal 1991. However, since the complete ms was not at hand we could not confirm the authenticity of the LC as a text providing the correct version of the Āś.[49]

Any way, since two references quoted by the LC on the name of Ātreya are attested in two different mss, we may say that these two mss form parts of one single text. Thus, the LC is certainly a very important secondary source in the text-critical study of the Āś.

I.12.0. The LC and the *Māheśvara Śikṣā*

In the preceding paragraphs we have seen how does the LC help in editing the Āś. Now, let us see how does it act as the prime secondary source in the reconstruction of the *Māheśvara Śikṣā* [Mś]. It will not be exageration if we say that the LC has added this particular name to the list of *śikṣās,* since even Aithal 1991 does not record it. Needless to say, all other authentic sources also do not take cognizance of it. Thus, we do not know whether it exists in ms form in some library. The analysis of its contents show that it is different from *Śambhu Śiksā* and also from the *Pāṇini Śikṣā.* In such a situation it would be indeed interesting to have a look in this particular text.

The LC quotes passages from the Mś is the following contexts :

1. The alphabets of the TS
2. Process of articulation and description of phonemes
3. *Pragṛhyas*
4. *Sandhis*
5. *Vikṛtis*
6. Elision
7. Augmentation
8. Doubling
9. *Svarabhakti*
10. Pronunciation of Praṇava

Now, let us deal with these issues one by one.

1.12.1. The Alphabets

Both these groups of mss of the LC reckon sixty phonems of the TS in contrast with some other commentaries as they reckon just fiftynine by omitting *svarabhakti.* The only difference between these sets of mss is (*i*) ms A/D deduce these sixty phonemess from various *sūtras* occurred in the TPr. (*ii*) Whereas the second group of ms B/C/E/F take support from the Mś. To quote them verbatim–

1. MSA/D–तथा हि, अ आ आ ३, इ ई ई ३, उ ऊ ऊ ३, ऋ ॠ, ऌ ए ऐ, ओ औ, इत्यचः षोडश। कादयो मावसानाः पञ्चविंशतिस्पर्शाः, यरलवा अन्तस्थाः, जिह्वामूलीय-शषसोपध्मानीयहकाराः इत्यूष्माणः। अनुस्वारः विसर्जनीयः, रङ्गः, दुश्लिष्टलकारः, यमाश्चत्वारः, स्वरभक्तिः, इति षष्टिसंख्या सूत्रत एवं स्पष्टाद्रष्टव्या।

2. **MSC/E/B/F**–तथाहि, अ आ आ ३, इ ई ई ३, उ ऊ ऊ ३, ऋ ॠ ऌ, ए ऐ, ओ औ इत्यचः षोडशः। क ख ग घ ङ, च छ ज झ ञ, ट ठ ड ढ ण, त थ द ध न, प फ ब भ म, एते स्पर्शाः। यरलवा अन्तस्थाः जिह्वामूलीय, शषसोपध्मानीय हकाराः इत्यूष्माणः। अनुस्वारः विसर्जनीयः रङग, दुश्लिष्टलकारः। चत्वार यमाः स्वरभक्तिः इति षष्टिसंख्याकसमूहो माहेश्वरशिक्षायां उक्तः।

Though the LC gives reference to the MŚ in this context, it does not quote the exact passage from it. Still, to bear the intention of it, the LC is certainly helpful.

I.12.2. The Process of Articulation and Description of Phonemes.

1. According to the TPr, any 'phone' *i.e.* sound in general is produced at the juncture of chest and throat. The different sounds are further resonated at various places. These places are enlisted by the TPr as follows–

> **तस्य प्रातिश्रुत्कानि भवन्ति उरः कण्ठः शिरः मुखं नासिके इति ॥2.3॥**

The Mś adds one more to the list and it is श्रवणे *i.e.* ears. One has to check these findings in modern theories. But, at least here the Mś comes forward with its own views.

2. **स्पर्शस्थानेषूष्माणः आनुपूर्व्येण** तैप्रा. २.४४ The *sūtra* describes places of articulating the fricatives. The TPr recognises six fricatives *viz., jihvāmūlīya, ś, ṣ, s, upadhmānīya,* and *h.* Out of these six, the initial five are produced in the same place that of

the stops respectively, *i.e. jihvāmūlīya*, as velar *ś* as the palatal, *ṣ* as retroflex, *'s'* as the dental, and *upadhmānīya* as labial. Here, the LC finds place to describe the nature of *jihvāmūlīya* and *upadhmānīya*. It describes

जिह्वामूलीयोपध्मानीययोः स्वरूपं तूक्तं माहेश्वरशिक्षायाम्-

जिह्वामूलीयो विसर्ग इव पूर्वः कखोर्ध्वयोः।

फफयोश्चोपध्मानीयोऽन्ते विसर्गो ह वै स्मृतः।

"*Jihvāmūlīa* is that sound, the *visarga* before k and kh. *e.g. Rāmaḥ karoti* and the *Upadhmānīya* is one which comes before P and ph. Ultimately, it is *visarga* only."

I really wonder why the commentator has not quoted this particular verse either in the enumeration of the alphabets or under the *sūtra* 1.9 परे षडूष्माणः।

3. नासिकाविवरणादानुनासिक्यम्।। तैप्रा २.५२

The *anunāsika* sounds are produced by expanding the nasal cavity.

Therefore, the sound produced is heard like the sound of bronze vessel. The Mś describes it as

"काँस्यध्वनिसमानश्च रङ्गसंज्ञ इतीर्यते" इति माहेश्वरशिक्षायाम्।

In fact, *anunāsika* and *raṅga* are two different types of sounds.

I.12.3. Pragṛhyas etc.

The following verse describes the situations wherein the *saṁhitā* text is shown marked with *iti*.

The TPr rule is इतिपरोऽपि 1.44. The *Pragṛahas i.e.* the units which do not undergo any euphonic combination are shown in the division *i.e.,* in the Pps, Kps etc. followed by iti. The LC quotes here the verse which enumerates the situations where iti is added to the *saṁhitā* word in the Pps etc. To quote–

सर्वोपसर्गप्रग्रहेङ्ग्यान्ते स्यादित्यसंहिते।

पुनरीङ्ग्य विरामश्चादौ तथा प्रग्रहः क्रमे।

इतियुक्तं विरामस्थं द्विधा नैवोपसर्गकः।
नीचावानो विरामस्थस्तदित्यूर्ध्वे ग्रहे क्रम इति।

To translate–In the non-*saṁhitā* text *i.e.* (in the Pps) all the *upasargas,* non-combinable vowels, the indicated units (*iṅgya i.e.* complex formations) similarly in the *Krama* texts, the end of complex formation, the *upasargas* and also *pragṛhya* are with iti. The unit that occurs at the end is always repeated, but never the *upasargas* which occur at the end, which are unaccented, अव, आ and नः if followed by तद्, the unit preceding pause are 'never repeated in the *Kp.*

This is a standard rule found in most of the *śikṣās.* The *Mś* adds just one point; तदित्यूर्ध्वे

I.12.4. Euphonic Combinations or Sandhis

1. The fifth chapter of the TPr guides the reader for reconstruction of the Sp on the basis of the Pp. The opening *sūtra* of it reads–अथ संहितायामेकप्राणभावे।। ५.१

It seems that even the Mś also designs some of its contents in the same direction. Therefore, the LC quotes an *adhikāra* rule of it,

वक्ष्यते सोधुनैकोश्वासाभावे तु पदान्तवत्।

I.12.5. Morphophonemic Changes

1. The TPr 5.28 discusses augmentation of nasal sound in certain situations. In *śikṣā* literature we find that these nasals are classified more accurately. The śikṣaś tell us of two types of nasals.

(*i*) **Permanent** (नित्य नासिक्य), which are, *yama, anusvāra* and the fifth phoneme of each class.

(*ii*) The other category is that of **conditional nasals** or निमित्त नासिक्य, the sounds which are nasalised in some situation come under this category. The *Vyāsa śikṣā* and the Mś both have to contribute on this issue. The LC quotes their views to explain the situation of TPr 5.28 as

अन्तस्थापरश्च सवर्णमनुनासिकम्।

The phoneme 'm' if followed by semivowels gets changed to homogeneous nasal of the semivowel. *e.g.* सम् + यत्ता: is uttered as–सँय्यत्ता: etc. The MŚ specifies-

यमोन्त्यानुस्वाराणां सास्यनासास्थानमुच्यते।

तदेव यलवहा चानिमित्तेन तु कीर्तितम् इति माहेश्वरवचनाच्च।

2. If त्रि, ट, अस्थूरि, धि, सुव: and नि: precede न then it is changed to ण. The Tr specifies conditions for such a change in the seventh chapter. A part of these conditions are mentioned in 7.2. The LC quotes similar view of the MŚ as त्रिटास्थूरिधिसुवर्नि:पूर्व इति माहेश्वरवचनात्।

3. The *visarga* is changed to '*s*' if it preceeds '*a*'; to '*ṣ*' if preceeds k, kh & p.

   This phenomenon is described in 8.23 of the TPr. The MŚ also has the same opinion. However, the quotation given by LC is not complete. It reads–षमेत्यवर्णपूर्व: समिति माहेश्वरवचनात्। leaving the condition of '*ṣ*' incomplete.

4. **उदथापरश्चोदथापरश्च।। तैप्रा 9.24**

   The phoneme '*n*' if followed by उत् and अथा is not changed to semivowels *i.e.* to *repha* or *yakāra*. The phoneme '*n*' is exception to this phenomenon as discussed in the 9th chapter of the *TPr.* The *MŚ* says the rules and negations of these are also applicable to other *vikṛtis*. It says एत्यार्षेयो यत्वरेफौ विलोम एव सोच्यतेति माहेश्वरवचनात्।

5. न श्येती मिथुनी।। तैप्रा १०.१५

   These two words do not undergo any change. [Cf. I.12.] The *LC* quotes the rule of the MŚ which is not at all different from the ĀŚ.

   नार्षे श्येती मिथुन्यपीति माहेश्वरवचनात्।

1.11.6 Elision

उत्पूर्वस्सकार: व्यञ्जनपर:: TPr. **5.14.**

The sound *'s'* is elided if preceded by *ut* and followed by a consonant, in the *Sp.* This phenomenon is discussed also in 1.12. The LC along with the ĀŚ, quotes opinion of the MŚ as follows : 'स्थास्तंभोरेव पूर्व सः' इति महोश्वरवचनाच्च।

2. The TPr 11.3 enlists certain *anuvākās* in which the vowel 'a' is not elided even if preceded by *'e'* or *'o'*. The LC adds one to the list of the *anuvākas* by taking support from the MŚ.

'ईयुर्याज्येयमेनम्' इति माहेश्वरवचनाह्योऽपरीषु पश्यान्।

3. The TPr 12-8 cites certain examples wherein elision of *'a'* takes place. To establish one of these examples, the LC takes support from the MŚ as ग्रयपूर्वोऽन्वतप्यश्चेति।

The example supported by the MŚ is as follows–

अग्नयोऽन्वतप्यप्त।

4. The elision of *'m'* is described in 13.4 [Cf. I.12.] The same phenomenon is discussed by the MŚ as नोर्ध्वे राजि सःसांक्विपि

5. In the same passage a situation is described wherein *'m'* is not elided. the opinion of the MŚ is as follows–

शान्त्यूर्ध्वं ॐ मित्यत्र मः सरूपतयेति अन्यदपि

The *'m'* of om is not elided when followed by शान्तिः।

1.12.7. *Vikṛtis*

The MŚ describes *jaṭā* in the same line of the *AŚ* and the *VŚ.* It says–

सकृतादिद्वितीयं द्विः आदि द्विश्च परं सकृत्
पठेदतुल्यपदयोः क्रमवत्संधिभिर्जटाम्।
त्रिक्रमे त्रिक्रमं त्युक्तः विलोमेनानुलोमतः।
इति माहेश्वरशिक्षायाम्।

The LC reads this verse under 8.12.

I.13.8. Doubling

The LC quotes the following passages from the MŚ in the context of doubling.

1. **स्वरपूर्वं व्यञ्जनं द्विवर्णं व्यञ्जनपरम्॥ तैप्रा १४.७**

Here the quotation of the MŚ does not make clear statement about the two phenomes which are reduplicated. However, from the quotation from the ĀŚ we can find out those and these are *'n'* and *'ṅ'* : cf. [I.12]

The LC also quotes another statement from the MŚ as follows–ह्रस्वपूर्वादनुस्वारयोगाद्वीं च।

i.e. The phoneme–*ṅ, ṇ* & *n* occurring at the end and preceded by a short vowel are reduplicated.

2. The 14.26 of the TPr denies doubling of *'l'* according to some grammarians. The MŚ supports the Pr view as ऐकादूर्ध्वलवयोर्योगस्तत्राप्यसंयुतेति माहेश्वरवचनात्।

3. The final *'n'* if followed by a consonant is not doubled, the TPr 14.28 says. However, the MŚ is not in favour of the TPr. It says in the following conditions *'n'* is doubled. The word used for द्वित्व is संयुक्त to quote-

संयुक्तौ न हकारौ चेदृकारः परतो यदि।
संयुक्तं तत्र विज्ञेयं नोभयोर्व्यक्तिरिष्यते॥

आसन्निषूहृत्स्वसः।

अनृकारस्वरोर्ध्वेषु यवहेषु परेषु च।
नोन्तगो संयुतं तत्र दीर्घवोत्तरे यदि।
तथैवङोन्तगौ यत्र हवयोः परभूतयोः।
इति माहेश्वरशिक्षायाम्।

1.12.8. Augmentation

The TPr 14.8 (cf. I.12) speaks of augmentation. We have also seen that the ĀŚ adds अप to the list. The MŚ also goes hand in hand with the ĀŚ and says–'पाथ एषोत्यातिभूते परमापोपसर्गतः' इति माहेश्वरवचनात्।

I.13.10. Svarita

The MŚ describes *svarita* as follows–

ह्रस्वो दीर्घश्च मध्येनान्त्येन चेद्वित्व उत्तरे।
द्विमात्रिके चावसाने दीर्घोन्त्यस्वरितो भवेदिति माहेश्वर-
वचनात्।

1.12.9. Description of *Praṇava*

The MŚ describes *Praṇava* as follows–

ब्रह्माविष्णुरुद्रोमस्त्रिव्यूहोहं समहत्यपि।
सशक्तौ लीयते सैवों परो नादो महेश्वरः।
अउमनादाः क्रमेण ज्ञेयाश्च प्रणवे स तु।
आदावुच्चश्चतुर्मात्रोन्ते च मध्ये त्रिमात्रिकः।
स्त्रवत्यादावनुक्तेन्ते रङ्गोऽन्ते नादसंज्ञकः।

1.12.10. Views on *Svarabhakti*

1. The MŚ describes the *svarabhakti* in the same line of the ĀŚ and that of the VŚ as follows–

स्वरोर्ध्वोष्मोर्ध्वश्च रोल स्वरभक्तिमवाप्नुयात्।
स्वरभक्तेस्स्वरूपं तु अर्धपादद्वयात्मकम्।
पूर्वार्धं संवृतो दीर्घो न्योर्ध्वेषु विवृतोपरे।
क्रमेण पादश्चत्वार उरज्ञरस्वरात्मकाः।
लकारस्यैव लो मध्ये होर्ध्वे लः कर्विणीचरः।
करेणु हरिणी रः शसोर्ध्वो लः शोर्ध्वहारितः।
रः षोर्ध्वः सा हंसपदाप्येव भक्तिश्च पञ्चधा।
(*ii*) धूर्षदं च स्वतंत्रता।

1.12.11. Observations

1. We have seen that the MŚ opines on various subjects which are generally discussed in a fullfledged *śikṣā* text.
2. It describes the subjects peculiar to the TS. Therefore, keeps similarity with the MŚ and the VŚ, with certain exceptions.
3. Since it upholds its own peculiar views, indicated by the exceptions, shows that it must be representing a particular

branch of the TS, which categorically is not known as different.

4. Thus, though from the versification and style of writing it looks quite modern *śikṣā,* however, represents the old views.
5. We do not know, which library or house it adorns now, but it is worthwhile to search for the mss of this particular *śikṣā.*

Footnotes

1. **ब्रह्म यस्त्वननुज्ञातमधीयानादवाप्नुयात्।**
स ब्रह्मस्तेयसंयुक्तो नरकं प्रतिपद्यते॥ 2.116 मनुस्मृति
Bhatt, Rameshwar (1985) "Manusmti" Chaukhamba Sanskrit Pratisthan, Delhi.
2. for details see
(*a*) Jha, V.N. (1992) "A Linguistic analysis of the Taittirīya Padapāṭha", Sri Satgura Publications, Delhi.
(*b*) Kulkarni, N.R. (1995) "A Grammatical Analysis of the Taittirīya Padapāṭ ha", Sri Satguru Publications, Delhi.
3. **जटा-माला-शिक्षा-रेखा-ध्वजो-दण्डो रथा घनः।**
अष्टा विकृतयः प्रोक्ता क्रमपूर्वा मनीषिभिः॥5॥
विकृतिवल्ली of **व्याडी**
Devasthali, G.V. (1978) *"Vedavikṛtilakṣaṇasaṅgrahaḥ"* BORI, Pune.
4. See '*ślokyāya namaḥ/avasānyāya namaḥ/*' TS 4.5.6.1, Vājasaneya Saṁhitā 16.33.
5. for details see
(*a*) Indra (1973) 'प्रातिशाख्यों में प्रयुक्त पारिभाषिक शब्दों का आलोचनात्मक अध्ययन, विश्वेश्वरानंद वैदिक रीसर्च इन्स्टिटयूट, होशियारपूर
(*b*) K.C. Chaterji (1964 2nd edn) "Technical Terms and Technique of Sanskrit Grammarians" University of Calcutta, Calcutta.
6. Aitareya Brāhmaṇa (1896) Ānandāśram Sanskrit Series no. 31, Pts. I-II, Pune, 5.3/6.29.
7. (ed) Chinnaswami Shastri (1935/1936) Tāṇḍamahābrāhmaṇa with Sāyana's Commentary, Kashi Sanskrit Series 105, Chowkhamba Sanskrit Series Office.
8. (ed) Gokhale, Gaṅeshshastri (1910) "Chāndogya Upaniṣad", Anandaśram Sanskrit Granthavali 63, Pune.
9. Keith, A.B. (ed & tr) (1909) Aitareya Āraṇyaka (with pts of Śāṅkhāyana

Āraṇyaka), Oxford University Press, London.

10. (ed) Sri Saccidananda Saraswati, (1961) "The Taittirīya Upaniṣad-Śikṣāvallī 1.2" Holenarsipur, Mysore.
11. प्राणो वंश इति विद्यात्। ऐ आ.2.3.6
12. यद्धि सन्धिं विवर्तयति तन्निर्भुजस्य रूपम्। अथ यच्छुद्धे अक्षरे अभिव्याहरति तत्प्रतृणस्य अग्रे उ एव उभयमन्तरेण उभयं व्याप्तं भवति। ऐआ 3.3
13. See for details Deshpande Madhav, (1997) "Śaunakīyā Caturādhyāyikā" Introduction, Dept. of Sanskrit and Indian Studies, Harvard University.
14. Op. cit.
15. Whitney, W.D. R 1973 (1863) "The Taittirīya Prātiśākhya and Tribhāṣyaratna" M. Banarsidass, Delhi, p. 6.
16. Aithal, K.P.S. R1993 (1991) "Vedalakṣaṇa–Vedic Ancillary Literature–A Descriptive Bibliography", M. Banarsidass, N. Delhi.
17. Taittirīya Upaniṣad, op. cit.
18. Shastri, Hardatta *"Ṛgvedabhāṣyabhūmikā Sāyaṇācāryakṛtā"*. Sanskrit Vishvavidyalaya, Varanasi, pp. 109-110.
19. Ghosh, Manmohan R. 1986 (1938) "*Paninīyaśikṣā*" Indian Books Centre, Delhi, Introduction, pp. xxvi-xxvii.
20. Kulkarni, N.R. (1987-88) "On Two Peculiar Terms of the Vyāsa Śikṣā", Oriental Journal, Tirupati.
21. Varma, Siddheshwar (19661) "Critical Studies on the Phonetic Observations of the Indian Grammarians" Munshi Ram Manohar Lal, Delhi. p. 55.
22. (ed) Varma, Virendrakumar (1972) "Ṛgveda Prātiśākhyam with the comm. Of Uvaṭa" Benares Hindu University Sanskrit Series, V., p. 37.
23. (ed) Pattabhiramasastri, (1976) "The Vyāsaśikṣā" The Kashi Sanskrit Series 225, Chaukhamba Sanskrit Samsthan, Varanasi.
24. Sharfe, H. (1977) "History of Grammatical Literature" Wiesbaden.
25. Op. cit. p. 21. He says–"As regards their relative chronological position, the Prātiśākhyas may be placed in the following order :
    1. *Ṛgvedaprātiśākhya*-the older
    2. *Taittirīya Prātiśākhya* (kernel)
    3. (*a*) *Atharva Prātiśākhya* (kernel) nearly contemporaries
       (*b*) *Vājasaneyī Prātiśākhya*
    4. Paṇini
    5. *Taittirīya Prātiśākhya* (later phase of)
    6. *Atharvaveda Prātiśākhya* (later phase of)
    7. *Ṛktantra* of the Sāmaveda
26. Scholars like Yudhisthir Mimamsaka though have handled the text of Maitrāyanī Prātiśākhya; it seems to be lost. See Yudhisthir Mimansak R 1984 (1961), "Sanskrit Vyākaran Śāstra Kā Itihās, Ramlal Kapoor Trust, Bahalgarh, Haryana, pp. 109-110.

27. (ed) Shringy R.K. (1991) Śaṁgitaratnākara, Munshiram Manoharlal, Delhi Sharma Prem Lata.
28. Allen, W.S. op. cit., "in a recent paper, however, Dr. A.A. Bake has pointed out that this interpretation is unfounded and that 'strange to say, there is no trace of the knowledge of the existence of the vocal cards in the texts on the theory of music" p. 33.
29. TPr.2.2
30. (ed) Sharma, V.V. (1930) Māhiṣeyabhāṣya or Padakramasadana of Māhiṣeya, Madras University Sanskrit Series-I, Madras.
31. (ed) Rangacarya K. & R. Shama Sastri, "The Taittirīya Prātiśākhyam (with the com. Tribhāṣyaratna of Somayarya and Vaidikābharaṇa of Gārgya Gopāla Yajvan" Mysore.
32. Op. cit.
33. This is an incomplete commentary deposited in mss form at GOML, Madras. Aithal has not taken a note of it.
34. This ms is not recorded in the New Catelogus Catalogorum.
35. Deposited in the Adyar Library, Madras.
36. (ed) Shastri Shivaramakrishna (1938-39) Journal of Annamalai University, Vol. 8.
37. Aithal, K.P. op. cit.
38. Kulkarni N.R. (1990) 'A note on the Lakṣaṇacandrikā "Vaṇiyotiḥ" Vol. 3, Bhubaneshvar.
39. Though Aithal declares it as incomplete it is not so. the *adhyāya* division in place of *praśna* might have puzzled him.
40. Yet we have to confirm that the ĀŚ deposited in Hamburg is identical with the ĀŚ quoted by the LC.
41. Kulkarni, N.R. (1993) 'Problems of editing the *śikṣā* texts in "Problems of Editing Ancient Texts" ed. V.N. Jha, Chaukhamba Sanskrit Pratishthan, Delhi, pp 52-62.
42. MS A & D quote an additional verse.

    लकारस्य वकारस्य संयोगे स्वरितो यदि।
    विशेषं तत्र जानीयाद्दित्वम् इत्यभिधीयते।।
    बिल्ल्वः।

    The word *bilva* should be pronounced as *billva*. The TPr rule under which the LC quotes the verse does not speak reduplication of a final phonemen or does it support non-doubling prescribed in the present verse. It seems to be off the context. It would have been proper if the mss had quoted the above verse to contradict opinion of Hārita, who is not in favor of doubling of '*l*' in the word *bilva*. The Tpr 14.21 restores Hārita's view as follows: लतवर्गौ यवकारपरौ।

The com Tribhāṣyaratna reads : हारितः सांन्निध्याल्लभाते। तन्मते लतवर्गौ न खलु यकारपरौ द्वित्वमाप्नुतः। यथा लकारः कल्याणी। बैल्वः।

Thus, according to Hārita doubling of '*l*' is not desired, whereas Ātreya favours it in the above verse. Present recitation is not contradictory to Ātreya's view. Most probably, such contradiction has prompted the commentator to lable the group of five rules of the TPr (14.18-22) as *aniṣṭapañcakam. i.e.* undesired rules.

Any way, it seems that the proper place of citing this particular rule is 14.21 MS C does not cite the verse under discussion.

43. MS A and D do not recognize this verse as from the ĀŚ though they quote it.
44. MS A & D wrongly scribe the comment under 10.19.
45. cf. P.8.3.23.
46. MS C does not read this verse.
47. MS A & D omit.
48. Kulkarni. N.R. (1988) 'On the Reconstruction of the ĀŚ' Aligarh Journal of Oriental Studies, Vol. V, nos 1-2, Vivek Publications, Aligarh.

अथ लक्षणचन्द्रिकाप्रारम्भः॥[१]

अथ प्रथमोऽनुवाकः॥

श्रीगणेशाय नमः। श्रीउमामहेश्वराभ्यां नमः।[२] अथ प्रातिशाख्यव्याख्या-प्रारम्भः।[३]

परब्रह्मशिवं शक्तिं ततश्चोमासदाशिवौ।
ईश्वरं पार्वतीं रुद्रं रुद्राणीं च जनार्दनम्॥
विरिञ्चिं च महासेनं हेरम्बं सूर्यभार्गवौ।
बृहस्पतिं च तत्पत्नीं तथान्यान् सकलान् गुरून्।
नत्वा च प्रातिशाख्यस्य व्याख्या लक्षणचन्द्रिका॥
महादेवाभिधेयेन यथामत्या विरच्यते।[४]

अथ वर्णसमाम्नायः॥१॥

अथ शब्दो मङ्गलार्थानन्तर्यार्थोऽधिकारार्थश्च।[५] आनन्तर्यं वेदाध्ययनानन्तरमित्यर्थः। पाठक्रमोऽधिक्रियत इति सूत्रान्वयः।[६] पूर्वशिष्टैर्यउपदिष्टो वर्णसमूहः स एव गृह्यत इति सूत्रार्थः।[७]

१.	MS A/D/E	अथ प्रातिशाख्यव्याख्याप्रारम्भः।
२.	MS A	श्रीसरस्वत्यै नमः। श्रीगुरुभ्यो नमः।
	MS D	श्रीगुरुभ्यो नमः।
	MS E	श्रीशङ्कराय गुरवे नमः।
३.	MS A/D/E	Omit.
४.	MS A/E	विनायकं गुरुं भानुं ब्रह्माविष्णुमहेश्वरान्। व्याख्यार्थे प्रातिशाख्यस्य भारतीं च नमाम्यहम्॥
	MS D	Adds the verse in the margin.
५.	MS A/D	प्रथमो मङ्गलार्थः। द्वितीयोऽनन्तर्यार्थः। तृतीयोऽधिकारार्थः।
६.	Ms A/D	add समित्यैके। आम्नायते आनुपूर्व्येण एकीभूता अकारादयो वर्णाः स्वरभक्त्यन्ताः।
७.	MS A/D	आनुपूर्व्येण पूर्वैः शिष्टैरुपदिष्टाः।

तथाहि–अ आ आ३, इ ई ई३ उ ऊ ऊ३ ऋ ॠ ऌ ए ऐ ओ औ इत्यचः षोडश। क ख ग घ ङ च छ ज झ ञ ट ठ ड ढ ण त थ द ध न प फ ब भ म एते स्पर्शाः।[१] य र ल वान्तस्थाः।[२] जिह्वामूलीय-शषसोपध्मानीयहकाराः इत्यूष्माणः।[३] अनुस्वारः विसर्जनीयः रङ्गः दुश्लिष्टलकारः चत्वार यमाः[४] स्वरभक्तिः इति षष्टिसंख्याकसमूहो माहेश्वरशिक्षायामुक्तः।[५]

अथ नवादितः समानाक्षराणि॥२॥

अथेति संज्ञाधिकारः। तस्मिन्नाद्या नववर्णाः समानाक्षरसंज्ञकाः स्युः।[६]

द्वे द्वे सवर्णे ह्रस्वदीर्घे॥३॥

तेषु द्वे द्वे ह्रस्वदीर्घे च परस्परं सवर्णसंज्ञे भवतः।[७]

न प्लुतपूर्वम्॥४॥[८]

प्लुतपूर्वं चेत्सवर्णसंज्ञकं न। अतः 'अग्ना३इ इत्याह' [तैसं. ६.५.८] इत्यत्र दीर्घादेशो न भवति।[९]

१. MS A/D कादयो मावसानाः पञ्चविंशतिस्पर्शाः।
MS E writes कादिमान्ताः and rulus out, adds in the margin एते स्पर्शाः।

२. MS E यादिवान्ता अन्तस्थाः।

३. MS E जिह्वामूलीय-शषस-उपध्मानीयहाः इत्यूष्माणः।

४. MS A/D यमाश्चत्वारः।

५. MS A/D इति षष्टिसंख्या सूत्रत एव स्पष्टा द्रष्टव्या। यजुर्वेदविषये एष एव निर्णयो निर्णीतः। वर्णानां समाम्नायो वर्णसमाम्नायायः।
MS E omits उक्तः। adds in the margin माहेश्वरशिक्षायाम्।

६. MS A/D तस्मिन्वर्णसमाम्नाये आद्या न [व] वर्णा समानाक्षरसंज्ञकाः स्युः। वन्ताः।

७. MS A/D स्तः।
MS E rubs out स्तः and replaces it by भवतः।

८. MS A/D read the present *sūtra* as न प्लुतपूर्वे।

९. MS A/D प्लुतपूर्वं समानाक्षरं सवर्णसंज्ञकं न स्यात्। समासोऽत्र बहुव्रीहिः। 'अग्ना ३(इ) इत्याह' इत्यत्र दीर्घादेशनिषेधे सति इवर्णोकाराविति यत्वे 'लुप्यते' [तैप्रा १०.१९] इति सूत्रेण यकारे लुप्ते सति 'न प्लुतः' इति सूत्रेण संधिकार्यं न। ततः अग्ना ३ इ इत्याहेति सिद्ध्यति।
MS E omits भवति।

षोडशादितः स्वराः॥५॥

तस्मिन्नाद्याः षोडशवर्णाः स्वरसंज्ञकास्स्युः।[१]

शेषो व्यञ्जनानि॥६॥

स्वरेभ्यः शेषस्यैषा[२] संज्ञा स्यात्।

आद्याः पञ्चविंशतिस्स्पर्शाः॥७॥

व्यञ्जनेष्वाद्याः च एतत्संज्ञकाः स्युः। कादिमान्ताः।[३]

पराश्चतस्रोऽन्तस्स्थाः॥८॥

स्पर्शेभ्यः प० चत्वारोऽन्तःस्थासंज्ञकाः स्युः।

परे षडूष्माणः॥९॥

आभ्यः परे षडूष्मसंज्ञकास्स्युः।

स्पर्शानामानुपर्व्येण पञ्चपञ्च वर्गाः॥१०॥

एषामानुपूर्व्येण पञ्चपञ्च वर्गसंज्ञकास्स्युः। कचटतपादयो ङञणनमान्ताः इत्यर्थः।

प्रथमद्वितीयतृतीयचतुर्थोत्तमाः॥११॥

एकैकस्मिन्वर्गे यथाक्रमेण वर्णाः प्रथमादिसंज्ञकास्स्युः।

संख्या नाम्नि सिद्धेऽपि संख्यान्तरानभिधानार्थं प्रथमादिसंज्ञाविधानम्। स्वरान्तःस्थादिषु संख्यासंज्ञानिषेधार्थम्।[४]

ऊष्मविसर्जनीयप्रथमद्वितीया अघोषाः॥१२॥

एते अघोषसंज्ञकास्स्युः।

---

१. MS A/D वर्णसमाम्नाये आद्याः षोडशवर्णाः स्वरसंज्ञकाः स्युः। आवन्ता इत्यर्थः।

२. MS A/D एतत्।

३. MS A/D add अत्र आद्या इति शब्दान्तरोऽर्थान्तरसूचकः। व्यञ्जनेषु आद्या इति।

४. MS A/D प्रतिषेधार्थम्।

न हकारः॥१३॥

स्पष्टम्।

व्यञ्जनशेषो घोषवान्॥१४॥

अघोषेभ्यो व्यञ्जनशेषो घोषवत् संज्ञस्स्यात्। उक्तेषु अघोषेषु[१] शेषस्य घोषवत्वं सिद्धम्। तथाप्यत्र[२] व्यवहारार्थं संज्ञा क्रियते। शेषादपि कण्ठोक्तेर्विशेषात्। अन्यथा हकारव्यञ्जनशेषस्वरा अपि न घोषवन्तो नाप्यघोषाः। तथा सति घोषवदिति यत्र वक्ष्यति तत्र सन्देहस्स्यात् घोषवन्नाम किमिति। तन्निराकरणायेदं सूत्रमारभ्यते।[३]

आप्रावोपाभ्यधिप्रतिपरिविनीत्युपसर्गाः॥१५॥

एते उपसर्गसंज्ञकास्स्युः। यजुर्वेदविषये एतावन्त एवेतीतिशब्दो नियामकः।

वर्णः कारोत्तरो वर्णाख्या॥१६॥

कारोत्तरो वर्णः वर्णस्याख्या भवति। समासोऽत्र बहुव्रीहिः।

अकारव्यवेतो व्यञ्जनानाम्॥१७॥

पूर्ववत्। व्यवहित इति विशेषः।

न विसर्जनीय जिह्वामूलीयोपध्मानीयानुस्वारनासिक्यानाम्॥१८॥

एषां कारोत्तरत्वं प्राप्तमनेन निवर्त्यते।[४] अत एव ज्ञापनादेतेषां वाचकात्कार-प्रत्ययः। अन्येषां तु वाच्यादेव।

एफस्तु रस्य॥१९॥

रस्य तु एफशब्दाख्या भवति। तु शब्दः कारोत्तरत्वमकारव्यवेतत्वं च निवर्तयतीति[५] भाष्ये।[६]

---

१. MS A/D यद्यपि ऊष्मादिषु अघोषूक्तेषु........

२. MS A/D add यथा उभयोर्मध्ये 'अयं बुधः' इत्युक्तेभ्योऽबुध इति सिद्ध.......

३. MS A/D add व्यञ्जनरूपः शेषः।

४. MS A/D निर्वर्त्यते

५. MS A/D निवारयति

६. MS A/D भाष्यकारेणोक्तम्।

ह्रस्वो वर्णोत्तरस्त्रयाणाम्॥२०॥

वर्णोत्तरो ह्रस्वो ह्रस्वादीनामाख्या भवति।

अकारो व्यञ्जनानाम्॥२१॥

व्यञ्जनानामकार आख्या भवति। 'शचछपर[१]' तैप्रा (५.२२) इत्यादि।[२]

ग्रहणस्य च॥२२॥

निमित्तिनं निमित्तं च ग्रहणमित्युच्यते। ग्रहणस्याकार आख्या भवति।[३] निमित्तिनो यथा–'किꣳशिल किꣳशिलं' (तैप्रा., ६.२५) निमित्तस्य यथा– 'जपरो जकारम्' (तैप्रा ५.२३) इत्यादि।

अःकार आगमविकारिलोपिनाम्॥२३॥

एषामःकार[४] आख्या भवति। अःकार[५] इति प्रथमाविभक्तेरुपलक्षणम्। आगमादीनां यथा–'त्रपुमिथुपूर्वः शकारश्चपरः' (तैप्रा. ५.४) अथ नकारो णकारम (तैप्रा. ७.१)॥[६] ईम्पूर्वो मकारः (तैप्रा. ५.१२)॥ अःकार इति निर्देशात् (तैप्रा. ५.१२) वर्णद्वयादपि[७] क्वचित्कारप्रत्ययो भवति। तेनान्कार इत्यादीनां सिद्धिः।

ग्रहणं वा॥२४॥

तेषाम् अःकारेण विनापि क्वचिद्ग्रहणं वा भवति।[८] यथा 'आदिरꣳहतिः[९] (तैप्रा. १६.२९)।

---

१. All mss read च छ प र. However, I have emended it as given above as per the actual rule of the *TPr* and the same quoted in other commentaries.

२. MS A/D add : अनया संज्ञया व्यञ्जनमात्रस्यैवग्रहणं न तु स्वरसहितस्य। यवनहपरस्वरपरेष्विति ज्ञापनात्।

३. MS A/D add एष्टरेतन्निति [तैप्रा १०.१४] निमित्तम्। यथा 'अशीयेष्टः' [तैसं ९.२.११]

४. MS B अकार

५. MS A/D अकार

६. MS A/D omit the succeeding portion and add the example तिष्ठन्त्येकया सपूर्वः।

७. MS B वर्णयोः वेदेपि......

८. MS A/D read : तेषां क्वचिद्ग्रहणं वा भवति। अःकारेण विना।

९. MS B also adds हन्यादुप्यमानं च।

आसन्नः सन्देहे॥२५॥

सन्देहे सति आसन्नं पदं वर्णं वा गृह्णीयात्। आपृषतीत्यादि (तैप्रा ४.१५) अनासन्नत्वादत्र न। 'सारस्वत्यः पृषती'[१] (तैसं. ५.६.१२)

अनेकस्यापि॥२६॥

सन्देहे अनेकस्य पदस्य वर्णस्य वा ग्रहणं भवति। 'इमे एव रसेन'[२] (तैप्रा. ४.२४, तैसं. ६.३.११)

प्रथमो वर्गोत्तरो वर्गाख्या॥२७॥

वर्गशब्दोत्तरः प्रथमः वर्गस्य आख्या भवति।[३]

अं विकारस्य॥२८॥

अमिति विकारस्य आख्या भवति।

पूर्व इति पूर्वः॥२९॥

पूर्व इत्यनेन पूर्वस्यैव ग्रहणम्।

पर इत्युत्तरः॥३०॥

पर इत्यनेन उत्तरस्यैव ग्रहणम्।

ऋकारल्कारौ ह्रस्वौ॥३१॥

इमौ ह्रस्वसंज्ञौ भवतः।[४]

अकारश्च॥३२॥

ह्रस्वसंज्ञः।[५]

---

१. MS B सारत्यः पृषति।
MS A/D omit; add एव प्रतितिष्ठति बृहदुत्तरे (तैसं ७.१.४)

२. MS A/D omit this example and add 'तिष्ठन्त्येकया सपूर्वः' (तैप्रा. ५.९८)

३. MS A/D/E स्पष्टम्।

४. MS A/D स्तः

५. MS A/D पूर्ववत्

तेन च समानकालस्वरः॥३३॥

अकारेण तुल्यकालस्वरो[१] ह्रस्वः। इकारऽकारश्चेत्यर्थः। ऋकारल्कारयोः कालसन्देहात्तन्निराकरणार्थं ह्रस्वावित्युक्तम्।

अनुस्वारश्च॥३४॥

ह्रस्वसंज्ञस्स्यात्। ह्रस्वार्धमात्रानिराकरणार्थमिदम्।[२]

द्विस्तावान् दीर्घः॥३५॥

द्विरूपो ह्रस्वो दीर्घसंज्ञस्स्यात्। द्विगुण काल इत्यर्थः।

त्रिः प्लुतः॥३६॥

त्रिगुणकाल[३] इत्यर्थः।

ह्रस्वार्धकालं व्यञ्जनम्॥३७॥

व्यञ्जनमेव ह्रस्वार्धकालं भवति।

उच्चैरुदात्तः॥३८॥

नीचैरनुदात्तः॥३९॥

एतयोर्लक्षणमग्रे वक्ष्यते।

समाहारस्स्वरितः॥४०॥

उदात्तानुदात्तयोर्वर्णधर्मयोः समाहारो यत्र स स्वरितसंज्ञस्स्यात्।[४]

---

१. MS B/D/E तुल्यं कालस्वरो

२. MS E adds अत्र विशेषः।
MS A/D/E add मात्राद्विमात्रोऽनुस्वारो द्विमात्रान्मात्र एव तु।
मात्रिकादपि संयोगे मात्रिकस्तु द्विरूपवत्॥
उदाहरणानि–'सꣳशितं मे; ताꣳहस्ते सꣳश्रवाह,
स्वरोद्ये त्वनुस्वारो भवेदध्यणुमात्रिकः। व्याशि ४५३
MS E omits [विरामश्चेतयोर्मध्ये वैशेषिकाच्च दीर्घयोः।] व्याशि ४५४
अचिपरे पादाधिकमात्रिक इत्यर्थः।

३. MS E त्रिगुण इत्यर्थः।

४. MS B omits स

तस्यादिरुच्चैस्तरामुदात्तादनन्तरे यावदर्धꣳह्रस्वस्य॥४१॥

उदात्तादनन्तरे यः स्वरः स्वर्यते तस्यादिरुदात्ततरो भवति यावध्रस्वस्यार्धम्। यथा 'स इधानः' [तैसं. ४.४.४]

उदात्तसमश्शेषः॥४२॥

शेषः उदात्तसमो भवति। समशब्दयोगात्किञ्चिन्न्यूनत्वमस्ति।

सव्यञ्जनोऽपि॥४३॥

व्यञ्जनसहितस्योक्तविधिर्भवति। यथा–'वरिव': [तैसं. ३.३.११]

अनन्तरो वा नीचैस्तराम्॥४४॥

स्वारस्योत्तरार्धो नीचतरो भवति।

अनुदात्तसमो वा॥४५॥

उत्तरार्धो नीचसमो भवतीत्यन्ये।[१]

आदिरस्योदात्तसमः शेषोनुदात्तसमः इत्याचार्याः॥४६॥

द्वौ समौ इत्याचार्या ब्रुवते।[२] यथा–वरिवः [तैसं. ३.३.११] तस्यादि-रित्यारभ्यास्मिन्विकल्पजाले सूत्रमेतदेवेष्टं, न तूपरितनमिति भाष्यम्।[३]

सर्वः प्रवण इत्येके॥४७॥

प्रवणो नाम स्वारः।[४] सव्यञ्जन इत्यारभ्य सर्वः प्रवणो भवति इत्येके ऊचिरे। वरिवः [तैसं. ३.३.११]

नानापदवदीङ्ग्यमसंख्याने॥४८॥

नानापदवदित्यस्य द्विरावृत्तिर्ज्ञेया। नानापदमिव नानापदवत्। तदेव ईङ्ग्यसंज्ञं स्यात्। ईङ्ग्यं नानापदवद् भवति असंख्यानविषये।

तस्य पूर्वपदमवग्रहः॥४९॥

तस्येङ्ग्यस्य पूर्वपदमवग्रहसंज्ञं स्यात्। अनयोर्नियतलिङ्गत्वादन्योन्यान्वयः।

१. MS A/D omit इत्यन्ये।

२. MS A/D add स्पष्टम्।

३. MS A/D भाष्ये व्यवस्था।

४. MS A/D प्रवण स्वारपर्यायः।

पदग्रहणेषु पदं गम्येत॥५०॥

पदग्रहणेषु सूत्रेषु गृहीतं पदमेव ज्ञातव्यं, न पदैकदेशः। अत एव 'क्रत्वे' [तैसं. ३.२.५] इत्यत्र प्रग्रहो न।

अपि विकृतम्॥५१॥

पदग्रहणेषु विकृतमपि पदमवगन्तव्यम्।[१]

अप्यकारादि॥५२॥

पदग्रहणेषु अकाराद्यपि पदं विज्ञेयम्।

अन्कारादि च॥५३॥

पदग्रहणेषु अन्काराद्यपि पदं विज्ञेयम्।[२]

एकवर्णः पदमपृक्तः॥५४॥

एकावर्णात्मकं पदं तदपृक्तसंज्ञस्स्यात्। व्यञ्जनेनासंयुत इत्यर्थः।

आद्यन्तवच्च॥५५॥

अपृक्तसंज्ञकं पदम् आद्यन्तवच्च कार्यभाग्भवति। आदिवद्यथा–'स उ वि' (तैसं. ४.३.३) तस्यादिरुच्चैस्तरामिति कार्यं भवति। अन्तवद्यथा–'ओ ते यन्ति' (तैसं. १.४.३३) इत्यत्र प्रग्रहकार्यं न भवति।

वर्णस्य विकारलोपौ॥५६॥

वर्णस्य विकारलोपौ[३] न तु सर्वपदस्य। लोपस्य 'स ते' (तैसं. १.२. १४)

विनाशो लोपः॥५७॥

वर्णविनाशो लोपसंज्ञः।[४] वर्णनित्यतानिराकरणायेदमिति भाष्ये।

---

१. MS A/D add 'अयमुष्ये' त्यत्र [तैसं ३.५.११] षत्वमापन्नेऽपि विसर्गलोपस्स्यादेव।

२. MS A/D add अन्कारा इति ज्ञापनाद्वर्णद्वयादपि क्वचित्कारप्रत्ययो भवति। अःकारागमेप्यत्राप्येवं बोध्यम्।

३. MS A/D add स्याताम्।

४. MS B लोसंज्ञः।

अन्वादेशोऽन्त्यस्य॥५८॥

निमित्तिनो निमित्तस्य वान्त्यस्यान्वादेशः कर्तव्यः। अनिर्दिष्टौ विकारलोपौ अप्यन्त्यवर्णस्यैव। अनेनावग्रह[१]आशीर्धूरि (तैप्रा ५.१०) त्यादीनां सिद्धिः।

उपबन्धस्तु देशाय नित्यम्॥५९॥

उपबन्धस्तु स्वदेशायैव नित्यं निर्देशकः स्यात्। स त्रिविधः। अधिकरणरूपः संख्यानविषयो मर्यादारूपश्च प्रदेश उच्यते। 'सोमाय स्व' [तैप्रा ४.४८] इत्यादि पूर्वः। 'गमयतो भवत' [तैप्रा ४.५२] इत्युत्तरः। 'इरावती' [तैप्रा ४. २२] इति तदुत्तरः। उपबन्धे यदुक्तं तदन्यत्र न स्यादिति तु शब्दार्थः।[२] कण्ठोक्तिं विनाऽन्यनिषेधः उपबन्धे न भवति इति नित्यशब्दार्थः इति भाष्ये।

नानापदीयं च निमित्तं प्रग्रहस्त्रादिषु॥६०॥

नित्यशब्दस्यान्वादेशश्चकारः।[३] प्रग्रहेषु स्त्रादिषु च नानापदसम्बन्धिनिमित्तं प्रग्रहानुस्वारकार्यम् असंहितायामपि न निवर्तते। यथा 'अर्धमास इत्यर्धऽमासे' [तैपपा. २.५.६] नावग्रहपूर्व [तैप्रा १६.११] इति निषेधोऽत्र न।

यथोक्तं पुनरुक्तं त्रिपदप्रभृति त्रिपदप्रभृति॥६१॥

यत्र[४] पुनरुक्तं[५] तत्र यथोक्तं करोति।[६] 'दैवी' मित्यनुवाके 'त्वमग्न' [तैसं. १.३.१४] इति मन्त्रस्य पुनरुक्तत्वादलोपः। 'वाग्वा' इत्यनुवाके 'त्वमग्र' इत्यस्य मन्त्रस्य विनियोगत्वात् तत्रापि तथैव। मन्त्रभिन्नसामान्यपदानां पुनरुक्तत्वात् तत्र त्रिपदप्रभृति नाम चतुर्थपदस्य कार्यं भवति। यथा पञ्चमकाण्डे सप्तमप्रश्ने 'द्यौस्ते' इत्युनुवाके 'अन्तरिक्षꣳ समुद्रः समुद्रोऽन्तरिक्षमिति (तैसं. ४.१.२) भवति। अलोपश्च त्रिपदप्रभृतित्वात्। त्रिपदं प्रभृति यस्य तत् त्रिपदप्रभृति[७] पुनरुक्तं यतः पञ्चपदमित्युत्तरं च हि।

१. MS A/D तेन

२. MS A/D add... आह देवी ह्येषा। अत्र त्रिपदन्यायेन पूर्वजे प्रभृत्येति प्राप्तिः।

३. MS A/D चकारस्तु शब्दनिगदितम्।

४. MS A/D add त्रिपदं प्रभृतिर्यस्य तत्रिपदप्रभृति।

५. MS A/B/D त्रिपदप्रभृति

६. MS A/D add पूर्वोक्तविधिं

७. MS A/D omit दैवी.......त्रिपदप्रभृति।?

पूर्ववद्भवति ज्ञेयं सर्वत्रापि विचक्षणैः।। इति व्यासः।।[१]

इत्युत्तुरं ब्राह्मणवाक्यम्। तत्र न्यूनत्वेपि कार्यं भवति।

एदोद्भयां वक्ष्यते तच्च यदनेकपदे पुनः।
जटोच्यतेऽन्यशब्देन तत्रानैक्यं न विद्यते।।

इति व्यासवचनादन्ययुक्तं चेत्पूर्वधर्मो न विद्यते।। यथा–

वाज्यध्वनो अध्वनो वाज्यध्वनः।[२]

अध्वन आक्रम्या क्रम्याध्वनोऽध्वन आ क्रम्य। (तैसं. प्र.१.२)

भवत्यत्यग्रे भवति भवत्यग्रे।

अग्रे बृहन्बृहन्नग्रे अग्रे बृहन्निति (तैसं. ५.२.१) सर्वत्र। ऋक्षु ब्राह्मण[३]वाक्येषु त्रिपदमात्राद्वा कार्यं भवतीति वररुचिमाहिषेयात्रेयैरुक्तम्।। तथैव भाष्ये।

इति प्रातिशाख्यव्याख्यायां प्रथमोऽनुवाकः।

१. MS A/D add पुनरुक्तं यतः............इति व्यासशिक्षायाम्।

२. MS A/B/E/D do give accented text.

३. MS A/D ब्राह्मणेषु।

॥ द्वितीयोऽनुवाकः॥

अथ शब्दोत्पत्तिः॥१॥

अथ इत्यधिकारः। वर्णानामुपादानकारणं शब्दः। तदुत्पत्तिरुच्यत इत्यर्थः।

वायुशरीरसमीरणात् कण्ठोरसोः सन्धाने॥२॥

शरीरे वायुः वायुशरीरम्।[१] तस्य समीरणं तस्मात् कण्ठोरसोः सन्धाने मध्यदेशे शब्दोत्पत्तिर्भवति।

तस्य प्रातिश्रुत्कानि भवन्त्युरः कण्ठः शिरो मुखं नासिके इति॥३॥

प्रकृतभूतस्य शब्दस्यैतानि स्थानानि प्रातिश्रुत्कानि भवन्ति।[२] इतिशब्दात् श्रवणस्यापि ग्रहणम्। मुखे च श्रवणेपि चेति माहेश्वरवचनात्। अग्रे सूत्रत्रयेण शब्दत्रैविध्यमुच्यते।

संवृते कण्ठे नादः क्रियते॥४॥

सङ्कुचिते कण्ठे यः शब्दः क्रियते स नादसंज्ञस्स्यात्।

विवृते श्वासः॥५॥

विस्तार इति विशेषः।

मध्ये हकारः॥६॥

उक्तयोर्मध्ये यः शब्दः स हकारसंज्ञः।

---

१. MS B — वायुःशरीरम्।

२. MS A/D — omit इतिशब्दात्........वचनात्।

MS E — adds this portion in the margin most probably in different hand.

ताः वर्णप्रकृतयः॥७॥

नादश्वासहकाराः ताः वर्णप्रकृतयः स्युः। अत्रान्योन्यान्वयो नियतलिङ्गात्।[१]

नादोऽनुप्रदानं स्वरघोषवत्सु॥८॥

एषु नादो मूलकारणं[२] स्यात्।

हकारो हचतुर्थेषु॥९॥

हकारो मूलकारणमेषु वर्णेषु।

अघोषेषु श्वासः॥१०॥

एषु वर्णेषु श्वासो मूलकारणम्।

भूयान्प्रथमेभ्योऽन्येषु॥११॥

प्रथमेभ्योऽन्येषु अघोषेषु श्वासोऽधिको भवति।

अवर्णे नाप्युपसंहृतमोष्ठहनू नातिव्यस्तम्॥१२॥

अवर्णे उच्चार्यमाणे ओष्ठहनू अतिसंश्लिष्टमतिविवृतं च न भवति।

ओकारे च॥१३॥

हन्वित्यस्यान्वादेशकश्चकारः। ओकारे उच्चार्यमाणे हनू अतिव्यस्ते न भवतः।[३]

ओष्ठौ तूपसंहृततरौ॥१४॥

ओकारे कार्ये ओष्ठावुपसंहृततरौ स्याताम्। सव्यञ्जनस्योक्तविधिर्न इति 'तु' शब्दार्थ इति भाष्ये।

ईषत्प्रकृष्टावेकारे॥१५॥

एकारे कार्ये ओष्ठौ सन्निकृष्टौ स्याताम्।

---

१. MS A नियतालिङ्गात्।
MS D rubs out नियतालिङ्गात् and replaces it by नियतलिङ्गात्।
MS E rubs out महाभाष्यानुसारेण and writes नियतलिङ्गात्।

२. MS B कारणम्

३. MS A/D स्तः
MS E writes स्तः rubs out and replaces it by भवतः।

उपसंहततरे हनू॥१६॥

एकारे कार्ये हनू उपसंहततरे भवतः।

जिह्वामध्यान्ताभ्यां चोत्तराञ्जम्भ्यान्त्स्पर्शयति॥१७॥

एकारे कार्ये जिह्वामध्यान्ताभ्यां उत्तराञ्जम्भ्यान्त्स्पर्शयति।[१] स्पृशेदित्यर्थः। हनुमूलप्रदेशा जम्भ्याः। जिह्वायाः मध्यं जिह्वामूलस्य अन्तौ।

उपसंहततरे च जिह्वाग्रमृकारल्कारेषु बर्स्वेषूपसंहरति॥१८॥

एतेषु हनू उपसंहततरे भवतः। जिह्वाग्रं च दन्तपङ्क्तेरुपरि निक्षिपेत्।[२]

एकेषामनुस्वारः स्वरभक्त्याश्च॥१९॥

एतयोर्यथासंख्येन पूर्वसूत्रोक्तौ विधी भवतः इति एकेषाम्। अन्येषां तु पूर्वस्यानुनासिकमात्रम्। स्वरभक्तेर्ऋकारतुल्यत्वमिति वररुचिमतम्। तच्चिन्त्यमिति भाष्ये। इदं सूत्रम् अनिष्टम्।

अनादेशे प्रण्यस्ता जिह्वा॥२०॥

अनुपदेशविषये जिह्वा तूष्णींभूता भवति। अकारे[३] उच्चार्यमाणे अनुपदेश-विषय इति भाष्यम्।

अकारवदोष्ठौ॥२१॥

ओष्ठयोर्यत्रानादेशस्तत्राकारवत्। अकारे यथा तथा ओष्ठौ भवतः। नात्युपसंहततरौ इत्यर्थः यथा–'इन्द्र' (तैसं. १.४.१८) इति।

तालौ जिह्वामध्यमिवर्णे॥२२॥

इवर्णे कार्ये जिह्वामध्यं तालावुपसंहर्तव्यम्। यथा 'इषे त्वा' (तैसं. १.१.१)

एकारे च॥२३॥

एकारे कार्ये पूर्वविधिर्भवति।[४] सव्यञ्जनस्यैकारस्य विधिरयमिति भाष्ये।

---

१. MSD/E जम्भ्यान्स्पर्शयति।

२. MSE adds अत्र संधिरुच्चारणसामर्थ्यात्। (in the margin) and in the main text reads शाखान्तरे इति भाष्ये। and rubs out.

३. MS A/D अवर्णे
MS E rubs out वर्णे and replaces कारे.

४. MS B न भ.......

ओष्ठोपसंहार उवर्णे॥२४॥

ओष्ठोपसंहार भवति उवर्णे कार्ये। अत्रोपसंहारशब्देन सन्निकृष्टौ ओष्ठौ दीर्घौ स्यातामित्यर्थः। ओष्ठौत्विति सूत्रेऽप्येवमेव।

एकान्तरस्तु सर्वत्र प्रकृतात्॥२५॥

सर्वत्र ओष्ठ्यस्वरेषु एकमात्रान्तरश्चेत् प्रकृतात् ओष्ठ्योपसंहारात्पृथ-गोष्ठोपसंहारः कर्तव्यः। 'भुज्युः' (तैसं. ३.४.७)

तु शब्दः एकान्तरत्वनियमं निवर्तयति। अन्ये सन्तीति ज्ञापयति।

तथा हि–

मध्ये वेवाप्यनुस्वारे विरामे संयुते स्थिते।
अप्यौकारे परे व्यक्तौ द्विरोष्ठयाविति निश्चितौ॥
संयुतश्चोष्ठमध्ये हो विसर्गादुत्तरश्च पः।
तालुभ्यां वायुमापूर्य माण्डुक्योष्ठ इति स्मृतः॥

इति व्यासः। क्रमेण[१] उदाहरणानि–बभुवुः [ऋ. ७.८८.५]

यो ँ शुम् [तैसं. ३.३.४] सुऽउन्नीयम् [तैसं. ६.२.४] उभौ[२] [तैसं. ५.६.२] अथोषधीषु [तैसं. ३.५.५.] जुह्वो घृतेन, वायुः पूतः [तैसं. १.८. २७] इ.

स्पर्शयोः संयुते यत्र पाठे चावसरे यदि।
आदेरीषच्छ्रुतिर्ज्ञेया विरामे मस्य चैव हि।

'विरामे व्यञ्जनस्य चे' त्यन्ये वदन्ति।

विरामे वर्ग्यपूर्वस्य प्रयत्नः क्रियते पृथक्।
ओमः पवर्ग्यूर्ध्वे चेन्न प्रयत्नपृथक्त्वितीति व्यासः।

अवसाने वर्गपूर्वस्य पुनः प्रयत्नः कर्तव्यः। तत् [तैसं. १.१.१४] ते [तैसं. १.१.२] तम् [तैसं. १.१.४] प्रत्नथा [तैसं. १.४.९] रुक्-कामः [तैसं.२.२.३] प्रणवात्परपवर्गस्य पुनः प्रयत्नो न। प्रयत्नो नाम स्थानकरणसम्बन्धः। ॐ पूर्णौ। अत्र विशेषमाह शिक्षाकारः।

१. MS A/D omit क्रमेण.

२. MS A/D वुभौ

मकारान्तं पदं पूर्वं पवर्गः परतो यदि।
पुनः प्रयत्नः कर्तव्यो मकारो परतो न च।।

तम् मा [तैसं. १.४.४५] इत्यादि।

अकारार्धमैकारौकारयोरादिः।।२६।।

अनयोरादिः अकारार्धं भवति।

संवृतकरणतरमेकेषाम्।।२७।।

अकारार्धं संवृतकरणतरं भवतीत्येकेषां मते।[1] सन्निकृष्टानि करणानि यस्य।

इकारोध्यर्धः पूर्वस्य शेषः।।२८।।

पूर्वस्यैकारस्य शेषोऽध्यर्ध इकारो भवति।[2] अधिकम् अर्धं यस्य।

उकारस्तूत्तरस्य।।२९।।

औकारस्य शेषः अध्यर्धउकारो भवति। इकार निषेधकस्तु शब्द इति भाष्ये।

अनुस्वारोत्तमा अनुनासिकाः।।३०।।

एते अनुनासिकाः स्युः।

स्वराणां यत्रोपसंहारस्तत्स्थानम्।।३१।।

यत्रोपसंहारस्तत्स्थानं स्यात्स्वराणाम्। उपश्लेष इत्यर्थः।

यदुपसंहरति तत्करणम्।।३२।।

यदुपसंहरति तत्करणं[3] स्यात्स्वराणाम्।[4] जिह्वाग्रमृकारेत्यादि।

अन्येषां तु यत्र स्पर्शनं तत्स्थानम्।।३३।।

यत्र स्पर्शनं तत्स्थानं स्याद्व्यञ्जनानाम्।

येन स्पर्शयति तत्करणम्।।३४।।

अध्येता येन व्यञ्जनानि प्रापयति तत्करणं स्यात्।[5]

१. MS A/B/D/E omit मते।
२. MS A omits पूर्वस्यैकारस्य शेषो।
३. MS E कर
४. MS D यत्र स्वरानुपसंहरति प्रापयति तत्करणं स्यात् स्वराणाम्।
५. MS A भवति।

हनुमूले जिह्वामूलेन कवर्गे स्पर्शयति॥३५॥

कवर्गे उच्चार्यमाणे जिह्वामूले हनुमूले स्पर्शयति।[1] प्रापयेदित्यर्थः। जात्यपेक्षायामेकवचनम्।[2]

तालौ जिह्वामध्येन च वर्गे॥३६॥

च वर्गे जिह्वामध्येन तालौ स्पर्शयेत्।

जिह्वाग्रेण प्रतिवेष्ट्य मूर्धनि टवर्गे॥३७॥

टवर्गे जिह्वाग्रेण वक्त्रविवरोपरिभागे स्पर्शयेत्। जिह्वाग्रं प्रतिवेष्ट्येत्यर्थः।

जिह्वाग्रेण तवर्गे दन्तमूलेषु॥३८॥

तवर्गे उक्तवत्।

ओष्ठाभ्यां पवर्गे॥३९॥

ओष्ठाभ्याम् अन्योन्यं स्पर्शयेत्। अत्रोत्तरोष्ठस्थानम्। अन्यत्स्पष्टम्।

तालौ जिह्वामध्यान्ताभ्यां यकारे॥४०॥

उभाभ्यां तालौ स्पर्शयेत्। जिह्वामध्यस्य अन्तौ।

रेफे जिह्वाग्रमध्येन प्रत्यग्दन्तमूलेभ्यः॥४१॥

प्रत्यगित्याभ्यन्तरऽपरिभाग इत्यर्थः।

दन्तमूलेषु च लकारे॥४२॥

लकारे जिह्वाग्रमध्येन दन्तमूलेषु प्रत्यक्। अयमर्थः–लकारस्य दन्तमूल-प्रत्यासन्नं प्रत्यक्प्रदेशस्थानमिति विज्ञेयं स्पर्शयेत्।

ओष्ठान्ताभ्यां दन्तैर्वकारे॥४३॥

अधरोष्ठान्ताभ्याम् उत्तरदन्ताग्रैः सह स्पर्शयति। दन्तैरिति स्थाननिर्देशः।

स्पर्शस्थानेषूष्माणः आनुपूर्व्येण॥४४॥

ऊष्माणः यथाक्रमेण स्पर्शस्थानेषूच्चारणीया भवन्ति। यथा जिह्वामूलीयः कवर्गस्थाने। यः करोति, यश्च, अष्टौ, स्तनाः उपध्मानीयः–यः पाप्मना [तैसं. २.३.१३]। जिह्वामूलीयोपध्मानीययोः स्वरूपं तूक्तं माहेश्वरशिक्षायाम्–

---

१. MS B omits

२. MS A जात्या

जिह्वामूलीयो विसर्ग इव पूर्वः कखोर्ध्वयोः।
पफयोश्चोपध्मानीयोऽन्ते विसर्ग ह वै[१] स्मृतः।। इति।[२]

पञ्चसूष्मसूक्तेषु हकारविशिष्टस्य[३] विधिरुपर्याचष्टे।

करणमध्यं तु विवृतम्।।४५।।

तेषां करणमध्यं तु विवृतं भवति। स्पर्शकरणसाम्यनिवृत्तिपरस्तु शब्दः। करणानां मध्यम्।

कण्ठस्थानौ हकारविसर्जनीयौ।।४६।।

कण्ठः स्थानं ययोस्तौ।[४] अनयोः करणाभावः।

उदयस्वरादिसस्थानो हकार एकेषाम्।।४७।।

एकेषां मते हकार आत्मन उपरि स्वरादिसस्थानो भवतीति वररुचोक्तं स्यादेतत्। आदिना सस्थान इत्यर्थः। उदयस्वरादिशब्देन ऐकारौकारयोर्ग्रहणम्। अनयोरादिरकारस्य संवृत्तकरणतरत्वमस्ति। सामान्यस्य तु आरम्भे उक्तमेव अतः पौनरुक्तिर्न। पूर्वसूत्रेण करणाभाव इत्युक्तम्। अनेन तु करणविधानम्। इदं तु मतान्तरमेव।

पूर्वान्तसस्थानो विसर्जनीयः।।४८।।

विसर्गः[५] आत्मनः पूर्वान्तस्थानकरणो भवति। अत्रापि पूर्ववत्। तैः[६] [तैसं. १.७.५] द्यौः [तैसं. १.३.१४] पूर्वान्तेन सस्थानः।

नासिक्याः नासिकास्थानाः।।४९।।

यमाः नासिकास्थानाः भवन्ति। यथा 'रुक्मम्' [तैसं. ५.१.१०] इत्यादि।

---

१. MS B/C हवस्मृतः। MS E–हवत्स्मृतः।

२. MS A/D omit जिह्वामूलीय.....इति।

३. MS A हकारो विशिष्टस्य
MS D/E हकारोऽवशिष्टस्य

४. MS B/A/D/E कण्ठ एव स्थानं ययोस्तौ।

५. MS A विसर्जनीयः।

६. MS A gives different example बाहुवोः।

मुखनासिक्या वा॥५०॥

ते मुखानासिकाभ्याम् उच्चारणीया वा स्युः।

वर्गवच्चैषु॥५१॥

सिंहावलोकनेन करणस्यानुकर्षकश्चकारः। नासिक्येषु वर्गवत्करणं भवति।

नासिकाविवरणादानुनासिक्यम्॥५२॥

घ्राणबिलादानुनासिक्यं रङ्गादिकर्त्तव्यम्। तथा हि–

श्लोकां सुमङ्गलां यद्धां उपहूतां ममांप्लुताः।
दीर्घास्तां इमि देवां उ स्वां अहं ममृवां अवाः॥
पञ्चरङ्गा प्लुता दीर्घाश्चत्वारस्तैत्तिरीयके॥
तेषां अन्तेषु[१] नासिक्यं रङ्गसंज्ञमितीर्यते॥
रङ्गे[२] स्वरे च मात्रैका प्रत्येकं रङ्गदीर्घयोः।
रङ्गे स्वरे च द्वे मात्रे तथा तत्प्लुतरङ्गयोः॥[३]
रङ्गप्लुतश्चतुर्मात्र इत्युक्तो यजुषां मते। इत्यारण्यशिक्षायाम्।
दीर्घप्लुता यथा रङ्गास्युस्तथेति त्वयं विधिः।
एकार्धमात्रशेषास्युर्हृदये मूर्ध्नि नासिके॥[४] इति कालनिर्णये।

कांस्यध्वनिसमानश्च रङ्गसंज्ञ इतीर्यते।[५] इति माहेश्वरशिक्षायाम्।[६]

॥ इति प्रातिशाख्यव्याख्यायां द्वितीयोऽनुवाकः॥

---

१. MS A/B/C/D/F मतेषु

२. MS A/D/E रङ्गस्वरे

३. MS A/D/E add hereafter, न च दीर्घस्यैकमात्रत्वं प्लुतस्य द्विमात्रत्वं कथमिति न च वाच्यम्। दीर्घस्यैवरङ्गविशिष्ट आद्यांश एकमात्रः रङ्गविशिष्ट-द्वितीयांश एकमात्रश्चेति न दोषः। एवं रङ्गप्लुतस्य आदिरङ्गविशिष्ट आद्यांशो द्विमात्रो रङ्गविशिष्ट द्वितीयांशो द्विमात्र इति। एवं मितित्वा रङ्गप्लुतश्चतुर्मात्र इत्यर्थः।

४. MS A/D/E add hereafter, ऊष्मरेफः स्वरेभ्यः प्रागनुस्वारोस्ति नान्यथा।

५. MS A/D/E read कांस्यध्वनिसमं रङ्गं हृदयादुत्थितं वदेत्।

६. MS A/D/E omit

॥ तृतीयोऽनुवाकः॥

अथ आदौ उत्तरे विभागे ह्रस्वं व्यञ्जनपरः॥१॥

अथेत्यधिकारः। पदादौ वर्तमानः संहितायां यो दीर्घोसौ विभागसमये व्यञ्जनपरो ह्रस्वमाप्नोति। उत्तरे पदान्ते वर्तमानः। अन्यत्पूर्ववत्। ह्रस्वान्तर भावित्वाद्देवाशीकादिग्रहणे प्लुतादर्शनाच्च दीर्घस्यैवोपलब्धिः। पदादौ दीर्घस्य पूर्वपदेन विभागः। पदान्ते दीर्घस्य उत्तरपदेन विभागः।[१] विभागपदस्यायमर्थः इति भाष्यकारेणोक्तम्।

देवा-शीका-सुम्ना-वयुना-हृदया-घोक्था-शुद्धा॥२॥

एतेष्ववग्रहेष्वन्त्यस्वरो विभागे व्यञ्जनपरो[२] ह्रस्वमापद्यते। देव[३]-यते [तैसं, ३.५.५] शीक-यते [तैसं. ७.५.११]। सुम्न[४]-यन्तः [तैसं. १.५.११]। श्व-वित् [तैसं. ५.५.२०] अप्यकारादित्यनेन। अश्व-वती[५]। [तैसं. ४.२.६] ऋत-यवः। [तैसं. २.२.५] वयुन-वित् [तैसं. १.२.१३]। हृदय[६]-विधः। [तैसं. १.४. ४५] अघ-यवः [तैसं. १.२.९]।[७] उक्थ-मदानाम्[८] [तैसं. २.४.११] शुद्ध-युवः।[९] [तैसं. १.३.८]

१.	MS A/D	omit this sentence.
२.	MS C	व्यंजपरो
३.	MS A/D	reads these examples with lengthening and without अवग्रह *e.g.*, देवायते etc.
	MS B	देवा-यते
४.	MS B	सुम्ना-यन्तः
५.	MS A/D	अश्वावन्ती
६.	MS B	हृदया-विधः
७.	MS A/D	अघायवो मा
८.	MS A/D	उक्थामदानाम्
	MS B	सुक्था-मदानाम्
९.	MS B/C/E	शुद्ध-युवः।

इन्द्रा वद्वन्वान्परः॥३॥

वत्, वन् वान् एवं परः इन्द्राशब्दः। अन्यत् पूर्ववत्। इन्द्र-वतीम्[१] [तैसं. ५.७.४], इन्द्र-वन्तः [तैसं. ४.७.५४], इन्द्र-वान् [तैसं. १.१.१२]

चित्रा वपरः॥४॥

पूर्ववत्।[२] अत्र वकार एव परनिमित्तम्। चित्रावसो[३] [तैसं. १.५.५.]

प्रस्थेन्द्रिया द्रविणा विश्वदेव्या दीर्घा वीर्या विश्वा वाता त्वा भङ्गुरा कर्णका वृष्णिया सुगोपर्क्सामाऽघा सत्रा वर्षा पुष्पा मेघा प्रा स्वा॥५॥

पूर्ववद्वयञ्जनपरत्वम्।[४] प्रस्थऽवत्[५] [तैसं. ४.२.५] इन्द्रिय-वते [तैसं. २.२.७] द्रविण-वतः [तैसं. ५.३.११] विश्वदेव्य-वते [तैसं. १.४.१] दीर्घ-धियः [तैसं. २.१.११] वीर्य-वन्तम् [तैसं. १.२.७] विश्व-मित्रस्य [तैसं. ५.२.३] वात-वत् [तैसं. २.४.७] त्व-वतः [तैसं. २.२.१२] भङ्गुरवतः [तैसं. १.५.६] कर्णक-वती [तैसं. १.५.७] वृष्णिय-वतः [तैसं. ३.५.६] सुगोप-तमः [तैसं. ४.२.११] ऋक्साम-भ्याम् [तैसं. १.२.३] अघ-श्वात् [तैसं. ३.१.७] सत्र-जितम् [तैसं. ४.१.२] वर्षा-ह्वाम् [तैसं. २.४.१०] मेघ-यते [तैसं. ७.५.११][६] पुष्प-वतीः [तैसं. ४.१.४] प्र-वनेभिः [तैसं. ४.२.४] स्व-धियम् [तैसं. १.३.१४]

लोक एवेष्टा॥६॥

लोके एव इति एवं पूर्वः इष्टा अन्यत्पूर्ववत्। 'लोक इष्टापूर्तेन'[७] [तैसं. ३.३.८], एवेष्टा-पूर्ती [तैसं. १.७.३]

---

१. MS A/D read all these example with lengthened form and without अवग्रह।

२. MS A/B/D/E/F omit

३. MS A/B/C/D/E read चित्रावसो

४. MS A/B/D/E/F omit व्यञ्जनपरत्वम्।

५. MS B/C प्रस्थावते।
MS A/D/E reads all examples lengthened and without *avagraha*.

६. MS B omits मेघायते.

७. MS A/D एवेष्टापूर्ती

शक्ती रथी त्विषी वाशी रात्र्योषध्याहुती व्याहृती
स्वाहाकृती ह्रादुनी शची चिती श्रोणी पृष्टी
पूत्यभी[१] चर्षणी पारी शत्रू विषू वसू
अनू हनू सू विभू इत्यवग्रहः॥७॥

एतेष्ववग्रहेषु अन्यत् पूर्ववत्। शक्तीवन्तः [तैसं. ४.६.६] रथीतमौ [तैसं. ४.७.१५] त्विषीमते [तैसं. ४.५.२] वाशीमन्तः [तैसं. २.१.११]

रात्रीभिः[२] [तैसं. २.४.१] ओषधीभ्यो वेहतम् [तैसं. २.१.५] आहुतीभिः [तैसं. २.६.९] व्याहृतीभिः [तैसं. १.६.१०] स्वाहाकृतीभ्यः [तैसं. ६.३.९] ह्रादुनीभ्यः [तैसं. ७.४.१३] शचीभिः [तैसं. ४.२.५] चितीभ्याम् [तैसं. ५.७.५] श्रोणीभ्याम् [तैसं. ७.३.१६] पृष्टीभिः [तैसं. ५.७.१७] पूतीगन्धस्य[३] [तैसं. २.२.२] अभीवृतः [तैसं. ३.५.११] चर्षणीधृतः [तैसं. ३.४.११] परीणसम् [तैसं. २.२.१२] अधीवासम्[४] [तैसं. ४.६.११] पारीणह्यस्य [तैसं. ६.२.१] शत्रूयतः [तैसं. १.५.६] विषूवान् [तैसं. ७.४.३] वसूयुः [तैसं. ४.३.१३] अनूराधाः[५] [तैसं. ४.४.१०] अननुयाजम् [तैसं. ६.१.५] हनूभ्याम् [तैसं. ७.३.१६] सूयवसिनी [तैसं. १.२.१३] विभुदाव्ने [तैसं. ३.५.८]

अवा सचस्वा नुदा मृडा वर्धा शिक्षा रक्षाऽद्या
भवा भजा यत्रा चरा पिबा ना धामा धारया
धर्षा धा वर्धया बोधाऽत्रा तत्रा मुञ्चाऽश्वस्या
पृणस्वा हिष्ठ त्वंतरा जनिष्वा[६] युक्ष्वाच्छा॥८॥

एतेष्वनवग्रहेषु।[७] अन्यत्पूर्ववत्। अवा नः। सचस्वा नः। [तैसं. ४.१.४] प्रणुदानः [तैसं. ४.३.१२] मृडा जरित्रे [तैसं. ४.५.१०] वर्धा नः। [तैसं. २.६.११] शिक्षा नः। [तैसं. ७.५.७] रक्षा नः। [तैसं. ४.५.१०] अद्या देवान्।

१. MS D/E correct पूत्यभिचर्षणी as पूत्यभीचर्षणी of the *sūtra*.
२. MS F रात्रिभिः
३. MS D reads पूतिगन्धस्य
४. MS B,C,F omit अधीवासम्
५. MS B अनुराधाः
६. MS जनिष्ठा
७. MS A अनग्रहेषु

[तैसं. ४.६.७] भवा पायुः। [तैसं. १.२.१४] भजा त्वम् [तैसं. १.६.१२] यत्रा नरः [तैसं. ३.१.११] चरा सोमम्[२] [तैसं. १.२.१०] पिबा सोमम्[३] [तैसं. २.४.१४] नाह देभुः [तैसं. १.२.१४] धामा ह [तैसं. ३.१.११] धारया वसूनि [तैसं. १.३.७] धर्षा मानुषान् [तैसं. १.३.८] घा स्यालात् [तैसं. १.१.१४] वर्धया त्वम् [तैसं. ४.६.३] बोधा नः[४] [तैसं. ४.२.३] अत्रा ते [तैसं. ४.६.७] तत्रारथम् [तैसं. ४.६.६] मुञ्चा स्वस्तये [तैसं. ३.२.८] अश्वस्या विशस्ता [तैसं. ४.६.९] पृणस्वा घृतेन [तैसं. १.५.३] हि ष्ठा मयोभुवः [तैसं. ४.१.५] त्वन्तरा मृधः [तैसं. ४.१.९] जनिष्वा हि [तैसं. ४.१.३] युक्ष्वा हि [तैसं. २.६.१२] अच्छा नक्षि [तैसं. १.५.६]

अधाग्नियाज्ये॥९॥

समासोऽत्र द्वंद्वः। अग्निरित्यग्निप्रकाशमन्त्राः। चतुर्थकाण्ड इत्यर्थः। उभा-वारभ्याग्निर्वृत्राणिपर्यन्ताः[५] प्रश्नोत्तमानुवाकायाज्यासंज्ञकाः। युक्ष्वेत्युनवाकश्च। अत्राधा शब्दः। अन्यत्पूर्ववत्। अधाह्यग्ने [तैसं. ४.४.४] अधा च नः [तैसं. ४.५.१०]

कुत्रा दक्षिणेना स्वेना हन्तना जगामा रुहेमा विद्मध्यामा
चकृमा क्षामा स्तरीमा भरेमा वर्षयथेरयथाऽऽरिथा
पाथा ऽथा सिञ्चथा जनयथा जयतोक्षताऽवता
याता शृणुता कृणुता बिभृता॥१०॥

एषूक्तवत्। कुत्राचित् [तैसं. २.१.११] दक्षिणेना वसूनि [तैसं. ३.४.११] स्वेना हि [तैसं. ७.४.१५] हन्तनां तम् [तैसं. ४.३.१३] जगामा परस्याः [तैसं. १.६.१२] रुहेमा स्वस्तये [तैसं. १.५.११]

---

१. MS A/B/D/E चरा सोम

२. MS B/F omit पिबा सोमम्।

३. MS A बोधानं

४. MS A/D वृत्राण्यन्ताः

विद्या[१] ते [तैसं. ४.२.२] ऋध्यामा[२] ते [तैसं. ४.४.४.] चकृमाकत् [तैसं. ४.७.१५] क्षामा रेहिहत्[३] [तैसं. १.३.१४] सुष्टरीमा जुषाणा[४] [तैसं. ५.१.११] भरेमा मनीषाम् [तैसं. १.६.१२] वर्षयथा पुरीषिणः [तैसं. २.४.८] मरुतः [तैसं. २.४.८] उदारिथा यजे [तैसं. ४.६.५] पाथादिवः [तैसं. ४.२.११] अथा सोमस्य [तैसं. १.१.१४] सिञ्चथा मधु [तैसं. ३.१.११] जनयथा चनः [तैसं. ४.१.५] जयता नरः[५] [तैसं. ४.६.४] उक्षता मधुवर्णम् [तैसं. ४.३.१३] अवता हवेषु [तैसं. ४.६.४] याता हिरण्ययैः[६] [तैसं. ४.७.१२] शृणुता हवम् [तैसं. ४.२.११] कृणुता बृहत् [तैसं. ५.७.२] बिभृतासु [तैसं. ४.२.३]

भरता याज्यासु॥११॥

भरता बृहत्।

अत्ता भवताऽनदता तरता तपता जुहुता
वोचताऽमुञ्चता चृता घुष्या जनया वर्तया सादया
पारया दीया हरा भराऽपा ससादा सृजा तिष्ठा येना॥१२॥

पूर्ववत्। अत्ता हवीꣳषि। [तैसं. २.६.१२] भवता मृडयन्तः [तैसं. १.४.२२] अनदता हते [तैसं. ५.६.७] तरता रजाꣳसि [तैसं. ३.५.४] तपसा सुवृक्तिभिः [तैसं. १.६.१२] जहुता विश्वकर्मणे [तैसं. ४.६.२] वोचता मे [तैसं. ४.७.१४] अमुञ्चता यजत्राः [तैसं. ४.७.१५] चृता बन्धम् [तैसं. ४.२.५] 'घुष्या विशस्ता'[७] [तैसं. ४.६.९] जनया दैव्यम् [तैसं. ३.४.२] वर्तया [तैसं. ३.३.१०]

---

१. MS B/C/F omit
२. MS A ऋध्वामा
३. MS F corrects in the margin
४. MS C जुणा
५. MS B omits जयता नरः
६. MS E हिरण्यैः
७. MS A/B/D/E घुष्या विशस्तः

उश्मसी क्रयी कृधी श्रुधी यदी॥१३॥[१]

पूर्ववत्। 'उश्मसि गमध्यै' [तैसं. १.३.६] क्रयी परम् [तैसं. १.८.१४] कृधी सु [तैसं. ४.७.१५] श्रुधी हवम् [तैसं. २.१.११] यदी भूमिम् [तैसं. ४.६.२]

सू तू नू मिथू मक्षू ऊ॥१४॥

पूर्ववत्। सू नः [तैसं. १.८.३] आ तू नः [तैसं. १.५.११] नू रणे [तैसं. ४.६.१] मिथू कः [तैसं. ४.६.९] मक्षू देववतः [तैसं. १.८.२२] ऊ नू[२] [तैसं. १.४.३३] ऊ षूणः [तैसं. ४.९.४]

व्युत्पूर्व आननुदात्तोऽनूष्मवत्यनूष्मवति॥१५॥

विऽत्पूर्वो वा आननुदात्तः ऊष्मरहित इत्यर्थः। विऽअनाय [तैसं. ४.२.९] उत्-अनाय [तैसं. ४.२.९] व्युत्पूर्व इति किम्? यदानृचुः [तैसं. ७.३.१] आनितिकिम्?[३] व्याघारयति। [तैसं. ५.२.७][४] अनुदात्त इति किं? व्यानट् [तैसं. ४.२.१०] उदानय [तैसं. ६.५.८] अनूष्मवतीति[५] किम्? व्यानशुः [तैसं. ५.७.७] उदानिषु [तैसं. ५.६.७]

॥ इति प्रातिशाख्यव्याख्यायां तृतीयोऽनुवाकः॥

---

१. MS A/D read 13 & 14 *sūtras* together-omit from पूर्ववत्। उश्मसि .....यदी भूमिम्

२. MS A/D omit

३. MS A/D/E आनीति।

४. MS C/B omits उदादाय

५. All mss read अनूष्मवति किम्?

॥ अथ चतुर्थोऽनुवाकः॥

॥अथ प्रग्रहाः॥१॥

प्रग्रहा उच्यन्त इत्यधिकृत्य।[1]

नावग्रहः॥२॥

अयं प्रग्रहो न। 'ऊकारः' [तैप्रा. ४.५] 'ओकारोऽसाꣳहितः' [तैप्रा ४.६] इत्याद्युद्दिश्य पुरस्तादपवादोनेन विधीयते। 'तनूनप्त्र' [तैसं. १.२.१०] इत्यादिषु अन्तः प्रग्रहो[2] न।

अन्तः॥३॥

पदस्यान्तः प्रग्रहसंज्ञः[3] स्यात्। 'ऊकार' [तैप्रा ४.५] 'ओकारो साꣳहित' [तैप्रा. ४.६] इत्यादि सामान्योक्तौ सत्यां सन्देहप्राप्तिस्तन्निवारणार्थम् इदं सूत्रम्।

इतिपरोऽपि॥४॥

अपि शब्दः सिंहावलोकनेन 'अथादौ इत्यत्र विभागपदम् अन्वादिशति। सोयं प्रग्रहः विभागे इतिपरः स्यात्। यथाउभे इति [तैसं. १.४.२२] इतिपरो यस्मादिति। अत्र विशेषोस्ति।

प्रग्रहेऽङ्ग्योपसर्गान्ते इति स्यादप्यसांहिते।
पुनस्त्वेङ्ग्यं क्रमे चादिर्विरामस्थं द्विधैक्यतः॥

एषामन्ते[4] पदाध्ययने इति शब्दः प्रयुज्यते। यथा 'द्वे इति' [तैसं. १.६.८] प्रजा इति प्र-जाः' [तैसं. १.२.६], उपेति [तैसं. १.१.१३] प्रेति [तैसं. २.२.१२] ईङ्ग्यं पदं पुनरुक्तं स्यात्पदक्रमयोः। आदिरिति प्रग्रह इत्यर्थः।

---

१. MS A/D अथेत्ययमधिकारः। प्रग्रहा उच्यन्त इति।

२. MS F इ.षु अतः प्रग्र.......

३. MS C ...अन्त....प्रग्रह adds ग्र in the margin

४. MS A/B/C/D/E read एषां मते

अधस्तान्प्रग्रहेङ्ग्येति सहोच्चारितत्वात्। क्रमकाले प्रग्रहसंज्ञः शब्दः पुनरुक्तं स्यात्। 'ते एनम्' 'ते इति ते' विरामस्थमवसानस्थं पदं क्रमे द्विधा स्यात्। क्रमकालेऽर्धानुवाकयोरन्तं पदं च क्रमात् इति शब्दसहितं अतः[१] पुनरुक्तं च भवेदित्यर्थः। 'सविता धियः' [तैसं. ४.१.१] धिय इति धियः। पशून्पाहि [तैसं. १.१.१] पाहीति पाहि। क्रम इति किम्? रयीणाम् [तैसं. १.१.१४] ऐक्यतः प्रग्रहादीनामुक्तविशेषपदाभ्यां एकवदुच्चारणं स्यात्। उक्तान्येवोदाहरणानि। पुनस्त्वेङ्ग्यमित्यत्र[२] तु शब्दप्रयोगेण ईङ्ग्यस्य द्वितीयोच्चारणे अवग्रहान्ते विरामं कृत्वा तदीङ्ग्यान्तमुच्यते। [तैसं. २.३.१४] यथा 'ज्येष्ठराजमिति ज्येष्ठ-राजम्' [तैसं. ७.१.८] 'सूद्गातेति सु-उद्गाता'

नोपसर्गो विरामस्थो निहतश्च द्वयोरधः।
अवा न त्रिषुमध्यस्थोऽ वग्रहोपि[३] च न क्रमे॥

अत्रोपसर्गशब्द इतिपरो न स्यात् पदकालेऽपि। क्रमेण उदाहरणानि। 'मर्त्येषु। आ' [तैसं. १.१.१८] अव। दिवः। द्वयोः पूर्वः। 'आ। प्रेति। यच्छ। अव।[४] नः। त्रिषु मध्ये स्थितः। अन्विति। सं। प्रेति। आकूत्या इत्या कूत्यै [तैसं. १.२.२] क्रमकाले तु सर्वेप्युसर्गा इतिशब्दपरा न सम्भवेयुः। प्र सः। सोऽग्ने इत्यादि। ते कत्युपसर्गा इत्याशङ्क्याह–

प्रोपावापर्यधिव्युत्सुन्यन्वपाप्यत्यभि प्रति।
परा निस्सं नवदशाप्युपसर्गा स्युरत्रहि॥

प्र।उप।अव।आ।परि।अधि।वि।उत्।सु।नि।अनु।अप।अपि।अति।अधि।[५] प्रति।परा।निः।सम्।।११।। एतेषां त्वेतन्निमित्तेयं संज्ञा इति व्यासशिक्षाविवरणे प्रपञ्चितम्। एवमेव[६] माहेश्वरशिक्षायाम्

---

१. All MS read अधः, however since it does not fit in the context it is emended as अतः।

२. MS F reads ...मित्युत्र

३. MS F A/û omits ग्र and reads अवहो

४. MS F अविन

५. MS A/B/C/D/E read अधि. However it is already stated in the list. I have chosen reading of Ms F.

६. MS B reads only एवम्

सर्वोपसर्गे प्रग्रहेऽङ्ग्यान्ते स्यादित्यसंहिते।[१]
पुनरीङ्ग्यविरामश्चादौ तथा प्रग्रहः क्रमे।
इतियुक्तं विरामस्थं द्विधा नैवोपसर्गकः।
नीचोऽवानो विरामस्थस्तदित्यूर्ध्वे ग्रहे क्रम इति।

ऊकारः॥५॥

पदान्ते ऊकारः सर्वत्र प्रग्रहो भवति। यथा–हनू वैते [तैसं. ६.२.११]

ओकारोऽसांहितोऽकारव्यञ्जनपरः॥६॥

असांहित ओकारः प्रग्रहस्स्यादकारपरो[२] व्यञ्जनपरो वा। 'सूनो असि' [तैसं. १.३.१४] 'विष्णो हव्यम्' [तैसं. १.३.३] असांहित इति किम्? सोऽब्रवीत् [तैसं. २.१.२] अकारव्यञ्जने परे यस्मात्।

समहदथपित्पूर्वश्च॥७॥

एतत्पूर्व ओकारः। उक्तनिमित्ताभावेऽपि प्रग्रहस्स्यात्। 'सो एव'[३] [तैसं. २.२.९] मो एषाम् [तैसं. ४.५.१०] हो इत्याह [तैसं. २.६.७] इन्दो इति [तैसं. ६.५.८] तथो एव [तैसं. ३.४.९] पितो आ [तैसं. ५.७.२]

अथैकारेकारौ॥८॥

अथेत्यधिकारः। इमौ प्रग्रहत्वेन विधीयते। एतदधिकृतत्वम्।

अस्मे॥९॥

अन्त्यस्वरः प्रग्रहः। 'अस्मे ते' [तैसं. १.२.७]

त्वे इत्यनिङ्ग्यान्तः॥१०॥

त्वे क्रतुम्। [तैसं. ३.५.१०] अनिङ्ग्यान्त इति किम्? अनागास्त्वे [तैसं. २.१.११]

देवते उभे भागधे ऊर्ध्वे विशाखे शृङ्गे एने मेध्ये
तृण्णे तृद्ये कनीनिके पार्श्वे शिवे चोत्तमे एवोत्तरे

---

१. MS E असांहिते
२. MS A/D read after ओकारः–एव परः प्रग्रहस्स्यात्।
३. MS F reads सी एव

शिप्रे रथन्तरे वत्सरस्य रूपे विरूपे विषुरूपे सदोहविर्धाने अधिषवणे अहोरात्रे धृतव्रते स्तुत-शस्त्रे ऋक्सामे अक्ते अर्पिते रैवते पूर्ते प्रत्ते विधृते अनृते अच्छिद्रे बहुले पूर्वजे कृणुध्वꣳसदने॥११॥

उक्तानि प्रग्रहसंज्ञकानि। यथा 'देवते समृध्यै [तैसं. २.१.९] 'उभे एव' [तैसं. ४.४.४] भागधे भागधाः [तैसं. २.५.६] भागेति किम्? उदधे या [तैसं. ५.५.९] ऊर्ध्वे समिधौ [तैसं. २.६.६] विशाखे नक्षत्रम् [तैसं. ४.४.१०] शृङ्गे त्वम् [तैसं. ६.२.८] मेध्ये एवं[१] [तैसं. ६.२.९] असंतृण्णे हि [तैसं. ६.२.११] संतृद्ये धृत्यै [तैसं. ६.२.११] कनीनिके अग्निष्टोमौ [तैसं. ७.२.९] पार्श्वे भूयिष्ठः [तैसं. ७.३.१०][२] शिवे नः [तैसं. ४.६.६.] विकर्णी चोत्तमे [तैसं. ५.३.७] चेति किम्? उत्तमे मासि [तैसं. ७.५.३] तथो एवोत्तरे [तैसं. ३.४.९] एवेति किम्? उत्तरे[३] तेन [तैसं. ७.१.४] शिप्रे अवे पयः [तैसं. १.४.३०] यद्बृहद्रथन्तरे[४] [तैसं. ७.५.३]

एव[५] संवत्सरस्य रूपे [तैसं. ७.५.१][६] विरूपे धापयेते [तैसं. ४.१.१०] विषुरूपे अहनी [तैसं. ४.१.११] वत्सरस्य वि विष्विति किम्? आ रूपे अन्तम् [तैसं. ४.३.१३] सदोहविर्धाने एव [तैसं. २.५.५] अधिषवणे जिह्वा [तैसं. ६.४.११] अहोरात्रे गच्छ[७] [तैसं. १.३.११] धृतव्रते [तैसं. १.८.१२] आविन्ना [तैसं. १.८.१२] स्तुतशस्त्रे एव [तैसं. ५.६.८] ऋक्सामे वै [तैसं. ६.१.३] अक्ते वृषणम् [तैसं. १.३.७] अर्पिते [तैसं. ४.७.१३] उद्रोदत्त, शाक्वररैवते सामनि [तैसं. १.८.१३] इष्टापूर्ते सम् [तैसं. ४.७.१३]

---

१. MS A/D एवैने

२. MS A/D पार्श्वे परः

३. MS A/D षोडश्युत्तरे

MS C In the main body of the text reads उत्तरे ते न, and adds षोडशी in the margin in different hand.

४. MS A/D read रथन्तरे अन्वर्जेयुः

५. MS A/D omit एव

६. MS C/D/E/F omit

७. MS A/D read प्राविशन्

प्रत्ते कामम् [तैसं. ५.४.९] विधृते सर्वतः [तैसं. ६.४.१०] मध्ये सत्यानृते[१] [तैसं. ५.६.८] अच्छिद्रे बहुले [तैसं. ४.१.३] पूर्वजे पितरा [तैसं. ४.१.११] कृणुध्वꣳसदने [तैसं. ४.१.११] कृणुध्वमिति किम्? सदने सीद[२] [तैसं. ४.३.७]

अमी चक्षुषी कार्ष्णी देवता फल्गुनी मुष्टी धी
नाभी वपाश्रपणी अहनी जन्मनी सुम्निनी
सामनी वैष्णवी ऐक्षवी दर्वी द्यावापृथिवी॥१२॥

पूर्ववत्। अमी वैते [तैसं. ३.३.७] चक्षुषी वै [तैसं. २.६.२] कार्ष्णी उपानहौ [तैसं. ५.४.४.] देवता फल्गुनी[३] [तैसं. ४.४.१०]। देवतेति किम्? सा फल्गुनी यत् [तैसं. २.१.२] मुष्टी करोति [तैसं. ५.२.१] प्रधी तौ [तैसं. ७.४.११] रजतनाभी [तैसं. ५.५.२४] वप्राश्रपणी प्र [तैसं. ६.३.९] अहनी द्यौः [तैसं. ४.१.११] पासि जन्मनी [तैसं. १.४.१२] सुम्निनी सुम्ने [तैसं. १.१. १३] सामनी प्रतिष्ठित्यै [तैसं. ४.४.२]* दर्वी श्रीणिषे [तैसं. २.२.१२] द्यावा-पृथिवी एव [तैसं. २.१.४] द्यावेति किम्? अल्पा पृथिवी [तैसं. ३.३.१०]

पूर्वश्च॥१३॥

द्यावापृथिवी शब्दात्प्रग्रहस्स्यात्। यावती द्यावापृथिवी [तैसं. ३.२.६]

न रुन्धे नित्यम्॥१४॥

रुन्ध इति शब्दस्य न। नित्यशब्दोऽन्यनिषेधार्थः। रुन्धे द्यावापृथिवी[४] [तैसं. ६.४.१] रुन्धे यदा [तैसं. २.१.५]

हरी सहुरी सहूती कल्पयन्ती आपृषती आहुती॥१५॥

पूर्ववत्। हरी ते [तैसं. ४.६.९] सहुरी सपर्यात् [तैसं. ४.२.११] सहूती

१. MS A/D read सत्यानृते अवपश्यन्
२. MS A/D अपां त्वा सदने
३. MS A/D read पितरो देवताफल्गुनी
४. MS A/D रुन्धे द्यावापृथिवीम्

* वैष्णवी बृहन् (तैसं. ७.३.२) रेक्षवी विश्ची (तैसं. ६.२.९)

वनतम् [तैसं. २.३.१४] कल्पयन्ती ऊर्ध्वम् [तैसं. १.२.१३] युञ्जापृषती [तैसं. ४.६.९][१] आपृषतीति किम्? पृषती स्थूलपृषती [तैसं. ५.६.१२][२]

पूर्वश्च॥१६॥

आहुती शब्दात्पूर्वः। एते आहुती [तैसं. १.५.२]

वाससी तपसी रोदसी॥१७॥

एतान्युक्तसंज्ञानि स्युः। वाससी इव [तैसं. १.५.१०] दीक्षातपसी प्र[३] [तैसं. ६.१.१] रोदसी तयोः [तैसं. ५.५.१]

परश्च॥१८॥

रोदसी शब्दात्परः। रोदसी वावशाने [तैसं. १.७.१३]

व्यचस्वती भरिष्यन्ती नः पृथिवी॥१९॥

व्यचस्वती सम् [तैसं. ४.१.३] अन्तर्भरिष्यन्ती [तैसं. ४.१.३] नः पृथिवी इमम् [तैसं. ४.१.११]

ये अप्रथेतामुर्वी ते अस्य यं क्रन्दसी छन्दस्वती ते आचरन्ती अन्तरैतासु॥२०॥

एतास्वृक्षु। उक्तविधिस्स्यात्।[४] ये अप्रथेताममितेभिः [तैसं. ४.७.१५] उर्वी रोदसी वरिवः [तैसं. ४.७.१५] ते अस्य योषणे [तैसं. ४.१.८] यं क्रन्दसी अवसा [तैसं. ४.१.८] छन्दस्वती उषसा [तैसं. ४.३.१९] ते आचरन्ती समनाः [तैसं. ४.६.६] अन्तरा मित्रावरुणा चरन्ति [तैसं. ५.१.११]

नोपस्थे॥२१॥

पूर्वसूत्रस्थ 'उपस्थ' इत्यस्योक्तविधिर्न। बिभृतामुपस्थे [तैसं. ४.६.६]

इरावती प्रभृत्या दाधार॥२२॥

इरावतीत्यारभ्य दाधारान्तं प्रग्रहस्स्यात्। इरावती [तैसं. १.२.१३] धेनुमती [तैसं. १.२.१३]

---

१. MS A/D omit आपृषती.....स्थूलपृषती.....

२. MS A/D add एते आहुती

३. MS A/D/E/F omit प्र

४. MS A/D omit

पूर्वजप्रभृत्यायम्॥२३॥

पूर्वजे प्रभृति अयं पर्यन्तं प्रग्रहस्स्यात्। पूर्वजे ऋतावरी [तैसं. २.६.७] 'पूर्वश्चासौ जे च पूर्वजे' इति विग्रहो भाष्यकारेणोक्तः।

इमे गर्भमुपैव रसेन परः॥२४॥

इमे अयं प्रग्रहस्स्यादेतत्परः।[१] इमे गर्भम्[२] [तैसं. ३.४.३] इमे उपावत्स्र्यतः[३] [तैसं. ६.१.३] इमे एव रसेन [तैसं. ६.३.११]

क्रूरमापस्सजूर्ब्रह्मजैतेषु च॥२५॥

एतेष्वनुवाकेषु 'इमे'[४] शब्दः प्रग्रहस्स्यान्निमित्तं[५] विना। 'इमे वै रोदसी' [तैसं. ५.१.५] 'इमे एवोपधत्ते'[६] [तैसं. ५.५.४] 'इमे अश्विना संवत्सरः' [तैसं. ५.६.४] न हि मे यजुषाप्तुम् [तैसं. ५.२.७][७]

पूर्णे च॥२६॥

'ब्रह्म जज्ञानम्' इति अनुवाके पूर्णे प्रग्रहस्स्यात्।[८] 'पूर्णे एवैनम्' [तैसं. ५.२.७]

दृढे॥२७॥

अयं प्रग्रहे निमित्तं विना। 'पृथिवी च दृढे [तैसं. ४.१.८]

घ्नी चक्रे पपरे॥२८॥

इमौ प्रग्रहौ स्तः। पपरे। वार्तघ्नी पूर्णमासे [तैसं. २.५.२] चक्रे पृष्ठानि [तैसं. ६.६.८]

न्वती[९]॥२९॥

ओमन्वती ते [तैसं. २.६.९]

---

१. MS F reads एते परः

२. MS A/D इमे गर्भः।

३. MS B/C/E/F read उपवत्स्र्यतः।

४. MS A/D add इति

५. MS B/F read प्रग्र

६. MS F read धते

७. MS A/D add जेति किम्? ब्रह्मवादिनः।

८. MS F read प्रगस्स्यात्......

९. MS B/C/E/F omit ओमन्वती ते

पपरो न॥३०॥

अयं प्रग्रहस्स्यात्। पपरो न। मूर्धन्वती पुरोनुवाक्या। [तैसं. २.६.२]

समीची॥३१॥ न परो न॥३२॥

अयं प्रग्रहस्स्यान्नपरो न। समीचीनामासि।

ची यत्प्रपरः॥३३॥

प्राची प्रेतम्। [तैसं. १.२.१३] तिरश्ची यत् [तैसं. ६.२.१]

आन्मही॥३४॥

आन्पूर्वो मही प्रग्रहस्स्यात्। महान्मही [तैसं. २.३.१४] आनिति[१] किम्? मही[२] द्यौः [तैसं. ३.३.१०]

पती श्रुतिः॥३५॥

पतीत्यस्य यत्र यत्र श्रवणं तत्र प्रग्रहः। द्वौपती [तैसं. ६.६.४] दम्पतीवामम् [तैसं. ३.२.८]

ग्नी॥३६॥ न हिपरः॥३७॥

'ग्नी' प्रग्रहस्स्याद्धिपरो[३] न। 'ऐन्द्राग्नी हि' [तैसं. ५.५.६]

वीड्द्वारौकृष्णश्चरावो यदापरः॥३८॥

एवं परः प्रग्रहस्स्यात्। सती वीडयेथाम् [तैसं. ७.४.७] देवी द्वारौ [तैसं. ३.२.४] अतिष्ठमाने कृष्णः [तैसं. ६.१.३] ये चरावः [तैसं. १.५.१०] नन्नमाने [तैसं. ४.६.२] द्वारौ[४] [तैसं. ३.२.४] यदा विना सर्वाणि हलन्तानि।

न ज्ञे अह्ने नित्यम्॥३९॥

एतयोः प्रग्रहो न। राज्ञे कृष्णः [तैसं. ५.५.११] एप्यह्ने[५] कृष्णः [तैसं. ७.५.१०] नित्यशब्दः प्राप्त्यन्तरप्रतिषेधकः[६] गमयतः [तैप्रा ४.५२] सोमाय स्वेत्यादिना [तैप्रा ४.४८] प्राप्तिः।

१. MS A/D omit from आनिति......द्यौः।

२. MS F महीं

३. MS F omits ह

४. MS A/D द्वारौ विना यदा.....

५. MS A/D अह्ले....

६. MS C प्राप्त्यन्तरप्रतिनिषेधकः

आकारएकारपूर्वस्तु बहुस्वरस्य ते थे॥४०॥

ते थे इत्येतयोः प्रग्रहस्स्यादुक्तनिमित्ते सति। यथा 'मृजाते[१] यः' [तैसं. २.२.६] 'मन्थिनौ गृह्येते [तैसं. ६.४.१०] रिरिचाथे [तैसं. ४.२.११] बहुस्वरस्येति किम्? 'तत्प्रवाते[२] [तैसं. ६.४.७] व्रीडादिनिमित्तसापेक्षता[३]निवर्तकस्तु शब्द इति भाष्ये।

न शार्याते॥४१॥

अयं प्रग्रहो न। पूर्वसूत्रेण प्राप्तः। शार्याते[४] अपिबः [तैसं. १.४.१८]

ते मा पातं नम एनमभि वायुर्भमुपाहस्तु परः॥४२॥[५]

ते इत्यस्य प्रग्रहस्यादेषु परेषु।[६] ते मापातम् [तैसं. १.२.२] ते [तैसं. ३.२.४] नमोऽग्नये [तैसं. १.५.१०] ते एनमभि [तैसं. २.५.६] ते वायुर्व्यवात् [तैसं. ३.४.३] ते गर्भमदधाताम् [तैसं. ३.४.३] ते उपामन्त्रयत [तैसं. ६.१.३] ते अहोरात्रयोः [तैसं. ६.१.३][७] इति ते त्वाव नोत्सृज्ये [तैसं. ७.५.७]

अनुदात्तो न नित्यम्॥४३॥

अनुदात्तश्चेत्प्रग्रहो न। उत ते नमः [तैसं. ४.५.१] नित्यशब्दः प्राप्त्यन्तर-निषेधकः।[८] नमस्ते अस्त्वायुधाय [तैसं. ४.५.१]

एते तनु वौ वै समे व हि यज्ञपदिष्टक्परः॥४४॥

द्विपदमेकम्। त्रीण्यन्तानि पदांशानि। प्रग्रहस्यादेषु परेषु। एते तनुवौ [तैसं. ५.७.३] एते वै संवत्सरस्य [तैसं. २.५.३] एते एव नमस्यन्[९] [तैसं. २.५.६] एते हि देवानाम् [तैसं. २.५.६] एते यज्ञस्य [तैसं. २.६.२] एते पदे [तैसं. ५.१.६] एते इष्टके [तैसं. ५.३.५]

---

१. All mss except C do not show accentuation.

२. All mss except C do not show accentuation.

३. MS A/D read साक्षेपता

४. MS F reads शार्वाते

५. MS F reads न शार्याते after this sūtra and rulus out.

६. MS A/D omit यथा

७. MS A/D read ते त्वाव

८. MS A/D ते अस्त्वायुधाय   ९. MS F तपस्यन्

परश्च द्वयोः॥४५॥

पत् इष्टक् एतयोः परः उक्तस्वरः प्रग्रहो भवति एते इति शब्दपूर्वे[१] सति। एते पदे [तैसं. ५.९.६] एते इष्टके [तैसं. ५.३.५]

स्थः परः॥४६॥

समासोऽत्र बहुव्रीहिः। श्जप्त्रे स्थः [तैसं. ७.२.१३]

परश्चोभयोः॥४७॥

निमित्तनिमित्तिनोः पर इत्यर्थः। 'शिल्पे स्थस्ते' [तैसं. १.२.२] उभयोरिति किम्? वृषणौ स्थ उर्वशी [तैसं. १.३.७] शब्दान्तरत्वेनार्थान्तरत्वम्।

सोमाय स्वैतस्मिन्॥४८॥

सोमाय स्वेत्यनुवाके प्रग्रहस्स्यात्[२] 'अवी द्वे धेनू' [तैसं. ५.६.२१] इत्यादि।

द्वे॥४९॥

प्रग्रहस्स्यात्। 'द्वे द्वे सम्' [तैसं. १.६.८]

परश्च॥५०॥

द्वे इत्यस्मात् परः प्रग्रहः। द्वे शुक्ले [तैसं. ५.३.१]

एकव्यवेतोऽपि॥५१॥

एकपदेन व्यवहित इत्यर्थः। द्वे वाव देवसत्रे [तैसं. ७.४.५]

गमयतो भवतोऽनूकारात्परं तनू यदकरोत् कुर्यादिष्टिष्वब्रूतां प्रवर्तास्ताꣳस्तभ्नीतां वाचयति बिभृतस्ताग्निं गायत्रं ताभ्यामेवोभाभ्यामवान्तरं पर आषष्ठात्॥५२॥

[३]अनूकारात्परं[४] भवतः। इष्टिषु कुर्यात्। इष्टिरूपाः दशमादयस्त्रयः प्रश्नाः। एवं परे आषष्ठात्पदात् पूर्वः प्रग्रहस्स्यात्। आङभिविधौ ते न सहेत्यभिविधिः। 'ते एवैनं प्रतिष्ठां गमयतः [तैसं. २.५.१२] 'उत्तरावती भवतः' [तैसं. ५.४.८]

१. MS F शब्दे पूर्वे

२. MS F प्रग्रहास्स्युः।

३. Ms A/D add अत्र नवपदं विना द्विपदग्रहणम्। MS C adds it with different hand in the margin

४. MS A पदं

अनूकारात्परमिति किम्? दीक्षन्तेऽन्तनामानावृत्[1] भवतः [तैसं. ७.४.८] एते वै महायज्ञस्यान्त्ये तनू यत् [तैसं. २.२.७] 'बुध्नवती अग्रवती याज्यानुवाक्ये अकरोत् [तैसं. २.३.४] मानवी ऋचौ धाय्ये कुर्यात् [तैसं. २.२.१०] ते ऽब्रूताम् [तैसं. २.५.२] हविर्धाने प्राची प्रवर्तयेयुः' [तैसं. ३.१.३] 'इमे वै सहास्ताम् [तैसं. ३.४.३] वैश्वदेवाग्निमारुते उक्थे अव्यथयन्ती स्तभ्नीताम् [तैसं. ४.४.२] उत्तमे औदुम्बरी वाचयति [तैसं. ५.१.१०] ते एव यजमानस्य रेतो बिभृतस्तस्मात् [तैसं. ५.६.८] एते दधाते ये अग्निं गायत्रम् [तैसं. ६.३.५] एते वै यज्ञस्याञ्जसायनीस्त्रुतीताभ्यामेव।[2] अत्र कुण्डलीदेवदत्तन्यायेन सिद्धिः।[3] अवयवधर्मेणेत्यर्थः। ये द्वे अहोरात्रे एव ते उभाभ्याम् [तैसं. ७.४.४.] उत्सृज्ये इत्याहुर्य[4] अवान्तरम्। [तैसं. ७.५.७]

न ग्रामी वर्चसी मिथुनी मासे लोके धत्ते॥५३॥

एते प्रग्रहा न स्युः। गमयत इत्यादिप्राप्तस्य[5] निषेधः।

'ग्राम्येव भवति' गणवती याज्यानुवाक्ये भवतः [तैसं. २.३.३] ब्रह्मवर्चस्येव भवत्युभयतो रुक्मौ भवतः [तैसं. २.३.२] अथ मिथुनी भवतः [तैसं. ६.५.८] पूर्णमासे प्रायच्छतावब्रूताम्।[6] [तैसं. २.५.२] लोके प्रतितिष्ठन्तो यन्ति द्वौ षडहौ भवतः [तैसं. ७.४.११] धत्ते ज्योतिष्मिन्तावस्मा इमौ लोकौ भवतः [तैसं. २.६.२]

अते समानपदे नित्यम् अवे चावे च॥५४॥

अनयोः पदैकदेशयोः गमयत इत्यादिपरोऽपि प्रग्रहो न। रुन्धतेऽतिरात्रावभितो भवतः [तैसं. ७.२.६] अनातताय धृष्णवे उभाभ्याम् [तैसं. ४.५.७] समानपद इति किम्? एव ते उभाभ्याम्[7] [तैसं. ७.४.४] नित्यशब्दः प्राप्त्यन्तरपरिहारार्थः। 'द्वे जाये विन्दते [तैसं. ६.६.४]

॥इति प्रातिशाख्यव्याख्यायां चतुर्थोऽनुवाकः॥

---

१. MS A न्वृतु
२. MS A/D स्क्र
३. MS C कुण्डलि.....सिधिः।
४. MS A/D ....स्याकु......
५. MS A/D omit
६. MS प्रायच्छनाव.....
७. MS F उभ्यांभो.......

॥ अथ पञ्चमोऽनुवाकः॥

अथ संहितायामेकप्राणभावे॥१॥

अथेत्यधिकारः। संहितायामेकप्राणभाव इत्यधिकृतं[1] वेदितव्यम्।[2] इत[3] उत्तरं यद्वक्ष्यामः। नानापदसंधानेति संहितार्थः। एकेन प्राणेन[4] उच्छ्वासेन उच्चार्यते वेदभागस्तावाने[5]कप्राणभाव इत्यर्थः। तस्मिन्। अत एव अवसाने पदविधिः। अत्र विशेषमाह—

नित्यं प्राक्पदसम्बन्धं चादिप्राक्पदमन्तरा।
परेण नित्यसम्बन्धं प्रादीन्परपदं तथा॥

इति कालनिर्णये। अस्यार्थः—चादीन्नित्यं पूर्वपदसम्बन्धं कुर्यात्। प्रादीनुत्तर-पदसम्बन्धं कुर्यात्। "कद्रूश्च वै [तैसं. ६.१.६] चात्वालाद्धिष्णियान् [तैसं. ६.३.१] उपवपति योनिर्वै[6] [तैसं. ६.३.१] इत्यादि। प्रादयस्तु प्रग्रहप्रकरणे उक्ताश्चादयस्त्वनन्ताः।[7] तथा च माहेश्वरशिक्षायाम्—"वक्ष्यते सोऽधुनैकौ नैच्छ्वा साभावे तु पदान्तवत्" इति।

यथायुक्ताद्विधिस्सा प्रकृतिः॥२॥

यथास्थितात्पदपाठात् कूटस्थाद कूटस्थादविचलितो यो विधिः सा प्रकृतिसंहिता विज्ञेया। प्रमा असि [तैसं. ४.४.१२] 'ज्या इयम्' [तैसं. ४.६.

---

१. MS F omits इ
२. MS F ...व्य
३. MS A/D omit इत
४. MS A/D omit प्राणेन
५. MS A वगदभावस्तावान्
MS F तवान्
६. MS A/D योनिर्वा
७. MS A/D omit तथा च........इति

६] अत्र परस्परान्वयो सूत्रनिर्देशात्।[१] एवं स्वरितयोर्मध्ये यत्र नीचमित्यादौ ज्ञेयम्। [तैप्रा १९.७]

तत्र पूर्वं पूर्वं प्रथमम्॥३॥

तत्र संहिताविधाने[२] पूर्वं सूत्र[३] पदं च प्रथमं कर्तव्यम्। यथा 'भक्ष।आ।इहि' [तैसं. ३.२.५] अत्र दीर्घादेशे कृते पश्चाद् एत्वे कृते भक्षेहि इति भवति। अन्यथा एत्वे कृते भक्षैहीति स्यात्तच्चानिष्टम्। पूर्वपदविषयमिदम्। 'षट् नवत्यै' [तैसं. ७.२.१५] अत्र णत्वे कृते पश्चाट्टकारस्य परसवर्णे कृते षण्णवत्या इति भवति। अन्यथा परसवर्णे कृते 'षणनवत्या' इति स्यात्। तन्निवृत्यर्थमिदम्। सर्वत्रायं न्यायः।[४]

त्रपुमिथुपूर्वः शकारश्चपरः॥४॥

एवं पूर्वः शकारागमस्स्याच्चपरः। 'त्रपुश्च मे' [तैसं. ४.७.५] 'मिथुश्चरन्तम्' [तैसं. ४.७.१७] एवं पूर्व एवं पर इति किम्? 'विभु च मे' [तैसं. ४.७.४] मिथू कः [तैसं. ४.६.९]

सुपूर्वश्च चन्द्रपरः॥५॥

पूर्ववत्। सुश्चन्द्र [तैसं. ४.४.४]

सम्पूर्वस्सकारः कुरुपरः[५]॥६॥

अत्र सकारागमः। संस्कुरुते' [तैसं. ५.६.६]

अकुर्व च प्रत्ययात्परः॥७॥

सम्पूर्वः सकारागमः स्यादकुर्वप्रत्ययात्परः। प्रत्ययो नाम अकार उच्यते।[६] 'त इषुंस्समस्कुर्वत' [तैसं. ६.२.३] प्रतीयते व्यञ्जनान्यनेनेति प्रत्ययः।

---

१. MS A/D सूत्रोच्चारणबलात्
२. MS F संहित विधाने
३. MS B पूर्वं पूर्वं सूत्रं विधिं च
पूर्वं पूर्वं पदं सूत्रं च
४. MS A/D अयं न्यायः सर्वत्रैव।
५. MS C omit रु
६. MS A/D read अभिव्यङ्ग्यते व्यञ्जनानि अनेन इति प्रत्ययः। तइषुंस्समस्कुर्वन।

नीचापूर्वोदिकार उच्चापरः॥८॥

दकारागमस्स्यात्। नीचादुच्चा [तैसं. २.३.१४]

असम्पूर्वोरमृकारः॥९॥

असम्पूर्वो[१] ऋकारः अरमा[२]पद्यते[३]। 'असमर्त्यैं' [तैसं. ३.३.८] अत्रैकपद[४] निमित्तं बोध्यम्।

अवग्रहआशीर्धूः सुवरिति रेफं परः सकारष्षकारम्॥१०॥

अवग्रहे आशीः धूः सुवः एषामवग्रहस्थानां विसर्गः[५] रेफम् आप्नोति। एभ्यः परः सकारश्चेत्षकारम्। 'आशीर्पदया' [तैसं. ६.२.९] धूर्षाहौ [तैसं. ७.२.८] सुवर्षाम् [तैसं. ४.४.४][६] कखपकारपराः [तैप्रा ८.२३] अघोषपरस्तस्येत्युभयोरपवादः।

अथ लोपः॥११॥

इत्याधिकृत्य। 'तिष्ठन्त्येकया' [तैप्रा ५.१९] इति सूत्रपर्यन्तोऽधिकारोऽयम्।

ईम्पूर्वो मकारः॥१२॥

ईमितिपदात् परो मो लुप्यते। ई मन्द्रासु [तैसं. ४.१.७] 'ग्रन्थान्तरेऽप्यनार्षे च यदृच्छा वर्तते' इति व्यासवचनात्। ब्राह्मणादिग्रन्थे यदृच्छा वर्तते।[७] 'स ई ममाद' [तैसं. ४.१.८] प्र नक्षत्राय[८] एके[९] महि साम मन्वत[१०] पूषꣳस्तव[११] अनार्षे[१२] च। अग्निष्टात्स्विष्टकृद्विद्वान्[१३] उशमसी पोषमित्यादि।[१४]

---

१. MS A/D एवं पूर्वो। २. MS B/C/E/F आरम्

३. MS A/D add विकारम् ४. MS A/D तत्रैकपदस्थं

५. MS A/D write अवग्रहेषु and correct in the margin as स्थानां

६. MS A/D add विसर्गोऽवग्रहेष्विति व्यासवचनात्।

७. MS A/D ग्रन्थान्तरे ब्राह्मणारण्यके।

८. MS A/D reads only प्रनक्ष

९. MS A/D adds before एके-अर्चन्त

१०. MS A/D omit मन्वत

११. MS A/D omit this example.

१२. MS A/D read अनार्षे सूत्रादिषु।

१३. MS A/D read अग्निष्टात् स्विष्टकृ

१४. MS A/D omit.

तु नु पूर्व उदात्तयोर्वकारः॥१३॥

उदात्तयोस्तुन्वोः सतोरिति विभज्य। तु पूर्वो नुपूर्वो वा वलोपस्यादव्ययस्थश्चेत्। 'चादीनामेव वो लोप' इति आत्रेयवचनाच्चादौ वश्चेति' व्यासवचनाच्च।[१] सत्वै [तैसं. २.६.६] इन्वै [तैसं. १.६.७] अव्ययस्थ[२] इति किम्? वाजस्य नु नु वाजस्य [तैसं. १.७.७]। वसतु नु नु वसत्वि[३]त्यादि [तैसं. ६.४.२]

उत्पूर्वस्सकारो व्यञ्जनपरः॥१४॥

उत्पूर्वः सकारो लुप्यते व्यञ्जनपरः। अत्र[४] लोपस्थास्तंभस्थश्चेत्। 'स्थास्तंभोरेव लोपः स'[५] इत्यात्रेयवचनात् 'स्थास्तंभोरेव[६] पूर्ब स' इति माहेश्वरवचनाच्च। एकमुत्थानम् [तैसं. ७.२.७] प्रत्युत्तब्ध्यै। स्थास्तंभश्च[७] इति किम्? स्वायुषोदुद्वायुषेति [तैसं. १.२.८] स्तोममुदुत्तोममिति [तैसं. १.७.११] च स्यात्।

एष स स्य इति च॥१५॥

व्यक्तिविषय इति शब्दः। एषां विसर्गो लुप्यते व्यञ्जनपरः।[८] एष ते [तैसं. ३.१.२] स ते [तैसं. १.२.१४] स्य वाजी [तैसं. १.७.८]

नासः॥१६॥

अप्यकारादिप्राप्तेर्निषेधः। 'हृत्स्वसो मयोभून्'[९] [तैसं. ४.२.११]

इद्विदग्न इमां न एनौषधीः परस्सः॥१७॥

एवं परः स इत्यत्र विसर्गो लुप्यते।[१०] सेदु [तैसं. १.१.१४] सेदग्ने

---

१. MS A/D व्यासवचनादव्ययस्थ त्वम्।

२. MS A/E omit अव्ययस्थ इति किम् etc.

३. MS B/C/D read वसन्वित्यादि।

४. MS A/D यत्र सलोपः

५. MS A/D add निमित्तेन यथा भवेत्।

६. MS A/D omit

७. MS A/D omit

८. MS A/D add श्चेत्। also add एषसस्य हलूर्ध्वे [हल्यूर्ध्वे?] च विसर्गो लुप्यते तथा। इत्यात्रेयवचनाद्विसर्ग एव नान्यः।

९. MS C मयोमभून्

१०. MS F लुप्येते

[तैसं. १.२.१४] सेमां[१] नः [तैसं. ४.६.६] द्विपदनिमित्तानीमानि। सैनाऽनीकेन [तैसं. ४.३.१३] सौषधीः [तैसं. ४.२.३]

अवग्रह इत्येकम्॥१८॥

इतिशब्दविशिष्ट एकमित्यवग्रहे मो लुप्यते। इत्येकैकं तस्य [तैसं. ५.८.१][२]

तिष्ठन्त्येकया सपूर्वः॥१९॥

'तिष्ठन्ति' शब्दविशिष्टएकयेत्यस्मिन्नन्त्यो वर्णः सपूर्वो लुप्यते। पूर्वेण[३] सह सपूर्वः। 'तिष्ठन्त्येकैकया' [तैसं. ७.५.८]

नकारः शकारं चपरः॥२०॥

नः शकारमापद्यते च परः।[४] अहीꣳश्च [तैसं. ४.५.७]

नायन्नैरयन्नाध्र्नुवन्ननड्वान्घृणीवान्वारुणानेवास्मिन्॥२१॥

पूर्वस्यापवादः। अन्यनिमित्तं द्विपदम्। 'आयन्चतस्रः' [तैसं. ५.२.३][५] ऐरयं चन्द्रमसि [तैसं. १.१.९] लोक आध्र्नुचरुणा [तैसं. ५.५.१] अनड्वां च मे धेनुः [तैसं. ४.७.१०] घृणीवां चेतति त्मना [तैसं. ३.५.११] वारुणां चतुष्कपालान् [तैसं. २.३.१२] एवास्मिन्चक्षुः [तैसं. २.२.९] द्विपदेन किम्?[६] आध्र्नुवं तस्मिꣳश्च।

तकारश्चकारꣳशचछपरः॥२२॥

शचछपरस्तकारश्चकारमापद्यते। तच्छंयोः [तैसं. २.६.१०] तच्चा ददुः [तैसं. ७.१.५] 'तच्छन्दसाम्' [तैसं. ५.५.६] स्पर्शपूर्वः।[७] शकारश्छकारमिति

---

१. MS F — सेमा नः।
२. MS A/D — add 'मश्चावग्रहइत्येकं या तिष्ठन्त्येकयोर्ध्वतः' व्यासः।
३. MS F — reads पूर्वे....
४. MS A/D — add चेत्
५. MS A/D — omit from ऐरयं....वारुणां चतुष्कपालान्।
६. MS C/E — add द्विपदेन किं etc. in the margin.
७. MS A/D — यदि
MS E — write यदि स्पर्शः etc, rubs it out and adds in the margin इत्यत्र....शकारग्रहणम्।

छत्वे कृते पश्चादस्य प्राप्तिरेव नास्ति। कुतः? पूर्वं पूर्वम् इति न्यायात्। अत एव सूत्रे शकारग्रहणम्।[१]

जपरो जकारम्॥२३॥

जपरस्तकारो जमापद्यते।[२] तज्जयानाम् [तैसं. ३.४.४]

नकार एतेषु ञकारम्॥२४॥

नकारो ञकारमापद्यते श च छ जे षु परेषु। एनाञ्छमयति [तैसं. ३.४.८] आयञ्चतस्र:[३] [तैसं. ५.२.३] ताञ्छन्दोभिः [तैसं. ७.५.९] आत्मञ्जायते [तैसं. ३.५.७]

लपरो लकारम्॥२५॥

लपरौ तनौ लकारमापद्यते। 'यल्लोहितम्' [तैसं. २.१.७] त्रींल्लोकान् [तैसं. १.७.७७]

नकारोऽनुनासिकम्॥२६॥

नकारो नाम तत्स्थानो लकार इत्यर्थः। सोऽनुनासिकं भजते। त्रीँल्लोकान् [तैसं. १.७.११]

मकारस्पर्शपरः तस्य सस्थानमनुनासिकम्॥२७॥

तस्य स्पर्शस्येत्यर्थः। 'यङ्काम (येत)' शञ्च [तैसं. ७.६.१०] 'तन्ते [तैसं. ३.२.७०] 'तम्प्र [त्लथा] [तैसं. ७.४.९]

ज्ञघ्नोत्तरो मकारश्चेदनुस्वारोऽत्र केवलः।

द्विमात्र इति विज्ञेयो ह्यन्यधर्मविवर्जितः॥ इति व्यासः। गकाररहित इत्यर्थः।[४] संज्ञानम् [तैसं. ४.२.४] तं घ्नन्ति [तैसं. २.१.११]

---

१. MS A/D omit

२. MS A/D अकारमाप्नोति।

३. MS D आपञ्चतस्र:

४. MS B is completed here.

अन्तस्थापरश्च सवर्णमनुनासिकम्॥२८॥

अन्तस्थापरो मकारः तस्याः सवर्णं सदृशमनुनासिकं भजते।[१] 'संयत्ताः [तैसं. १.५.१] सुवर्गं लोकम् [तैसं. १.५.४] संव्वत्सरः [तैसं. १.५.१]

विज्ञेया नित्यनासिक्या यमानुस्वारपञ्चमाः।
अजन्तस्था हकारश्च निमित्तेन तु कीर्तिताः॥ इति व्यासवचनात्।
यमोन्त्यानुस्वाराणां[२] सास्यनासास्थानमुच्यते।
तदेव यलवहा चा निमित्तेन तु कीर्तितमिति माहेश्वरवचनाच्च।

न रेफपरः॥२९॥

पूर्वप्राप्तस्य निषेधः। साम्राज्याय [तैसं. १.८.१६]

य वकारपरश्चैकेषामाचार्याणाम्॥३०॥

यपरो वपरो मकारः उक्तं[३] न भजत इत्येकेषाम्।[४] संयताः [तैसं. १.५.१]

उत्तमलभावात्पूर्वो ऽनुनासिक इत्यात्रेयः॥३१॥

नस्य मस्य च लभावात् पूर्वस्वरोऽनुनासिको भवतीत्यात्रेयो मन्यते। सूत्र-द्वयमनिष्टम्।

ङपूर्वः ककारः सषकारपरः॥३२॥

ङपूर्वः ककारागमः स्यात्सपरो वा षपरो वा।

प्रत्यङ्क्[५] सोमः [तैसं. १.८.२७] 'प्रत्यङ्क् षडहः'[६] [तैसं. ७.४.२]

---

१. MS A/D — read as follows : संयत्ता, सुवर्गं लोकम् [१.५.४] संष्वत्सरः [१.५.१] आसामानुनासिकत्वं कथम्? धर्मवाचकः शब्दः धर्मिणं कथयति। शुक्लं पटः इत्यादिवत्। अन्यदपि-विज्ञेया कीर्तिता। इति व्यासवचनात्। अनुनासिकाननुनासिकभेदेन यवला द्विधा इति व्याकरणे।

MS E — reads the text as given in the main body in the margin.

२. MS A/D — omit

३. MS A — reads युक्तं   ४. MS A/D omit मतम्।

५. MS A/D — read प्रत्यङ्ख in both the examples.

६. MS D — reads क्षडहः

टनकारपूर्वश्च तकारः॥३३॥

टनपूर्वस्तकारागमः[१] सषपरः।[२] 'षट् त्सम्' (तैसं. ६.६.३) 'तान्त्सुब्धान्' [तैसं. २.४.१] कृत्वः[३] षट्त्षट् कृत्वः षष्ठे हन्न हन्त्षष्ठे[४]

स्पर्शपूर्वश्शकारश्छकारम्॥३४॥

स्पर्शपूर्वः शकारः छकारमापद्यते। 'तच्छयोः'[५] [तैसं. ४.३.२]

न मकारपूर्वः[६]॥३५॥

पूर्वस्यापवादः। 'सꣳशितम्' [तैसं. ४.७.७०]

पकारपूर्वश्च वाल्मीकेः[७]॥३६॥

पकार इति विशेषः। 'अनुष्टुप्शारदी' [तैसं. ४.३.२]

व्यञ्जनपरः पौष्करसादेर्न पूर्वश्च अकारम्॥३७॥

व्यञ्जनपरः शकारः स्पर्शपूर्वोऽपि छत्वं[८] नापद्यते। शात्पूर्वो नकारो अकारम् नापद्यते। 'पापीयान् श्रेयसे' [तैसं. १.५.७] नैतत्सूत्रद्वयमिष्टम्।[९]

---

१. MS A/D read only सषपरः।

२. MS A/D after सषपरः read अन्यत् पूर्ववत्।

३. MS A/D omit this example.

४. MS C reads the following verse which does not fit in the context.

स्यातां सोर्ध्व खथोर्ध्वे च ङ नौ ह्रस्वाद्विमात्रिकौ।
षपरा नित्यखथोर्ध्वे हकारे हल्परे तथा।
असंयुतश्च नो दीर्घान्मात्रिको यवहोत्तरे। ह्रस्वान्न।

In fact this verse should be cited under *sūtra* 32.

५. MS A/D शरच्छ्रौत्री (तैसं. ४.३.२)

६. MSF carelessly writes नमस्कारपूर्वः

७. MS E/F वाल्मिकेः

८. MS F छत्वमानापद्यते

९. MS C ....द्वयमनिष्टम्।

प्रथमपूर्वो हकारश्चतुर्थं तस्य सस्थानं प्लाक्षिकौण्डिन्य-गौतम-पौष्करसादीनाम्॥३८॥

प्रथमपूर्वो[१] हकारः प्रथमसस्थानं[२] चतुर्थं भजते।

अविकृत एकेषाम्॥३९॥

हकारो विकृतस्यादित्येके[३] ब्रुवते। 'अर्वाक् ह्येनम्' [तैसं. ६.३.३]

चतुर्थोऽन्तरे शैत्यायनादीनाम्॥४०॥

एषां मते उभयोर्मध्ये प्रथमसस्थानश्चतुर्थागमस्स्यात्।[४] 'अर्वाक्घ्ह्येनम्' [तैसं. ६.३.३] आदिशब्देन भारद्वाज-कौहलेय-कौण्डिन्य'[५]-पौष्करसादयः।

मीमांसकानां च मीमांसकानां च॥४१॥

एषां मते पूर्वोक्तमेव स्यात् नैतत्सूत्रत्रयमिष्टम्।

॥ इति प्रातिशाख्यव्याख्यायां पञ्चमोऽनुवाकः॥

---

१. MS C प्रथ (omits म)

२. MS A/D तस्य सस्थानं
   MS C प्रभसस्थानं

३. MS A/D omit इत्येके ब्रुवते।

४. MS A/D प्रथमस्थान

५. MS A/D कौहलीपुत्र

॥ अथ षष्ठोऽनुवाकः॥

अथ षकारः सकारविसर्जनीयौ॥१॥

इत्याधिकृत्य।

स्वानासो[1] दिव्यापोह्ययमुकमुमोप्रोत्रीमहिद्यवि पद्यवग्रहपूर्वः॥२॥

चत्वारि पूर्वं द्विपदानि।[2] एवं पूर्वोऽवग्रहपूर्वश्च सकारः षकारमापद्यते। 'स्वानासो दिविषन्तु' [तैसं. १.२.१४] 'आपो हि ष्ठा' [तैसं. ४.१.१] 'अयमुष्यः' [तैसं. ३.५.११] कमुष्विद् [२.६.११] 'ऊ षु ण' [तैसं. ४.१.४] 'मो षू णः' [तैसं. १.८.३] प्रोष्वस्मै [तैसं. १.७.१३] त्रिषधा[3] [तैसं. २.४.११] महिषत् [तैसं. ३.२.८] द्यविष्ठ [तैसं. २.४.१४] पदिषिताम् [तैसं. ४.७.१५] शुचिषत् [तैसं. १.८.१५] गोष्टोमम् [तैसं. ७.४.११]

असदामासिञ्चंश्च॥३॥

अवग्रहपूर्वयोः एतयोः सः षमापद्यते। 'न्यषदाम' [तैसं. ७.५.२] अभ्यषिञ्चन् [तैसं. ७.५.२]

उपसर्गनिष्पूर्वो ऽनुदात्ते पदे॥४॥

पदकाले[4] सर्वानुदात्तपद इत्यर्थः। परिषिञ्चति[5] [तैसं. ५.४.४] विष्यामि [तैसं. १.१.१०] निष्टनिहि [तैसं. ४.६.६] निष्पूर्वस्येदम्। सर्वानुदात्त इति किम्? 'विसीमतः' [तैसं. ४.२.८] पदे पदकाले[6] इत्यर्थः।

१. MS F carelessly writes स्वानांसो
२. MS A/D पूर्वं
३. MS E/F त्रिषधस्था
४. MS A/D omit पदकाले
५. MS D adds निषुपूर्वस्यैवेदं प्रतिभाति। अवग्रहस्थनिषेधस्य वक्ष्यमाणत्वात्।
६. MS E/F omit पदे पदकाले इत्यर्थः।

रासस्सप्तेऽग्निर्विदुर्मीढुः पायुभिः वेंस्सुमतिर्माकिरीयुरायुरा-भिस्सधिर्नकिस्तकारपरो नित्यम्॥५॥

रासः पूर्वः अग्निः सप्ते पूर्वोऽग्निः निरित्यादयश्चैषां[१] विसर्गः षकारमापद्यते तपरश्चेत्। 'अविदुष्टरासः अग्निष्टत्' [तैसं. १.१.१४] सप्ते[२] अग्निष्ट्वा [तैसं. ५.१.११] निष्टपामि [तैसं. १.१.१०] 'विदुष्टरꣳसपेम' [तैसं. २.५.१२] अप्यकारादिति वचनात्। अविदुष्टरासः [तैसं. १.१.१४] मीढुष्टम [तैसं. ४.५. १०] पायुभिष्ट्वꣳ [तैसं. १.४.२४] वेष्टꣳहि [तैसं. ४.३.१३] सुमतिष्टे [तैसं. १.४.४५] माकिष्टे [तैसं. १.२.१४] ईयुष्टे [तैसं. १.४.३३] आयुष्टे [तैसं. २. ५.१२] असंख्यानत्वा[३]द्विलोमेत्वत्रापि। भूतेभ्यस्त्वा विश्वायुः [तैसं. १.२.१२] आभिष्टे[४] [तैसं. ४.४.४] सधिष्टव [तैसं. १.४.३३] नकिष्टम् [तैसं. २.१. ११] नित्यशब्देन अवग्रह इत्यादिनिषेधनिषेधार्थम्। कण्ठोक्तिविदुरित्यस्यैव नत्वविदुरित्यस्येति दौर्बल्यात् तत्संरक्षणार्थो नित्यशब्दः।[५] अघोषपरस्तस्येत्य-स्यापवादोऽयम्।

अथ न॥६॥

इत्यधिकृत्य।

अवर्णव्यञ्जनशकुनि पत्न्यृतुमृत्युमलिम्लुबृहस्पतिपूर्वः॥७॥

अवर्णपूर्वो व्यञ्जनपूर्वश्चेत्यादिपूर्वः सकारः षकारं नापद्यते[६]। 'अन्तरिक्ष सत्' [तैसं. १.८.१५] 'आसिञ्चस्व' [तैसं. १.४.१९] 'ऋक्सामे वै [तैसं. ६.१.३] 'शकुनि सादेन' [तैसं. ५.७.१४] 'पत्नी संयाजानाम्' [तैसं. २.६. १०] 'ऋतुस्थाः' [तैसं. ५.७.६] 'मृत्युसंयुतः' [तैसं. १.५.९] 'मलिम्लुसेना' [तैसं. ६.३.२] बृहस्पतिसुतस्य [तैसं. १.४.२७]

---

१. MS A/D निरित्यादि एतेषु।

२. MS C च सप्ते।

३. MS D/A omit असंख्यानत्वात्

४. ---"--- अभिष्टे

५. ---"--- इतिभाष्ये। add

६. MS A आपद्यते।

ऋकाररेफवती॥८॥

ऋकाररेफौ विद्येते यस्मिन् तत् तस्मिन्पदे वर्तमानः सकारः[१] षकारं नापद्यते। विसृजते [तैसं. १.७.६] विस्रस्यः [तैसं. ६.२.९]

अवग्रहः॥९॥

अवग्रहस्थः सकारः[२] षकारं नापद्यते उपसर्गनिमित्तश्चेत्। अयं निषेधो न त्वाद्यसूत्रस्य त्रीग्रहणज्ञापनात्।[३] 'मञ्चा क्रोशन्ति' इति न्यायेन अवग्रहस्थः। 'अधि संवसन्तः' [तैसं. ३.५.१] 'अभि संविदाने [तैसं. ५.१.११]

सवस्थानम्॥१०॥

सवेति पदैकदेशो बहूपादानार्थः। 'अग्निसवः' [तैसं. ५.६.२] 'सवने सवने [तैसं. ६.४.११] 'प्रसवाय'[४] [तैसं. ६.६.५] 'गोस्थानम्' [तैसं. १.१. ९]

न धिपूर्वे॥११॥

प्रतिप्रसवोऽयम्। 'अधिषवणे [तैसं. १.१.५] 'अधिष्ठानम्'[५] [तैसं. ४. ६.२]

सन्तानेभ्यस्सप्तभिस्सम्मिताऽस्तनाऽसीतऽस्पशस्सक्सनिस्सनीस्स-भेयस्सत्वा सस्यायै॥१२॥

परिसन्तानेभ्यः [तैसं. ७.४.२१] त्रिसप्ताभिः [तैसं. ५.२.६] वेदिसम्मिताम् [तैसं. ५.६.८] द्विस्तनाम् [तैसं. ५.१.६] अनुसीतम् [तैसं. ५.२.५] प्रतिस्पशः [तैसं. ५.७.३] सगिति पदैकदेशः। पृश्निसक्थः [तैसं. २.१.३] पृश्निसक्थाय [तैसं. ७.३.१८] एतद्गोसनि[६] [तैसं. ७.५.२] अश्वसनिः [तैसं. ३.२.५]

---

१. MS F — सः
२. MS D — सः
३. MS D, E — add this line in the margin.
Ms E, F — read it with the following variation....न त्वाघस्य
४. MS E, F — omit this example
५. Ms F — अधिस्थानम्
६. MS F — ...गोसति

वृष्टिसनिः [तैसं. ५.३.१] सुसभेयः [तैसं. ७.१.८] अभि सत्वा सहोजाः [तैसं. ४.६.४] सुसस्यायै [तैसं. १.२.२][१]

न स्वरस्पर्धा[२]स्स्तरीमसाहस्त्रसारथिस्स्फुर
न्तीस्सुब्ज्योतिरायुश्चतुः[३]पूर्वस्स्तो॥१३॥

प्रतिप्रसवोऽयम्। अम्ब निष्वर[४] [तैसं. १.४.१] विष्पर्धा[५] [तैसं. ४.३.१२] सुष्टरीमा जुषाणा [तैसं. ५.१.११] ग्रहणस्य चेति वचनादकारगृहीतम्। द्विषाहस्त्रम् [तैसं. ५.६.८] त्रिषाहस्त्रः[६] [तैसं. ५.६.८] सुषारथिः [तैसं. ४.६.६] विष्फुरन्ती [तैसं. ४.६.६] सष्टुप्[७] [तैसं. ४.३.१२] ज्योतिरित्यादीनां स्तो इत्यस्य सम्बन्धः। ज्योतिष्टोमम् [तैसं. ७.४.११] आयुष्टोमम् [तैसं. ७.४.११] चतुष्टोमस्तोमः [तैसं. ५.३.१२] स्तरीमादीनामवग्रहपूर्वत्वात्प्राप्तिः। अजस्तोमाय[८] ज्योतिः इत्यत्र तु न शङ्कनीयम्।

तर्हाँ॰स्तस्मिन्लोकान् विद्वाँ॰स्ताँ॰स्त्रीन्युष्मानू
र्ध्वानम्बकानृतूनश्मन्कृण्वन्पितॄननान्कपालाँ॰
स्तिष्ठन्नाद्युदात्ते नेमिर्देवान्त्सवने पशूँ॰स्तकार-
परस्सकारं प्राकृतो नित्ये प्राकृतो नित्ये॥१४॥

एषु ग्रहणेषु पदसमये तकारपरो[९] नकारः सकारमापद्यते।[१०] शततर्हाँ॰स्तृँ॰हन्ति [तैसं. १.५.७]। तस्मिँ॰स्त्वा [तैसं. १.६.५] लोकाँ॰स्तीर्त्वा [तैसं. ३.५.४] विद्वाँ॰स्त्रैधातवीयेन [तैसं. २.४.११] यस्तामविद्वान्, इत्यत्र न

---

१. MS A/D	add प्रथमषष्ठत्रयोदशानां उपसर्गत्वात् अन्येषामवग्रहपूर्वत्वात्प्राप्तिः।
२. MS F	स्वर्त्धा
३. MS F	पो
४. MS F	निष्थर
५. MS F	विष्पत्र्धा
६. MS A/D	द्विषाहस्त्रः
७. Ms F	सुष्टुप्
८. MS F	अतस्तोमाय
९. MS A/D	नकारः तकारपरः
१०. MS A/D	add नकारः प्राकृतश्चैव नित्यतोर्ध्वं समाप्नुयादिति व्यासवचनात्।

अनुस्वारागमो भवेत्। तामविद्वानविद्वान् ताम्।[१] अप्यकारादिप्राप्तेर्निषेधः। व्यासशिक्षाविवरणे[२] तु–तामविद्वानविद्वाःँस्ताँ[३] ताःँस्ते दधामि[४] त्रीःँस्तृचान्, युष्माःँस्तेनु ऊर्ध्वाःँस्तान्। त्र्यम्बकाःँस्तृतीयसवनम्, ऋतुःँस्तन्वंते, अश्मःँस्ते [तैसं. ४.६.१] कृण्वःँस्त्वा, पितॄँस्तन्तुः, प्राणाःँस्तस्य, अपिविकृतमिति वचनात्। द्वादशकपालाःँस्तृतीयसवने [तैसं. ७.५.६] तिष्ठःँस्तिष्ठति। [तैसं. २.५.९] आद्युदात्त इति किम्? 'प्रत्यतिष्ठन्ताः' [तैसं. ५.३.६] 'नेमिर्देवाःँस्त्वम्' [तैसं. २.५.१] 'सवने पशुःँस्तृतीयसवने [तैसं. ३.२.९] द्विपदेन किंम?[५] गच्छ देवान्त्वमित्यादि तान्तेन [तैसं. ५.७.३] अयं विकृतः। नित्य इति किम्? सन्त्सदृङ्ः।

॥ इति प्रातिशाख्यव्याख्यायां षष्ठोऽनुवाकः॥

१. MS A/D ता ताम्।

२. MS A शीक्षा

३. MS A/D ....add तामविद्वान्।

४. MS E omits दधामि

५. MS C adds in different hand प्रजां पशून तेनावर्धत।

॥ अथ सप्तमोऽनुवाकः॥

अथ नकारो णकारम्॥१॥

इत्यधिकृत्य।

षुषूकृधिसुवस्समिन्द्रास्थूर्युरुवाष्षट्त्रिग्रामनिष्पूर्वः॥२॥

तृतीयं चतुर्थं च द्विपदम्। 'ऊ षु णः' [तैसं. ४.१.४] 'मो षू णः [तैसं १.८.३] कृधि सुवर्ण [तैसं. २.२.१२] समिन्द्रणः [तैसं. १.४.४४] अस्थूरिणः [तैसं. ५.७.२] उरुणः [तैसं. २.६.११] वार्णाम [तैसं. ५.६.१] षण्णवत्यै [तैसं. ७.२.१५] अत्र षड्ग्रहणेन टकारग्रहणम्।

त्रिटास्थूरिधिसुवर्निःपूर्व इति माहेश्वरवचनात्।[१]

धिसुवस्त्रिटपूर्वो निःपूर्वो इति व्यासवचनाच्च 'त्रिणवः' [तैसं. ४.३.१] ग्रामणीः[२] [तैसं. ७.४.६] निर्णेनिक्ते [तैसं. ७.२.१०][३]

हन्यादुप्यमानं च॥३॥

निरितिशब्दोत्तरयोरेतयोर्नो णत्वमापद्यते।[४] 'निर्हण्यात्' [तैसं. ५.६.९] 'निरुप्यमाणम्' [तैसं. १.६.८]

पारीपरिपरीप्रपूर्वः[५]॥४॥

'पारीणह्यस्य' [तैसं. ६.२.१] 'परिणः' [तैसं. ४.५.१०] परीणसम् [तैसं. २.२.१२] प्रणः [तैसं. १.८.२२]

---

१. MS A/D omit

२. MS A/D ग्रामीणयम्।

३. MS A/D निर्णेनिजति।

४. MS A/D निःशब्दो.......

५. MS C/D/E पारि

अवर्णव्यवेतोऽपि॥५॥

पूर्वोक्तं स्यात्।[१] 'पर्यणयत्' [तैसं. २.३.४] 'प्राणाय' [तैसं. ७.१.१९]

वाहनउह्यमानो यानमयन्यवेनवंश्च[२]॥६॥

अयंच वंश्च[३] पदैकदेशः। प्रपूर्वेषु एतेषु उक्तं स्यात्। प्रवाहणः [तैसं. १.३.३] प्रोह्यमाणः [तैसं. ७.१.१९] प्रयाणम् [तैसं. १.६.११] प्रायणीयः [६.१.५] प्रायणम्[४] प्रायणीयस्य [तैसं. ६.१.५] प्रयवेण [तैसं. ४.३.११] प्रवणंस्यात् [तैसं. ६.२.६] वनस्पतयः प्रवणस्पतयः।

प्रापूर्वश्च॥७॥

प्रावणेभिः [तैसं. ४.२.४]

इन्द्रोऽयजुःपूर्व एनं केन॥८॥

यथासंख्येन। 'इन्द्र एणम्' [तैसं. ४.६.७] अयजुष्केण [तैसं. ५.१.२] तृप्त एवैनमिन्द्रइत्यत्रापि विलोमे।[५]

नृश्रीपूर्वो मनाः॥९॥

'नृमणा अजस्रम्' [तैसं. १.३.१४] श्रीमणाः [तैसं. ४.६.३]

अङ्गनामोनेगानिगानांग्यानि यामेन॥१०॥

'त्र्यङ्गाणां' [तैस ६.३.१०] दुरोणे [तैसं. १.२.१४] दुर्गाणि [तैसं. १.१.१४] पुरोगाणाम् [तैसं. ३.२.४] सुवर्ग्याणि [तैसं. ५.३.५] अन्तर्यामेण [तैसं. ६.४.६] रष इति सूत्रस्थरेफस्य देहलीदीपन्यायेन पूर्वसूत्रस्यापि सम्बन्धः।

रषः पूर्वो हवन्यह्नेहन्॥११॥

हन्निति[६] पदैकदेशः।[७] 'अग्निहोत्रहवणी च' [तैसं. १.६.८] अपराह्णे [तैसं. २.१.२] रक्षोहणम् [तैसं. १.२.१४] वृत्रहणम् [तैसं. ३.५.११]

---

१. MS A/D भवति
२. MS A/D वेनवश्च।
३. MS A/D अयं च वं च।
४. MS A/D omit
५. MS A/D omit the complete line.
६. MS A/D add अकारो व्यञ्जनानामित्यत्र परिभाषा न प्रवर्तते। रषः पूर्व इति निर्देशात्। अन्यथा 'वाघाषपूर्व' इत्यादिवत् रष पूर्व इत्युच्चारणम्। अतो रपूर्वं षःपूर्वं च पूर्वनिमित्तज्ञेयम्।
७. MS E omits also हन्निति पदैकदेशः।

रुपूर्वो मयान्यनी॥१२॥

अन्त्यपदैकदेशः। दारुमयाणि [तैसं. ६.४.७] पूर्वणीक [तैसं. १.३.१४]

वाघाषापूर्वस्तष्टम्॥१३॥

वाघापूर्वषपूर्वस्तष्टमापद्यते।[१] 'दार्वाघाटः' [तैसं. ५.५.१५] आयुष्टे [तैसं. २.५.१२]

थश्च ठम्॥१४॥

गोष्ठम्[२] [तैसं. १.१.१०]

न तकारपरः॥१५॥

विकृतस्यैव।[३] पर्यन्तरिक्षात् [तैसं. ३.१.१०]

नह्यति नूनं नृत्यन्त्यन्योऽन्याभिरन्यान्यन्तश्चान्तश्च॥१६॥

अयं निषेधः। पर्यानह्यति [तैसं. ६.१.११] 'प्र नूनम्' [तैसं. १.८.५] परिनृत्यति [तैसं. ७.५.१०] प्रान्यः शंसति [तैसं. ७.५.९] प्रान्याभिः [तैसं. ५.१.६] प्रान्यानि [तैसं. ६.५.११] वृत्रहन् [तैसं. १.४.३७]

'उच्चोन्योन्यशब्दलक्ष्यान्नोद्विगस्तोत्तरोन्तग' इति माहेश्वरवचनात्[४] 'नकारो द्वित्वगोलक्ष्यात्तकारोर्ध्वेपि वान्तगः' इति व्यासवचनाच्च।[५] अन्यं परिश्येन इत्यादिषु 'अन्नं प्रयच्छति' इत्यादिषु च णत्वं न।[६] 'अन्वारभ्य परीत्यत्र णत्वं शिष्टा न वदन्ति।[७] तथा[८] निशितायां निर्णिशितायां इत्यत्रापि वदन्ति।

॥इति प्रातिशाख्यव्याख्यायां सप्तमोऽनुवाकः॥

१. MS A/D भजते
२. MS A/D/E add पूर्ववत्।
३. MS A/D adds तकारपरः नकारः णत्वं नापद्यते। अयं निषेधो.......
   MS D omits तकारपर.....etc. and reads विकृतस्यैवायं निषेधः।
४. MS A/D omit उच्चो.....माहेश्वरवचनात्।
५. MS A/D omit च।
६. MS A/D add वान्तग इत्यत्र वकारः समीपगः इति विग्रहात्।
७. MS A/D add इति मम भाति।
८. MS A/D read निशितायां निरित्यत्र तृतीयनकारस्य णत्वं प्राप्तं तथापि शिष्टाः न वदन्ति।

॥ अथ अष्टमोऽनुवाकः॥

अथ प्रथमः॥१॥

इत्यधिकृत्य। विसर्जनीयपर्यन्तोऽधिकारोऽयम्।

उत्तमपरः उत्तमः सवर्गीयम्॥२॥

उत्तमपरः प्रथमः सवर्गीयमुत्तममापद्यते। 'वाङ्मे' [तैसं. ५.५.९] 'यन्मे' [तैसं. ५.५.९]

तृतीयः स्वरघोषवत्परः॥३॥

एवं परः प्रथमः सवर्गीयं तृतीयं आपद्यते।[१] वागसि[२] यद्वै [तैस. ३.२.९]

ककुच्चमकारपरः॥४॥

पूर्ववत्। 'ककुद्मान्'[३] [तैसं. २.७.७.] उत्तमपरः इत्यस्य अपवादः।

अथ विसर्जनीयः॥५॥

इत्यधिकृत्य। 'स्वरपरो यकारम्' [तैप्रा ९.१०] इत्यन्तोऽधिकारोऽयम्।

रेफमेतेषु॥६॥

विसर्गो[४] रेफमापद्यते स्वरघोषवत्परेषु[५] तदग्निराह [तैसं. ४.२.८] आशीर्मे [तैसं. ३.२.८]

न रेफपरः॥७॥

रेफः परः यस्मात्। 'रू रू रौद्रः'[६] [तैसं. ५.५.१३]

---

१. MS A/D भजते।

२. MS A/D ऋध.....गुत।

३. MS F ककुन्नान्।

४. MS A/D add स्वरेषु घोषवत्सुच परतः

५. MS A/D omit स्वरघोषवत्परेषु।

६. MS A/D अन्ता रुक्मः।

व्हारभार्वाहारबिभरजीगगरकरनन्तर्विषस्सुवः पुनरहरहः प्रातर्वस्तश्शमितस्सवितस्सनुतस्स्तनुतस्स्तोतर्होतः पितर्मातर्यष्टरेष्टर्नेष्टस्त्वष्टः॥८॥

एषां[१] विसर्गो रेफमापद्यते स्वरघोषवत्परः। द्वार्मित्रस्य [तैसं. १.१.४] अभारुवा [तैसं. ४.२.५] वार्णाम [तैसं. ५.६.१] हारस्ति [तैसं. २.४.१२] तमबिभरबिभस्तम्[२] [तैसं. २.५.१] अजीगरित्यजिगः [तैसं. ४.६.७] अर्वाकरकर[३]र्वार्वाकः [तैसं. ४.१.२] अनन्तरित्यै [तैसं. ५.२.५] विवरिति विवः [तैसं. ४.२.८] सुवर्देवान् [तैसं. ५.७.६] पुनरूर्जा [तैसं. १.५.३] अहरहर्हविर्धानिनाम् [तैसं. २.५.६] प्रातरुपसदः [तैसं. ६.३.३] दोषावस्तर्धिया [तैसं. १.५.६] शमितरिति [तैसं. ६.३.१०] सवितरेतत्ते[४] [तैसं. ३.२.७] सनुतर्युयोतु [तैसं. १.७.१३] स्तनुतरिति शाखान्तरे 'स्तोतरेतेन' [तैसं. ७.४. २०] होतर्यविष्ठ[५] [तैसं. १.२.१४] मरुतां पितः पितर्मरुताम् [तैसं. ३.३.९] मातर्मा [तैसं. ३.३.२] अशीयेष्टरेष्टः[६] [तैसं. १.२.११] नेष्टर्नेष्टः[७] पत्नीं [तैसं. ६.५.८] त्वष्टरिहा[८] [तैसं. ३.१.११] 'अवर्णपूर्वस्तु लुप्यते [तैप्रा ९.९] 'अथ स्वरपरो यकारम् [तैप्रा ९.१०] 'ओकारमः' [तैप्रा ९.७] सर्व इत्येताः प्राप्तीः प्रतिषेद्धुं व्हारभाराद्यारम्भः।

करावरनुदात्ते पदे॥९॥

कर्भागधेयम् [तैसं. १.३.७] आवरित्यावः [तैसं. ४.२.८] अनुदात्तत्वादत्र[९] न। कोऽस्य [तैसं. २.६.७] आवो वाजेषु [तैसं. १.३.१३]

---

१. MS A/D एतेषाम्।

२. MS A/D अबिभस्तन्तमबिभरबिभस्तम् [तैसं. २.५.१]

३. MS A/D अर्वाकरकररर्वा.......

४. MS A/D सवितरेतत्।

५. MS F होतवर्यविष्ठ

६. MS F आशीयेष्ट........

७. MS A/D नेष्टर्नेष्टः

८. MS A/D त्वष्टारिह

९. MS A/D अनुदात्त इति किम्?

अन्तरनाद्युदात्ते॥१०॥

'अन्तर्यामेण'[१] [तैसं. ६.४.६] आद्युदात्तत्वादत्र न। एषोन्तोन्तम् [तैसं. ७.२.७]

आवृत्परः॥११॥

विसर्गो[२] रेफमापद्यत्ते।[३] 'जिन्वरावृत्स्वाहा' [तैसं. २.४.७] उग्रावृत् [तैसं. २.४.७][४]

इतिपरोऽपि॥१२॥

इदमेव जटाया ज्ञापनम्। आवृत्परः विसर्ग इतिपरो रेफमाप्नोति। 'इति श्रुतः' 'श्रुतरितिश्रुतः' [तैसं. २.४.७] प्रसङ्गात्तस्याः लक्षणमाह।[५]

सकृदादिद्वितीयं द्विरादि द्विश्च पदं सकृत्
पठेदतुल्यपदयोः क्रमवत्संधिभिर्जटाम्॥
त्रिक्रमे त्रिक्रमं ह्युक्ता विलोमेनानुलोमतः।
इति माहेश्वरशिक्षायाम्।[६]
सकृदादिद्वितीयं द्विः पठेच्चादिपदं [७] सकृत्।
सन्धितः क्रमवच्चेति प्रोच्यते हि जटा बुधैः।
त्रिक्रमस्य[८] जटा ज्ञेया ह्युक्त्वा[९] पूर्वं क्रमं तथा।
पुनरन्तर्मध्यं चादिं पुनराद्यन्तन्तरं परम्।

---

१. MS A/D read न आद्युदात्तम् अनाद्युदात्तम्, तस्मिन्। अन्तरग्रे [तैसं. ४.१.९] अन्तर्यामे [तैसं. १.४.३]

२. MS A/D विसर्जनीयो ३. MS A/D आप्नोति

४. MS A/D omit this example.

MS A scribes by over sight the following portion, which actually should occur in the preceeding *sūtra*.
अनाद्युदात्त इति किम्? एषो तोन्तः।

५. MS A/D वक्ष्यते

६. MS A/D omit this portion of the माहेश्वराशिक्षा।

७. MS A/D परम्

८. MS F विक्रमस्य

९. MS F ह्युक्त्वा

अनुलोमः स्वपाठस्स्यात् विलोमः सन्धिनिर्मितः।
पदं पदं पठेत्ताभ्यां त्रिवारं चोर्ध्वतः पुनः। इति व्यासः।
आदिः[१] सकृर्द्धितीयं द्विवारं चकारात्पुनः।[२]
आदिद्धिवारं पुनर्द्वितीयमेकवारं यथा–

'इषेत्वा त्वेष इषे त्वा' [तैसं. १.१.१] 'मो षू णो नः षू मो मो षू णः' [तैसं. १.८.३] समवर्णस्वरयोस्तु क्रमवज्ज्ञेया।

स्वरवर्णादभेदस्य यत्पद्वितयस्य च।
जटाविचक्षणैरुक्तं क्रमोच्चारणमत्र तु।।

इति आत्रेयवचनात्।

पठेदतुल्यपदयोरिति माहेश्वरवचनाच्च।[३] यथा 'गायत्री गायत्री' [तैसं. १.५.८] तत्तत् [तैसं. १.१.१४] इत्यादि। अत्र विशेषमाहतुर्व्यासात्रेयौ–

"संहितावत्क्रमो ज्ञेयो जटा च विकृतादिषु।
पदद्वयनिमित्तं यदेकाभावेऽपि यत्र तु।"
"संहितावत्क्रमो ज्ञेयस्तद्वज्ज्ञेया जटा बुधैः।।"

अस्यार्थः–विकारागमलोपेषु[४] यथासाःहितं[५] कार्यं स्यादेकाभावेऽपि च, यथा–'आपो हि ष्ठा मयोभुवः' [तैसं. ४.१.५] आपो हि। हि ष्ठ। हि ष्ठ स्थ हि हि ष्ठ। 'मयि गृह्णाम्यग्रे अग्निम् [तैसं. ५.७.९] गृह्णाम्यग्रे अग्रे गृह्णामि। गृह्णाम्यग्रे अग्रे गृह्णामि गृह्णाम्यग्रे।[६] गावोन्वनुगावो गावो नु इत्यादि। कोऽवा[७] क्रमः कोऽवा त्रिक्रमः[८] इत्याशङ्क्याह।

---

१. MS A/D आदि
२. MS A/D चकात्
३. MS A/D omit
४. MS D विकारामरागमलो.......
५. MS D यथासःहितम्।
६. MS A/D अग्रे अग्निमग्निमग्रेऽग्रे अग्निम्
७. MS A/D add अत्र
८. MS E कोऽवा क्रमः कोऽवा विक्रमः इत्याशङ्क्याह।

संहितावत्क्रमो ज्ञेयो द्वितीयं पदवद्वयोः।
इति गन्त्वादिचेदुक्त्वा द्वितीयं चोत्तरं तथा।
आदन्तं तु यदुच्चान्तमोपसर्गपरं यदि।
परेण त्रिक्रमस्तस्य षुपदं नः परं त्वधः। इति व्यासः।

अहारहस्सुवरनिङ्ग्यान्तः॥१३॥

अहार्जातवेदाः [तैसं. ३.२.५] अहर्मांꣳसेन [तैसं. ५.७.२०] सुवर्देवान् [तैसं. १.७.९]ः इङ्ग्यान्तत्वादत्र न।[१] त्र्यहाः [तैसं. ७.३.१] देवसुवस्स्थ[२] [तैसं. १.८.१०]

न भिर्भ्याम्परः॥१४॥

अहरित्यत्र विसर्गो रेफं नापद्यते भिर्भ्याम्परः।[३] अहोभिः [तैसं. ७.५.१] अहोभ्याम् [तैसं. १.३.९]

अꣳहश्च सर्वेषाम्॥१५॥

'अꣳह इन्द्रम्[४]' [तैसं. २.२.७] 'अꣳहोमुचे' [तैसं. १.६.१२]

विधेर्मध्यस्थनासिक्यो न विरोधी भवेत्स्मृतः।
तस्मात्कुर्वन्ति कार्याणि वर्णानां धर्म एव तु।

इति वचनादत्र प्राप्तिः। अस्याः परिभाषाया इदमेव सूत्रं ज्ञापकम्। तन्निषेधार्यमिदम्।[५]

अनवर्णपूर्वस्तु रेफपरो लुप्यते॥१६॥

'रेवती रमध्वम्' [तैसं. १.३.७] अनवर्णपूर्वत्वेन ह्वारभारादीनां विसर्गलोपस्य अप्राप्तिस्तां निवर्तकस्तु शब्दः। तस्माद्ह्वारादीनां[६] विसर्गो

---

१. MS A/D अनिङ्ग्यान्त इति किम्?

२. MS A/D देवसुवः

३. MS A/D एवम्परः।

४. MS C add in the margin सर्वेषांमत्ते अꣳह इत्यस्मिन् ग्रहणे विसर्जनीयो न रेफमाप्नोति।

५. MS A/D तन्निषेध्या....दम्। अस्याः........सापकम्।

६. MS A/D ....द्ध्वारभारादीनां

लुप्यते।[1] 'रुन्धे पुनः पुनारुन्धे'[2] सुवो रोहावि त्यत्र[3] [तैसं. १.७.५] द्विरुक्तत्वादोत्वमेव। 'अहोरात्रे धृतव्रत' [तैसं. २.४.१०] इति निर्देशादहोरात्र-योरित्यादिष्वोत्वमेव। 'न धि पूर्वे' इति सूत्रं विशेषत्वेन [तैप्रा ६.११] स्थानशब्दस्य सिद्ध्यर्थमेव[4] इति निर्णयो भाष्ये कृतः।[5]

दीर्घं च पूर्वः॥१७॥

लुप्ताद्विसर्गात्पूर्वस्वरो दीर्घमापद्यते। 'रुरूरौद्रः' [तैसं. ५.५.१९]

एष्टश्च॥१८॥

लोपदीर्घौ स्याताम्। 'एष्टा[6] रायः' [तैसं. १.२.११] इदं सूत्रं वक्ष्यमाणमत-भेदानां निरासार्थम्।

नैकेषाम्॥१९॥

एकेषां मते उक्तविधिर्न। 'एष्टो रायः' [तैसं. १.२.११] ओत्वमेवेति वाररुचम्।

द्वावुत्तमोत्तरीयस्य रेफम्॥२०॥

उत्तमोत्तरीयशाखिनः मते विसर्गरेफौ रेफमापद्येते।[7]

'एष्टर्रायः'[8] [तैसं. १.२.११] इति वाररुचम्। माहिषेयं तु-द्वावुत्तमोत्तरीय-स्यर्षेर्मते विसर्गोऽरमापद्यते। 'एष्टर्रायः' [तैसं. १.२.१२]

सांकृत्यस्योकारम्[9]॥२१॥

अस्य मते विसर्गः उकारमापद्यते, इति माहिषेयम्। 'एष्टो रायः' [तैसं. १.२.११]

---

१. MS A/D add hereafter रेफोर्ध्वो लुप्यते रेफस्तत्पूर्वो दीर्घमाप्नुयात् इति व्यासवचनाद्यस्य विसर्गस्य रेफप्राप्तिस्तस्यैव लोप इत्यर्थः।

२. MS A/D add रुन्धे पुनः।

३. MS A/D 'सुवो रोहा ये'

४. MS A/D सिद्ध्यर्थ एव।

५. MS A/D इमा व्यवस्थाः भाष्ये उक्ताः।

६. MS F एष्ट रायः।

७. MS A/C/D/E आपद्यते

८. MS F एष्टरायः।

९. MS F सांत्यस्यो.....

उख्यस्य सपूर्वः॥२२॥

अस्य मते पूर्वेण सह विसर्गः उकारमापद्यते इति माहिषेयम्। 'एष्टु रायः' [तैसं. १.२.११] वाररुचं तु पूर्वेण सह विसर्गः रेफमापद्यते। 'एष्टृरायः' इदं सूत्रचतुष्कमनिष्टम्।

कखपकारपरष्षमकारपूर्वस्समवग्रहः॥२३॥

स्वरघोषवत्पूर्वमिति निवृत्तम्। अवग्रहस्थो विसर्गः कखपकारपरः[१] षकारमापघते। अवर्णपूर्वश्चेत्सम्। 'कखपोत्तरः षमेत्यवर्णपूर्वः समिति माहेश्वरवचनात्।[२] कखपोर्ध्वः षमवर्णपूर्वः[३] संयात्यवग्रह' इति व्यासवचना[४]च्चावर्णत्वम्।[५] 'पते धनदा धनदास्पत' इत्यादि। हविष्कृतानाम् [तैसं. ६.४.३] निष्खिदति [तैसं. ६.१.९] बहिष्पवमाने [तैसं. ६.४.९] नमस्कारैः [५.५.७] पथस्पथः[६] [तैसं. १.१.१४]

आविर्निरिडश्शश्वतोऽपसो[७] देवरिषोऽंहसोऽ तिदिवो विश्वतोऽश्मनस्तमसः॥२४॥

एषां षष्ठमष्टमं द्विपदम्। अनवग्रहार्थमिदम्। आविष्कृणुष्व [तैसं. १.२.१४] निष्पिबति [तैसं. २.३.११] इडस्पदे [तैसं. २.६.११] परिधिरिडस्परिधि [तैसं. १.१.११] इति विलोमे। शश्वतस्कः [तैसं. २.२.१२] अपसस्पारे अस्य[८] [तैसं. ३.२.११] देवरिषस्पाहि [तैसं. १.८.१४] विश्वतस्परि [तैसं. १.६.१२] अश्मनस्परि [तैसं. ४.१.१२] वयं तमसस्परि [तैसं. ४.१.७]

कृधिपिन्वपथे परः॥२५॥

एवं परो विसर्गः। 'उरुणस्कृधि' [तैसं. २.६.११] 'अपस्पिन्व' [तैसं. ४.३.४] नमस्पथे [तैसं. ४.७.१३]

---

१. MS D/E कखपपरः

२. MS A/D omit

३. MS A/D read कख षं तथावर्णपूर्वः........

४. MS A/D व्यासवचनात्

५. MS A/D/E add तस्य फलं त्विदमेव।

६. MS A/D add परिपतिम्

७. MS F शश्वतेऽपसो

८. MS E omit अस्य

न सक्रघकारपरे॥२६॥

स, क्र, घ एवं परे कृध्यादौ परे सति विसर्गः सं नापद्यते।[१] 'आमनसः कृधि स्वाहा' [तैसं. २.३.९] नः कृधि क्रत्वे [तैसं. ३.३.११] 'नः कृधि घृतम्' [तैसं. १.३.४]

पत्नी वेपती पते पतये पतिष्यतिम्परः॥२७॥

एवम्परो विसर्गः समापद्यते।[२] 'ब्रह्मणस्पत्नी वेदिम्' [तैसं. ३.५.६] शुभस्पती [तैसं. ३.२.१०] वास्तोष्पते [तैसं. ३.४.१०] वाचस्पतये [तैसं. १.४.२] वाचस्पतिर्वाचम् [तैसं. १.७.७] वाचस्पतिं विश्वकर्माणम् [तैसं. ४.६.२]

दिवस्सहसस्परिपुत्परः॥२८॥

यथासंख्यं न।[३] युदित्येकदेशः। केतवे दिवस्पुत्राय [तैसं. १.२.९] सहस्रपुत्रः [तैसं. ४.१.९] दिवस्परि [तैसं. १.३.१४]

रायस्पोपरः॥२९॥

पो इत्येकदेशः। 'रायस्पोषस्य' [तैसं. ३.२.३] 'रायस्पोषेण' [तैसं. १.७.९]

नमस्करो[४] परः॥३०॥

पूर्ववत्। नमस्करोति [तैसं. २.६.९]

वसुष्ककारपरः॥३१॥

वसुष्कविरन्निः[५] [तैसं. ४.४.४]

नाध्वरं विश्वतोऽन्तर्जातो विविशुः परुः पुनः॥३२॥

प्रथमं चतुर्थं च द्विपदम्। उक्तविधिर्न। 'अध्वरं विश्वतः परिभूः' [तैसं.

---

१. MS A/D भजते

२. MS A पूर्वविधिं भजते।
MS D सम्भजते।

३. MS A/D/E write दिवस्परि before पुदित्त्येक........।

४. MS F नमस्कारो परः।

५. MS A/D read इधानो वसुष्कविः [तैसं. ४.४.४]

४.१.११] 'अन्तः पार्श्वेन' [तैसं. १.४.३६] जातः पतिः [तैसं. ४.२.८] 'आविविशुः परुः परुः' [तैसं. ४.२.६] पुनर्पुनर्हि [तैसं. ६.५.१]

नष्टमाकृधीत्यत्र विलोमे सत्त्वमेव।[१] पुनरिति निषेधस्तु[२] परुः साहचर्यादवग्रहाहते निषेधादर्शनाच्चावग्रहस्थस्यैव निषेधः। अयमेवार्थस्तु व्यासशिक्षाविवरणे सत्त्वविधानात्।[३]

धषवति॥३३॥

धषौ विद्येते यस्मिन्। उक्तविधिर्न। 'बहिः परिधिः' [तैसं. २.६.६] 'परुषः प' [तैसं. ६.६.३] 'उभयतः क्ष्णूः' [तैसं. ५.१.१]

परिवा प्रपरः॥३४॥

परिव, प्र उक्तविधिर्न। प्रेत्युपसर्गरूपः[४] पदैकदेशः।[५] 'दिवः परि वाजेषु [तैसं. ४.२.११] इतः प्रदानम्।[६] [तैसं. ४.२.११] बहिः प्राणो वै [तैसं. ६.१.१]

न निर्ण निः॥३५॥

प्रतिप्रसवोऽयम्। प्राञ्चौ निर्णिष्प्राञ्चौ [तैसं. ६.४.१०]

॥ इति अष्टमोऽनुवाकः॥

---

१. MS F — सत्यमेव

२. MS A/D — read hereafter अवग्रहाहते निषेधादर्शनात्। परुः साहचर्याच्च अवग्रहस्थस्यैव निषेधः।

३. MS D — writes in the main body the following verse & rubs out.
कृध्युत्तरे पुनः शब्दे विलोमे सत्त्वमेव।
नाध्वरमिति सूत्रेणावग्रहस्थो निषिध्यते।

४. MS A/D — write all the example before प्रेत्यु.....।

५. MS A/D — read प्रेत्युपसर्गरूपः पदैकदेशस्य निषेधः।

६. MS E/D — adds after इतः प्रदानम् and rubs out.
उदथेत्यत्रदीर्घश्च ह्रस्वस्याप्युपलक्षकः।
तथा प्रपर इत्यत्र ह्रस्वो दीर्घोपलक्षक इति वचनात्।

॥अथ नवमोऽनुवाकः॥

ऊष्ममरोऽघोषपरो[१] लुप्यते काण्डमायनस्य॥१॥

अघोषपरः ऊष्मा[२] तत्परः विसर्गः लुप्यते इत्यस्य[३] मतम्। 'वायव स्थ' [तैसं. १.१.२] अस्य ग्रहणं विकल्पार्थम्। अन्येषां मते घोषपरः ऊष्मा, अन्यत्पूर्ववत्।[४] 'शुक्लास्स्यु' [तैसं. २.३.१] एवं विकल्पाश्रयणे[५] सति लक्षणान्तर्गतं[६] येषु लुप्यते तानि पदानि वक्ष्याम इति वचनं सरलं भवतीति भाष्ये।

अघोषपरस्तस्य सस्थानमूष्माणम्॥२॥

अघोषपरो विसर्गस्तस्याघोषस्य सस्थानम् ऊष्माणम् आपद्यते।[७] 'नः कृधि', यश्च [तैसं. २.३.५] यस्ते [तैसं. ३.१.१०] यः पाप्मना [तैसं. २.१.३]

न क्षपरः॥३॥

उक्तविधिर्न। 'मनः क्षेमे' [तैसं. ५.२.१] द्यौः क्षाम' [तैसं. १.३.१४]

कपवर्गपरश्चाग्निवेश्यवाल्मीक्योः॥४॥

एतयोः शाखिनोराचार्ययोर्मते कपवर्गपरो[८] वा पूर्वविधिं[९] नापद्यते। 'नः कृधि', अग्निः पशुः [तैसं. ५.७.२६] कपयोः वर्गौ।

---

१. MS A उष्म....

२. MS A उष्म

३. MS A/D काण्डमायनस्य मतम्।

४. MS A/F instead of अन्यत्पूर्ववत्, तत्परो विसर्गो लुप्यते।

५. MS A/C/D/E श्रवणे

६. MS F adds ततः

७. MS A/D भजते

८. MS A/D/E कवर्गपवर्गपरो

९. MS F पूर्वविधि......

ऊष्मपर एवैकेषामाचार्याणाम्।।५।।

एषां मते ऊष्मपर विसर्गश्चेदुक्तविधिर्न। 'वाजाः सम्' एवेति नियमेन[१] अत्र तु भवत्येव। 'नमस्ते' [तैसं. ४.५.९]

न प्लाक्षिप्लाक्षायणयोः।।६।।

कपवर्गपर ऊष्मपरविसर्गश्चैतयोः शाखिनोर्मते उक्तं नापद्यते।[२] 'यः करोति', यः पाप्मना' [तैसं. २.१.३] 'यः सोमम्'। एतत्सूत्रत्रयमनिष्टम्।[३]

ओकारमस्सर्वोऽकारपरः।।७।।

सर्वः अः ओत्वमापद्यते[४] अकारपरः।[५] 'प्रेद्धो अग्ने' [तैसं. ४.६.५] सोऽब्रवीत् [तैसं. २.१.२]

घोषवत्परश्च।।८।।

अः ओत्वमापद्यते[६] घोषवत्परः। 'मा नो मित्रः' [तैसं. ४.६.८] पृथक्करणम् उत्तरसूत्रे अनुवृत्त्यर्थम्।

अवर्णपूर्वस्तु लुप्यते।।९।।

अवर्णपूर्वो[७] घोषवत्परो विसर्गो[८] लुप्यते। 'परा ता[९] भगवः' [तैसं. ४.५.१] सोमा ३ न [तैसं. ६.१.९] अवर्णत्वेन दीर्घप्लुतयोः ग्रहणमवशेषात्। अकारपर इत्यस्य निवर्तकस्तु शब्दः।

१.	MS F	नियमे मात्र तु......
२.	MS A/D	उक्तविधिर्न।
३.	MS D/E	add in the margin एतत्सूत्र.....निष्टम्।
४.	MS A/D	भजते
५.	MS A/D	add अकारेण सहित इत्यर्थः।
६.	MS A/D	भजते
७.	MS A/D	अवर्णपरो
८.	MS A/D	विसर्जनीयो
९.	MS A/D/E	cite different examples as देवा गातुविदः [तैसं. १.१.१३] & सोमा ३ न [तैसं. ६.१.९]
	MS E	adds one more example to these of A. ता भगवः।

अथ स्वरपरो यकारम्॥१०॥

स्वरपर इत्यधिकृत्य।[1] अवर्णपूर्वः स्वरपरो विसर्गः यत्वमापद्यते।[2] 'आप उन्दन्तु' [तैसं. १.२.१] विसर्गो निवृत्तः।

एकारोऽयम्॥११॥

पदान्ते एकारः अयमिति विकारमापद्यते स्वरपरः। 'त एनम्' [तैसं. २.३.११]

ओकारोऽवम्॥१२॥

ओकारोऽवमापद्यतेऽच्परः। 'विष्णवे हि' [तैसं. २.४.१२]

नाकारपरौ॥१३॥

अकारपरौ अयवौ उक्तं नापद्यते।[3] 'ते अस्याम्' [तैसं. १.६.१२] 'समिद्धो अग्ने'[4] [तैसं. ५.१.११]

ऐकार आयम्॥१४॥

पदान्त ऐकार आयमापद्यतेऽच्परः।[5] 'आसामहा एव' [तैसं. ७.५.२]

औकार आवम्॥१५॥

आवमापद्यतेऽच्परः। 'अहावनदत' [तैसं. ५.६.१]

उकारोऽपृक्तः[6] प्रकृत्या वकारोऽन्तरे॥१६॥

अपृक्त उकारः प्रकृत्यावतिष्ठते अच्परः।[7] उकारस्वरयोर्मध्ये वकारागमस्स्यात्। 'अदन्त्युवैव' [तैसं. २.३.७]

न तत्तस्मात्साꣳहितः॥१७॥

एताभ्यां साꣳहित उकारोऽपृक्तः पूर्वविधिं नाप्नोति। 'तद्वाहुः' [तैसं. ७.

१. MS A/D अथेत्यधिकारः।

२. MS A/D भजते

३. MS A/D भजते

४. MS A/D अञ्जन्

५. MS A/D स्वरपरः पदान्ते ऐकारः आयुमिति विकारमापद्यते।

६. MS A/C/D/E उकारऽपृक्तः

७. MS A/D स्वरपरः

५.७] तस्माद्वाश्यम् [तैसं. ६.१.११] सांहितं युक्तमित्यर्थः। अयुक्तत्वादत्र न। 'उ बाहुः' [तैसं. ७.५.७]

ह्रस्वपूर्वो ङकारो द्विवर्णम्॥१८॥

ह्रस्वपूर्वः पदान्तो ङो द्वित्वं भजते अच्परः।[1] दध्यङ्‌ङृषिः[2] [तैसं. ४.१. ३]

नकारश्च॥१९॥

पूर्ववत्।[3] निरवपन्निन्द्राय [तैसं. २.४.२]

अनितिपरो ग्रहोख्ययाज्यापृष्ठ्यहिरण्यवर्णीयेष्वीकारोकारपूर्वो[4] रेफमाकारपूर्वश्च यकारम्॥२०॥

ग्रहोख्यादिषु ईपूर्व-ऊपूर्वो वा नकारो रेफमापद्यते। नत्वितौ।[5] आकार-पूर्वश्चेद्यकारम्। ग्रहो नाम अयं वा मित्रावरुणयो[6] इत्यारभ्य सर्वः[7] प्रश्नः, अग्निकाण्डस्य आद्यं प्रश्नद्वयम् उत्तमानुवाकवर्ज्यम् उख्यसंज्ञकम्।[8] उक्ता याज्या। 'समिद्दिशाम्' [तैसं. ४.४.१२] जीमूतस्य [तैसं. ४.६.६-९] यदक्रन्दो [तैसं. ४.६.६] ये वाजिनम् [तैसं. ४.६.६] अग्नेर्मन्वे [तैसं. ४.७.१५] यदक्रन्दो (तैसं. ४.६.६) या नो मित्रः (तैसं. ४.६.६) ये वाजिनम् (तैसं. ४. ६.६) समिद्धो अञ्जन् [तैसं. ५.१.११] गायत्री [तैसं. ५.२.११-१२] कस्त्वा [तैसं. ५.२.११-१२] इत्यनुवाकनवकं पृष्ठ्यसंज्ञकम्। ग्रहादिषु यथा–शत्रूंरप [तैसं. १.४.४२] मरुत्वाँइन्द्र [तैसं. १.४.१९] वनस्पतींरनु [तैसं. ४.२.८] मधुमाँअस्तु [तैसं. ४.२.९] ऋतुंर ऋतुपते [तैसं. ४.३.१३] अभवाँइभेन

---

१. MS A/D स्वरपरः

२. MS A/D add स्वरपरत्राभावेनात्र न। सदृङ् समानैः [तैसं. २.२.८]
MS C adds this line in the margin.

३. MS A/D add नकार इति विशेषः।

४. MS F हिरण्यहवर्णीये.....

५. MS A/D इतीत्येतस्मादन्यस्वरपरः

६. MS F मित्रावरुणेत्यारभ्य

७. MS F सर्वप्रश्नः

८. MS A/D संज्ञम्

[तैसं. १.२.१४] शत्रूँ॒रनपव्ययन्त [तैसं. ४.६.६] सर्वाँ॒अग्नीँ॒रप्सुषदः [तैसं. ५.६.१][1]

मर्त्यानुदयानमृतान्दुर्यानसोमपूर्वः सोऽस्मानविमान् गोमान्मधुमान् हविष्मान् हूतमानार्षे चिकित्वानिडावान् कक्षीवान् बाणवान् हि पयस्वान् वशान्विदत्रानमित्रानरान्[2] पोषान्महाँ॒श्च॥२१॥

मर्त्यान्, उदयान्, अमृतान्, असोमपूर्वो दुर्यान्, सो अस्मान्, अविमान्, गोमान्, मधुमान्, हविष्मान्, हूतमानार्षे,[3] चिकित्वान्, इडावान्, कक्षीवान्, बाणवान्,[4] हि पयस्वान्, वशान्, विदत्रान्, अमित्रान्, अरान्, पोषान्, महान्, एतेषु नकारः अनितिपरः यत्वमापद्यते।[5] मर्त्याँ॒ आविवेश [तैसं. ५.७.९] इ०

इन्द्रो मेऽकरूद्वमिहाऽप्येत्वगन्मेडे न्यानायजिष्ठ, आचर्त्वकुर्वतदुहददितिरग्रेऽधरान्त्सपत्नानलम्परश्च॥२२॥

आकारान्वादेशकश्चकारः।[6] 'इन्द्रो मे अकः, ऊद्वम्, इह, अप्येतु, अगन्म, ईडेन्यात्, अयजिष्ठः, आ च, ऋतु, अकुर्वत, अदुहत, अदितिः, अग्रे, अधरान्त्सपत्नान्, अलम्, एतानि परनिमित्तानि। 'सपत्नाँ॒ इन्द्रो मे' [तैसं. १.१.१३] इत्यादि।

न रश्मीञ्छ्रपयान्यमान्पतङ्गान्त्समानानर्चान्यजीयान्॥२३॥

रश्मीन्, श्रपयान्, यमान्, पतङ्गान्, समानान्, अर्चान्, यजीयान्, एतेषूक्तविधिर्न।। रश्मीननु [तैसं. ४.१.२] इत्यादि।

उदथापरश्चोदथापरश्च॥२४॥

उत्, अथ। उक्तविधिर्न। 'अमित्रानुत्' [तैसं. ४.१.१०] विद्वानथ

---

१. MS A/D add अनितीति किम्? इडावानितीडावान्

२. MS F विशान्

३. MS A adds अनितिनिषेधबाधनार्थम् आर्षग्रहणम्। तेन देवहूतमाँ॒ इत्याहेति भवति।

४. MS F reads बाणमान्

५. MS D write यकार, but makes it यत्व by scrubing out कार.

६. MS A/D चकारस्तु आकारपूर्वत्वान्वादेशकः।

७. MS F नर

[तैसं. ३.२.११] इतिं माहेश्वरवचनात्।[१] एत्यार्षेयो यत्वरेफौ विलोम एव सोच्यथेति उक्तौ विधिनिषेधौ च यत्वे रत्वे स्वरे परे।

विलोमेष्वपि तौ ज्ञेयौ प्रकृतौ नैव नो हलीति व्यासवचनाच्च।[२] नकारस्यार्षेयत्वरेफौ तस्यैव विलोमे यत्वरेफौ स्यातामचिपरे। यथा–'अन्यान-धरानधरानन्याः अन्याः अधरान्।' [तैसं. ३.२.८] हविष्मान्हविष्मानाप आपो हविष्मान्। अध्वरो हविष्माः हविष्माः अध्वरः अध्वरो हविष्मानित्यादि[३] [तैसं. १.३.१२][४]

॥ इति नवमोऽनुवाकः॥

---

१. MS A/D omit.

२. MS A/D व्यासवचनात्

३. MS A/D omit अध्वरो हविष्मानित्यादि।

४. MS D adds & rubs out
यस्यैवार्षयत्वरेफौ स्यातां तस्यैव पौरुषे।
सति स्वरपरेतद्वन्निषेधो नान्यथा भवेत्।

॥अथ दशमोऽनुवाकः॥

अथैकमुभे॥१॥

उभे एकमापद्येते इत्यधिकृत्य।[१]

दीर्घं समानाक्षरे सवर्णपरे॥२॥

आत्मनः सवर्णपरे ते उभे एकं दीर्घमापद्येते।[२] 'असीन्द्राण्यै' [तैसं. १.१.२] प्रार्पयतु [तैसं. १.१.१] सूत्रीयम् [तैसं. ६.२.४]

अथावर्णपूर्वे॥३॥

इत्यधिकृत्य।

इवर्णपर एकारम्॥४॥

अवर्णपूर्वे इवर्णपरे ते उभे एकारमापद्येते।[३] नेष्टिः[४] [तैसं. २.५.५]

उवर्णपर ओकारम्॥५॥

उभे ओत्वमापद्येते[५] 'त्वोर्जे' [तैसं. १.१.१]

एकारैकारपर ऐकारम्॥६॥

पूर्ववत्। ऐति सोमच्युतम् [तैसं. १.४.४३] सोमैन्द्राः[७] [तैसं. ५.६.१५]

---

१. MS A/D अथेत्यधिकारः। उभे एकामापद्येते इति।

२. MS A/D आप्नुतः।

३. MS A/D आप्नुतः। MS E read....उभे एत्वमापद्येते।

४. MS A/D add एयातां ब्राह्मणाय ब्राह्मणायेयातामेयातां ब्राह्मणाय

५. MS A/D omit

६. MS A/D omit read पृच्यस्वैकताय [तैसं. १.१.८] MS E writes only पूर्ववत् omits the rest.

७. MS A/D read सोमेन्द्राः

ओकारौकारपर औकारम्॥७॥

ब्रह्मौदनम् [तैसं. ५.७.३] अपौम्भन् [तैसं. २.४.१३][१]

अरमृकारपरे॥८॥

अरमापद्यते।[२] आग्नेय्यर्चा [तैसं. ३.१.६]

उपसर्गपूर्व आरम्॥९॥

अवर्णान्त–उपसर्गपूर्वे ऋकारपरे ते उभे आरमापद्येते।[३] उपार्च्छत्यथ[४] [तैसं. १.५.९]

उदात्तमुदात्तवति॥१०॥

उदात्तवति एकीभावे उदात्तमापद्यते।[५] इति[६] याज्या कार्येति। 'प्रोक्षितं' [तैसं. ७.१.१२][७] 'यजतैक:' [तैसं. ७.२.१०]

अनुनासिकेऽनुनासिकम्॥११॥

अनुनासिके एकीभावे सोनुनासिकमापद्यते।[८] इदमनिष्टम्।[९]

स्वरितानुदात्तसन्निपाते स्वरितम्॥१२॥

स्वरितशब्देनात्र[१०] नित्यस्वरित एव गृह्यत इति भाष्यम्। 'कन्येव' [तैसं. ३.१.११] 'याज्यैषा' [तैसं. २.६.२] 'क्वास्य[११]' [तैसं. ५.७.४]

---

१. MS A/D/E omit पूर्वो द्वन्द्वः उत्तरः कर्मधारयः।

२. MS A/D omit

३. MS A/D आप्नुतः

४. MS A/D cite different example ऋतव्या उपोपार्तव्या ऋतव्या उप। [तैसं ५.३.१]

५. MS A/D भवति

६. MS A/D omit इति

७. MS A/D add गोपायत

८. MS A/D अनुनासिकं स्यात्।

९. MS A/D add उक्तान्येवोदाहणानि

१०. MS A/D omit....नात्र F–स्वरितशब्दो नात्र

११. MS F कास्य

न धामापासिपरो बुध्नि याज्याऽपूषाऽमिनन्तार्षे॥१३॥

धा-मा-पा एभ्योऽसिपरश्चदेकीभावोनार्षे।[१] बुध्निया, ज्या, आ पूष।, अमिनन्त। एभ्य स्वरपरश्चेदेकीभावोनार्षे।[२] आर्षग्रहणं जटाया ज्ञापकम्। 'स्वधा असि' [तैसं. १.१.९] 'मा[३] असि' [तैसं. ४.४.११] प्रजा असि [तैसं. २.५.१२] अनसिपरत्वादत्र न।[४] माह ओजः, बुध्निया ईरते [तैसं. ४.३.१३] आ पूषा एतु [तैसं. २.४.५] 'ज्या इयम्' [तैसं. ४.६.६]।[५] आर्षग्रहणाद्विलोमे भवत्येव।[६] असि स्वधा स्वधास्यसि स्वधा। इव प्रपा प्रपेवेव प्रपा इत्यादि।[७]

एष्टरेतनेमन्नोद्मन्नोष्ठेवः परो लुप्यते॥१४॥

एवम्परः पूर्वोऽवर्णो[८] लुप्यते। 'अशीयेष्टः' [तैसं. १.२.११] उपेतन [तैसं. ३.१.४] 'त्वेमन्' [तैसं. ४.३.१] त्वोद्मन्[९] [तैसं. ४.३.१] स्वाहोष्ठाभ्याम्[१०] [तैसं. ७.३.१६] अभिमतेवः [तैसं. ५.३.५] अवर्ण इति किम्? शित्योष्ठः [तैसं. ५.६.१४]

इवर्णोकारौ यवकारौ॥१५॥

अवर्णपूर्व इति निवृत्तः। इवर्णोकारौ यथासंख्येन यवावापद्येते स्वरपरौ।[११] 'अभ्युत्'[१२] [तैसं. ६.२.९] एत्वा।

---

१. MS A/D ...एष्वन्त्यस्वरः असिपरः।

२. MS A/D एष्वन्त्यस्वरः स्वरपरश्च पूर्वविधिं नाप्नोति आर्षपाठे।

३. MS A/D प्रमा असि।

४. MS A/D असिपर इति किम्? आर्ष इति किम्?

५. MS A/D write all these examples after स्वधा।

६. MS A/D omit

७. MS A/D omit

८. MS C/E/F read पूर्वो वर्णो

९. MS A/D omit त्वोद्मन्

१०. MS A/D read अधरेणोष्ठेन

११. MS A/C/E/F स्वरपरः

१२. MS A/D अभ्यस्थात्।

उदात्तयोश्च परोऽनुदात्तस्स्वरितम्॥१६॥

उच्चयोरिवर्णोकारयोः परो नीचः स्वारम् आपद्यते।[१] व्येव [तैसं. ५.३.११] अप्स्वग्ने [तैसं. ४.२.११] उदात्त इति किम्?[२] धक्ष्यतसम् [तैसं. १.२.१४]

ऊभावे च॥१७॥

उच्चपूर्वस्य नीचपरस्योभावे स स्वरितमापद्यते।[३] उदात्तमुदात्तवतीत्यस्यापवादः। मासूत्तिष्ठन् [तैसं. ७.५.२]

न श्येती मिथुनी॥१८॥

एतयोरन्त्यस्य[४] यत्वं न।[५] 'श्येती अकुरुत' [तैसं. ५.५.८] 'मिथुनी अभवन्' [तैसं. ५.३.६] 'नार्षे श्येती मिथुन्यपीति माहेश्वरवचनात्। यमिवर्ण-उकारश्च वकारं भजति स्वयम्। मिथुन्यत्र भवेदेव ह्यनार्षे तु स्वरे परे॥'' इत्यात्रेयवचनाच्च विलोमे यत्वं भवत्येव। अथ मिथुनी मिथुन्यथाथमिथुनी।[६]

लुप्येते त्ववर्णपूर्वौ यवकारौ॥१९॥

आप उन्दन्तु [तैसं. १.२.१] इम एव [तैसं. २.४.१०] विचित्या३इति [तैसं. ६.१.९] अवर्णपूर्वत्वाभावादत्र न।[७] 'हृत्स्वसः' [तैसं. ४.२.११]

नोख्यस्य॥२०॥

अस्य शाखिनः पक्षे यवौ न लुप्येते।

---

१. MS A/D स्वरितम्

२. MS A/D उदात्ताभावेनात्र न।

३. MS A/D उदात्तपूर्वो नीचपरस्योभावे स्वरितं भजते।

४. MS A/D add न धामेत्यत्रार्षपदस्य सिंहावलोकनन्यायेन अत्रान्वादेशः।

५. MS A/D add आर्षे

६. MS A/D omit नार्षे.....अथ मिथुनी। However, reads यमिवर्णउकारश्च वकारं भजति स्वयम्। ...भवत्येव। तस्य फलं त्विदमेव। अथ मिथुनी मिथुन्यथोथ। in १०.१९

७. MS A/D अनवर्णपूर्वत्वेनात्र न।

वकारस्तु साङ्कृत्यस्य॥२१॥

अस्य मते वकारो न लुप्यते। 'वायविष्टये' [तैसं. २.२.१२] इदमेवेष्टम्। न तु पूर्वद्वयं परद्वयं च।

उकारौकारपरौ[१] लुप्येते[२] माचाकीयस्य[३]॥२२॥

अवर्णपूर्वौ उकारौकारपरौ यवौ[३] लुप्येते। 'आप उन्दन्तु' [तैसं. १.२.१] 'या ओषधयः' [तैसं. ४.२.६]

लेशो वात्सप्रस्यैतयोः॥२३॥

अवर्णपूर्वयोर्यवयोर्लेशस्स्यात् उवयोः परयोः। उक्तान्येवोदाहरणनि।[४]

न प्लुतप्रग्रहौ॥२४॥

इमौ सन्धिविधिं न भजेते 'अग्ना३इति' [तैसं. ६.५.८] 'ते एनम्' [तैसं. २.५.६]

परश्च परश्च॥२५॥

य लोपे पर सन्धिर्न। त एव।

॥इति दशमोऽनुवाकः॥

---

१. MS F उकारो

MS F omits

२. MS F माचकीयस्य

३. MS F यनौ

४. MS A/D omit.

MS F उक्तान्येतानि ध उदाहरणानि।

॥अथ एकादशोऽनुवाकः॥

लुप्यते त्वकार एकारौकारपूर्वः॥१॥

तेऽब्रुवन् [तैसं. २.५.१] सोऽब्रवीन् [तैसं. २.१.२] स्वरपरइत्यधिकार-निवर्तकस्तु शब्दः।

अथालोपः॥२॥

इतः परमलोप एवेत्यधिकृत्य।

धातारातिरुपवाजपेयजुष्ट-श्येनायोख्यध्रुवक्षितिरियमेवसाया-ऽग्निर्मूर्द्धारुद्रप्रथमोपोत्तमविकर्षविहव्यहिरण्यवर्णीययाज्या महापृष्ठे॥३॥

एकारौकारपूर्वो वाकारो न लुप्यत एषु। त्वष्टा नो अत्र[१], आरे अस्मे[२] [तैसं. १.५.५] देवः सवितः प्रसुव [तैसं. १.७.७] इत्यादि षडनुवाकानां वाजपेयसंज्ञा। अग्रे अश्वमयुञ्जन्[३] [तैसं. १.७.७] द्रप्सो[४] अंशुः [तैसं. ३.१.१०] पितृभ्यो अभि [तैसं. ३.२.८] विश्वे अमृतस्य पुत्राः[५] [तैसं. ३.२.८] ये अन्तरिक्षे ये[६] [तैसं. ४.२.८] ऊर्मिद्रप्सो अपाम् [तैसं. ४.३.४] द्विपदग्रहणादत्र न। अग्ने स्विष्टकृतः [तैसं. १.६.२] स्विष्टकृतोऽग्नेरित्यादि। वो अन्यामति [तैसं. २.४.१२] अस्यानुवाकस्य शेषभूता या ऋक् सापि स्वीकृतेति भाष्ये।[७]

---

१. MS A/D read another example. निधिपतिर्नो अग्निः [तैसं. १.१.४४]

२. MS A adds च

MS F adds प्र

३. MS A/D ते अग्रे [तैसं. १.७.७-८]

४. MS A/D ते अꣳशुः [तैसं. ३.१.१०]

५. MS A/D omit पुत्राः

६. MS A/D omit write नमो अस्तु सर्पेभ्यः [तैसं. ४.२.८]

७. MS A/D omit इति भाष्ये।

'ईयुर्याज्येयमे नवम' इति माहेश्वरवचनाद्ये[१] अपरीषु पश्यान्।[२] [तैसं. १.४.३३] 'अथो ये अस्य' [तैसं. ४.५.१०][३] उत्तमस्य समीपः उपोत्तमः। पुष्टं ग्रामे अस्मिन् [तैसं. ५.१०.७][४] 'अश्मन्नूर्जं पर्वत' [तैसं. ४.६.१] इत्याद्याः पञ्चानुवाका विकर्षसंज्ञकाः। पावकोऽस्मभ्यम् [तैसं. ५.४.४]। वाजो न [तैसं. ४.७.१२] इत्याद्यास्त्रयोऽनुवाका विहव्यसंज्ञकाः।[५] 'नाकेऽग्निमेतम्'[६] एको देवोऽपि [तैसं. ५.६.१] कृतो अभ्यानट् [तैसं. १.१.१४] समिद्दिशां [तैसं. ४.४.१२] जीमूतस्य [तैसं. ४.६.६-९] यदक्रन्दो [तैसं. ४.६.६-९] मा नो मित्रो [तैसं. ४.६.६९] ये वाजिनमग्नेर्मन्वे [तैसं. ४.७.१५] एते महापृष्ठ्यसंज्ञकाः। विवस्वद्वाते अभि [तैसं. ४.४.१२]

अँहसोऽंꣳहतिरनिष्टृतोऽवन्त्वस्मानवद्यादहनि च॥४॥

चतुर्थं द्विपदम्। धातारातिरादिस्थानाम् एषाम् अकारो न लुप्यते। यवनह पर [तैसं. १२.४] इत्यस्य अपवादः। 'प्रमुञ्चन्तो नो अंꣳहसः' [तैसं. ४.३.१३] परिद्वेषसो अंꣳहतिः [तैसं. २.६.११] ते अनिष्टृतः[७] [तैसं. ४.१.७] ते अवन्त्वस्मान्' [तैसं. २.६.१२] 'मित्रमहो अवद्यात्' [तैसं. १.२.१४] शुक्रे अहनी [तैसं. ४.४.१२]। धातारातिरादिस्थानामिति किम्? पाप्मनोऽंꣳहसोंꣳहसस्पाप्मनः पाप्मनोंꣳहस इ०।[८]

अनुधर्मास आपोमर्तोरथस्त्वोदत्ते वातःपूर्वः॥५॥

एवं पूर्वोन्वित्यत्राकारो न लुप्यते। 'घर्मासो अनु [तैसं. ४.३.११] आपो अनु स्थ न [तैसं. ५.६.१] मर्तो अनु [तैसं. ४.६.७] रथो अनु मर्यं [तैसं.

१. MS A/D omit up to वचनात्।
२. MS A/D add अग्ने अङ्गिरसः
३. MS A/D add द्रापे अन्धसः
४. MS A/D omit
५. MS A/D add देवासो अधिवोचतां मे [तैसं. ४.७.१४]
६. MS A/D omit नाके...एतम्।
७. MS A/D अग्निष्टृतः
८. MS A/D पाप्मनोंꣳहसो मुञ्चति [तैसं. २.२.७]

४.६.७][१] पीयति[२] त्वो अनु [तैसं. ४.२.३] दत्ते अनुहाय [तैसं. ३.२.२] वातो अनु[३] [तैसं. ५.५.७]

अभि वा त्वपश्च॥६॥

पूर्वं द्विपदम्। एतयोरकारो न लुप्यते वातःपूर्वः। 'वातो अभिवातु' [तैसं. ७.४.१७] द्विपदेन किम्? वातोऽभिपवते।[४] यद्वातो अपः[५] [तैसं. ७.४.२०]

अन्वगमश्च॥७॥

एतयोरकारो न लुप्यते अपःपूर्वः। अपो अन्वचारिषम्। [तैसं. १.४.४५] अपो अगमत् [तैसं. ७.४.२०]

आपः पूर्वोद्भिरपान्नपादस्मान्॥८॥

एषामकारो न लुप्यत आपः पूर्वः द्वितीयं द्विपदम्। समापो अद्भिः [तैसं. १.१.८] आपो अपां नपात् [तैसं. १.२.३] नपादिति किम्? वारुणीरापोपां च।[६] आपो अस्मान् [तैसं. १.२.१]

राये स इन्द्रः पूर्वश्चाकारपरे॥९॥

एवं पूर्वः अस्मान्नित्यस्याकारो न लुप्यते, अस्मान् इतिशब्दात्परे अकारे सति। 'सोऽस्माꣳअवहाय' [तैसं. ५.७.९] इन्द्रो अस्मान् अस्मिन् [तैसं. ३.१.८] अकार इति किम्? सोऽस्मान् पातु तस्मै।[७] [तैसं. ५.५.५] पूर्वपदस्य उदाहरणं शाखान्तरे इति भाष्यम्।

तेपूर्वोऽद्यान्धोऽꣳशुरग्रे॥१०॥

एषामकारो न लुप्यते ते पूर्वः। 'ते अद्य' [तैसं. ३.१.४] उपो[८] ते अन्धः [तैसं. १.४.४] ते अꣳशुः [तैसं. १.२.६] यत्ते अग्ने [तैसं. ३.५.३]

---

१. MS A/D omits मर्यः
२. MS A/D omits पीयति
३. MS A/D add वातु
४. MS A/D omit from द्विपदेन...पवते।
५. MS A/D read वातो अपो अगमत्
६. MS A/D omit नपादिति....अपां च।
७. MS A/D omit अकार.....तस्मै।
८. MS A/D omit

मेपूर्वश्च॥११॥

अग्ने इत्यत्र अकारो न लुप्यते मेपूर्वः। यन्मे[१] अग्ने [तैसं. १.६.२]

अस्याश्विनाऽपरा च॥१२॥

एषामकारो न लुप्यते मे पूर्वः। 'मे अस्य' [तैसं. १.५.१०] पुनर्मे अश्विना [तैसं. ३.२.५] मे अपरागतम् [तैसं. २.६.७]

नःपूर्वोऽसदग्निरघान्तमोऽभ्यस्मिन्नद्यपथि॥१३॥

अन्त्यं द्विपदम्। एषामकारो न लुप्यते नःपूर्वः। नो असद्वशे [तैसं. १.२.३] अयं नो अग्निः [तैसं. १.३.४] नो अघशꣳसः [तैसं. १.४.२४] नो अन्तमः [तैसं. १.५.६] स्विष्टिन्नो अभि [तैसं. ३.१.९] शिक्षा नो अस्मिन् [तैसं. ७.५.७] नो अद्य पथिभिः[२] [तैसं. ७.५.२४]

नमःपूर्वोऽग्रेऽश्वेभ्योऽग्रियाय॥१४॥

एषामकारो न लुप्यते नमःपूर्वः। 'नमो अग्रे वधाय' [तैसं. ४.५.८] नमो अश्वेभ्यः [तैसं. ४.५.३] नमो अग्रियाय [तैसं. ४.५.५]

आविन्नस्सोमः पूर्वोऽग्निपरः॥१५॥

एतत्पूर्वोकारो न लुप्यतेऽग्निपरः। 'आविन्नो अग्निः' [तैसं. १.८.१२]

अग्निष्टोमः सोमः सोमो अग्निष्टोमोऽग्निष्टोमः सोमः। अग्निपरत्वादिदमपि। ग्नीति पदैकदेशः शाखान्तरविषय इति भाष्ये।

धीरासोऽदब्धास-एकादशास-ऋषीणां पुत्रश्शार्यातेऽषाढः पितारः पृथिवी यज्ञ, आसते ये, गृह्णाम्यग्रे, वाङ् एष, जज्ञे, सꣳस्फानः, युवयोर्यः, पृष्ठे पतिर्वः, गो, शुष्मः, पुवस्समिद्ध-ऋषभः, पाथो, वचो, वर्षिष्ठे, जुषाणो, यो रुद्रो, वृष्णः, पूर्वः॥१६॥

एवं पूर्वोकारो न लुप्यते। 'धीरासो अनुदृश्य' [तैसं. १.१.९] अदब्धासो अदाभ्यम्' [तैसं. १.१.१०] एकादशासो अप्सुषदः [तैसं. १.४.११] ऋषीणां

---

१. MS A/D read only मे

२. MS E adds hereafter in the margin पथीति किम्? नोधवसु वसतीतीन्द्रः।

पुत्रो अधिराजः [तैसं. १.३.७] शार्याते अपिबः [तैसं. १.४.१८] अषाढो अग्निः [तैसं. १.५.१०] त्वत्पितारो अग्ने [तैसं. १.५.१०] पृथिवी यज्ञे अस्मिन् [तैसं. १.६.५] आसते ये अन्तरिक्षे [तैसं. ३.५.४] गृह्णाम्यग्रे अग्निम् [तैसं. ५.७.९] वाऽएषो असुरः [तैसं. १.६.६] जज्ञे अग्निः [तैसं. २.२.४] सऽस्फानो अभि [तैसं. ३.३.८] युवयोर्यो अस्ति [तैसं. ३.५.४] पृष्ठे अधिरोचने [तैसं. ३.५.५] यज्ञपतिर्वो अत्र [तैसं. ५.७.७] गो अर्धम् [तैसं. ६.१.१०] अगोअर्धम् [तैसं. ६.१.१०] अप्यकाराद्यनया। 'उच्छुष्मो अग्ने' [तैसं. १.६. २] पुवो अग्रेगुवः [तैसं. १.१.५] समिद्धो अञ्जन् [तैसं. ५.१.११] द्याम् ऋषभो अन्तरिक्षम् [तैसं. १.२.८] अश्वऋषभो वृष्णिरित्यत्रानार्षे।

'पाथो अपीहि' [तैसं. ३.३.३] उग्रं वाचो अपां [तैसं. १.२.११] वर्षिष्ठे अधि [तैसं. १.१.८] स्वाहा जुषाणो अप्सुः [तैसं. १.३.४] यो रुद्रो अग्नौ [तैसं. ५.५.९] वृष्णो अश्वस्य [तैसं. २.४.७] चतुर्थाष्टमनवमदशमैकादशचतुर्दशषड्विंशतिश्च द्विपदम्।

अरतिमस्य-यज्ञस्य-अतिद्रुतो-अतियन्त्य नृणो-विष्यन्ननमीवो-ऽन्नेष्वर्चिरजीतानज्यानिमह्नियाअम्बाल्यर्वन्तमस्त्वकृणोदङ्गिरोऽप्सु यो अस्कभायदच्युतोऽश्व- सनिरस्थभिरशिश्रेदङ्गेऽघ्निया॥१७॥

एषामकारो न लुप्यते। 'दिवो अरतिम्' [तैसं. १.४.१३] अग्ने अस्य यज्ञस्य' [तैसं. १.६.२] सोमो अतिद्रुतः [तैसं. १.८.२१] पश्यन्तो अतियन्ति [तैसं. ३.२.२] तदग्ने अनृणः [तैसं. ३.३.८] यवसे अविष्यन् [तैसं. ४.४. ३] स्वावेशो अनमीवः [तैसं. ३.४.१०] ये अन्नेषु [तैसं. ४.५.११] यो अर्चिः [तैसं. ५.७.८] शरदो अजीतान् [तैसं. ५.७.२] यो अज्यानिम्' [तैसं. ५.७.२] तिरो अग्नियाः [तैसं. ७.३.१३] अम्बे अम्बालि [तैसं. ७.४.१९] यो अर्वन्तम् [तैसं. ७.४.१५] बहिस्ते अस्तु [तैसं. ३.३.१०] इत इन्द्रो अकृणोत् [तैसं. १.१.१२] अग्ने अङ्गिरः [तैसं. १.२.१२] अङ्गिरोभ्यः स्वाहा इत्यत्र विलोमे। 'यो अप्सु यः' [तैसं. ५.५.९] 'यो अस्कभायत्' [तैसं. १. २.१३] रसो अच्युतः [तैसं. १.२.६] भक्षो अश्वसनिः [तैसं. ३.२.५] दधीचो अस्थभिः [तैसं. ५.६.६] वरुणो अशिश्रेत् [तैसं. १.८.१०] अङ्गे अङ्गे [तैसं. १.३.१०] अघ्नियैति पदैकदेशः। ते अघ्निये [तैसं. ७.१.६] पयो अघ्नियासु [तैसं. १.२.८] द्वितीय-तृतीय-चतुर्थाष्टादशैकविंशतिर्द्वाविंशतिद्विपदानीमानि।

अध्वरस्वरपदे॥१८॥

देवो अध्वरः [तैसं. १.३.१२] सत्यधर्माणो अध्वरे [तैसं. १.२.१]

स पूर्वस्यार्धसदृशमेकेषामर्धसदृशमेकेषाम्॥१९॥

यो लुप्तोकारः स पूर्वस्यार्धमात्रसदृशं कालं भजते इत्येकेषां मतम्।

॥ इत्येकादशोऽनुवाकः॥

॥अथ द्वादशोऽनुवाकः॥

अथ लोपः॥१॥

इतः परं लोप एवेत्यधिकृत्य। 'धातारातिरि' [तैप्रा. ११.३] त्यादिविषयोऽयमारम्भः।

असि॥२॥

अस्याकारो लुप्यते। 'प्रथोऽसि' [तैसं. ४.२.९] सुपर्णोऽसि [तैसं. ४.१.१०]

न गर्भस्सन्नद्धो[१] यमो भद्रः पूर्व॥३॥

पूर्वस्यापवादः। 'गर्भो अस्यौषधीनाम्' [तैसं. ४.२.३] 'सन्नद्धो असि' [तैसं. ४.६.६] 'यमो अस्यादित्य' [तैसं. ४.६.७] 'त्वं भद्रो असि' [तैसं. ४.३.१३]

यवनहपरः स्वरपरेषु॥४॥

यवनहपरोऽकारो लुप्यते तेषु स्वरपरेषु सत्सु।[२] 'हिरण्यशृङ्गो यः[३] [तैसं. ४.६.७] ताभिर्नोऽविता[४] [तैसं. ४.१.११] वरेण्यो नु [तैसं. ४.१.१०] जम्भयन्तोऽहि [तैसं. १.७.८]

जकारग्नापर उदात्तः॥५॥

जपरोग्नपरश्चोदात्तोऽकारो लुप्यते। 'ओजोऽजायथाः' [तैसं. १.६.१२] 'वन्द्योऽग्ने' [तैसं. १.३.१४]

---

१. MS F गर्भे

२. MS C reads something after सत्सु, but it is not clear.

३. MS A/D read this example at the end.

४. MS A/D नोविता
   C भिर्नोविता

५. MS A/D हिम्

मोवचो दधानस्स्थे पूर्वश्च॥६॥

एवं पूर्वो ग्नपरोकारो लुप्यते। म इति पदैकदेशः। 'इमोऽग्निम्'[१] [तैसं. ४.१.२] 'वचोऽग्नये' [तैसं. ३.२.११] दधानोऽग्निः [तैसं. ४.१.३] सधस्थेऽग्निम् [तैसं. ४.१.३]

अभ्यावर्तिन्नपूपमपिदधाम्यद्यान्वदितिश्शर्माग्नेर्जिह्वा मग्नयः पप्रयोऽस्माकमस्मे धत्ताश्माश्वा श्रुतिरश्यामा-माऽर्यमन्नस्मत्पाशानस्मिन्[२] यज्ञेऽस्ताऽव्यथमानाऽ भिद्रोहमधाय्यदोऽथो दुग्धा अरिष्टा अरथा अर्चन्त्यन्तर-स्यामत्रस्थान्नायाङ्गिरस्वदकरम्॥७॥

एषामकारो लुप्यते। 'अग्ने अभ्यावर्तिन्' [तैसं. ४.२.१] 'भद्रे शोचेऽपूपम्'[३] [तैसं. ४.२.२] 'अग्नेऽपिदधामि' [तैसं. ४.१.१०] 'नोऽद्यानुमतिः' [तैसं. ३.३.११] नोदितिः शर्म [तैसं. ४.६.६] नोग्नेर्जिह्वाम् [तैसं. ४.१.८] नोऽग्नयः प्रपयः [तैसं. १.७.७] नरोऽस्माकम् [तैसं. ४.६.६] विश्वेऽस्मे धत्त [तैसं. १.४.४४] नोश्मा भवतु[४] नः [तैसं. ४.६.६] अश्वेति दीर्घस्य यत्र यत्र श्रवणं तत्र तत्र लोपः। 'भरन्तोऽश्वाय' [तैसं. ४.१.१०] प्रचेतसोऽश्वानजनि [तैसं. ४.६.६] वाजयन्तोऽश्याम [तैसं. १.३.१४] ते मैषाम् [तैसं. ४.७.१४][५] तेर्यमन्[६] [तैसं. २.३.१४] तेऽस्मत्पाशान्[७] [तैसं. ४.३.१३] पिता तेऽस्मिन्यज्ञे [तैसं. २.६.१२] द्रुणानोस्ताः [तैसं. १.२.१४] सुपर्णोऽव्यथमाना [तैसं. ४.२.९] जनेऽभिद्रोहम् [तैसं. ८.४.११] सुमन्मेऽधायि [तैसं. ४.६.८] येऽदो रोचने[७] [तैसं. ४.२.८] 'अग्रेऽथो सीद' [तैसं. ४.१.९] 'नोनुमो दुग्धाः' [तैसं. २.४.१४] पूर्वेऽरिष्टाः [तैसं. ४.७.१४] पवयोऽरथाः [तैसं. १.६.१२] गायत्रिणोर्चन्ति [तैसं. १.६.१२]

---

१. MS F ....ग्नि।   २. MS F ......त्या

३. MS F adds दे।

४. MS A/D omit भवतु नः।

५. MS A/D omit

६. MS A/C/F omit

७. MS A/D omit

८. MS A/D read येऽदः

शूशुचोऽन्तरस्याम् [तैसं. ४.१.९] येऽत्रस्थपुराणाः[1] [तैसं. ४.२.४] पोषोऽन्नाय[2] [तैसं. १.७.९] सधस्थेङ्गिरस्वत् [तैसं. ४.१.६] तेभ्योऽकरम् [तैसं. ४.५.१] एकं तृतीयं चतुर्थं पञ्चमं षष्ठं सप्तमं नवमं पञ्चदशं षोडशमेकोनविंशतिः सप्तविंशतिरष्टाविंशश्चयुगलम्।

गाहमानो-जायमानो-हेतयो-मन्यमानो-
वनस्पतिभ्यः-पते-स्त्रिधस्[3]-तपसस्-
स्वधावो भामितोऽग्नय-आयो-ध्वर्यो क्रतोपूर्वः॥८॥

एवं पूर्वोकारोऽलुप्यते। 'गाहमानोऽदायः' [तैसं. ४.६.४] जायमानोऽह्नाम् [तैसं. २.४.१४] हेतयोऽन्यम् [तैसं. ४.५.१०] मन्यमानोऽमर्त्यम् [तैसं. १.४. ४६] वनस्पतिभ्योऽधि [तैसं. ४.६.१] पतेऽन्नस्य [तैसं. ४.२.३] स्त्रिधोऽति [तैसं. ४.१.७] तपसोऽधिजातः [तैसं. ४.२.१०] स्वधावोऽमृतस्य [तैसं. ३. १.११] भामितोऽमित्रस्य [तैसं. १.६.१२] अग्नयोऽन्वतप्यन्त [तैसं. ४.२.६] 'अग्नयग्रहणम्।' अन्वतप्यन्तेत्यस्याकारस्यलोपनिमित्तमेवेति भाष्यम्। तथा[4] च माहेश्वरशिक्षायाम् ग्नयपूर्वोन्वतप्यचेति। तप्यन्ताग्नयों[5] अग्नयोऽन्वतप्यन्त।[6] पञ्चमं नवमं च युगलम्। 'अदब्धायोऽशीततनो' [तैसं. १.१.१३] अध्वर्यो वै [तैसं. ६.४.३] शतक्रतो नु [तैसं. २.५.१२]

यद्यत्प्रग्रहपूर्वश्च अकारो लुप्यते त्विति।
आर्षे तु लोप एवस्स्यान्न तस्यानार्षे एव च॥

इत्यात्रेयवचनाद्विलोमे लोपो न।[7]

---

१. MS A/D omit पुराणाः
२. MS F reads.....अन्नान
३. MS F स्निधस्
४. MS A/D omit तथा च......चेति।
५. MS A/D add अग्नयोऽत्वतप्यन्त [४.२.६]
६. MS A/D omit अन्वतप्यन्त
७. MS A/D omit इत्यात्रेय.......न।

तस्मिन्ननुदात्ते पूर्व उदात्तस्वरितम्॥९॥

अकारे नीचे लुप्ते सति पूर्वोच्चः स्वारमापद्यते।[१] तेऽब्रुवन् [तैसं. २.५.१] सोऽब्रवीत् [तैसं. २.१.२]

उदात्ते चानुदात्त उदात्तम्॥१०॥

उच्चेकारे लुप्ते सति पूर्वो नीच उच्चमापद्यते।[२] रुन्धतेऽसत्रम् [तैसं. ७.३.८]

स्वरितश्च सर्वत्र स्वरितश्च सर्वत्र॥११॥

उच्चेकारे लुप्ते सति पूर्वस्वरित उच्चमापद्यते।[३] सर्वत्रेति वचनान्नित्यादीनां ग्रहणम्। ओजोऽजायथाः [तैसं. १.६.१२] उक्योथातिरात्रः [तैसं. ७.१.५]

॥इति द्वादशोऽनुवाकः॥

॥इति प्रथमः प्रश्नः॥

---

१. MS A/D स्वरितं भजते

२. MS A/D अकारे उच्चे लुप्ते सति पूर्वनीचः उच्चमाप्नोति।

३. MS A/D तस्मिन्नुच्चे लुप्ते सति पूर्वस्वरित उच्चमाप्नोति।

॥अथ त्रयोदशोऽनुवाकः॥

अथ मकारलोपः॥१॥

इत्यधिकृत्य।

रेफोष्मपरः॥२॥

एवं परः पदान्तो मो लुप्यते। सꣳशितम् [तैसं. ४.१.१०] तꣳषट् [तैसं. ५.५.२] सꣳसमित् [तैसं. २.६.११] प्रत्युष्टꣳरक्षः [तैसं. १.१.२] त्वꣳह [तैसं. २.६.११]

यवकारपरश्चैकेषामाचार्याणाम्॥३॥

यपरो वपरो मो लुप्यते इत्येकेषाम् मतम्।[१] पञ्चमानुवाके[२] सवर्णापत्तिं ये निषेधन्ति तेषां मतमिदम्। सिंहावलोकनेन[३] चान्वा[४]देशकः।[५]

न सꣳसामिति रापरः॥४॥

मो लोपः। 'क्विपि राजिन' इत्यात्रेयवचनात्। 'नोर्ध्वे राजि सꣳसांक्विपीति माहेश्वरवचनाच्च।[६] सꣳसामित्येतयोर्मौ न लुप्यते क्विबन्त राजति स्थरापरश्चेत्। 'सम्राजे' [तैसं. १.६.१२] 'साम्राज्येन' [तैसं. १.७.१०] क्विपि राजीति नियमादत्र लोप एव। राज्ञे सꣳ सꣳराज्ञे' या साꣳराजेत्यादि।[७] पदान्तश्च व्यञ्जनपर इति वक्ष्यमाणं द्वित्वनिषेधं इतिशब्दो निवारयति। अतोऽत्र द्वित्वमेव।[८] अन्यत्रापि क्वचिन्मकारो न लुप्यते तदाह माहेश्वरशिक्षायाम्।

---

१. MS A/D omit मतम्।
२. MS A/D read अध्याये
३. MS F is completed here.
४. MS A/D चकारो
५. MS D adds in a different hand एतत्सूत्रमनिष्टम्।
६. MS A/D omit
७. MS A/D omit या साꣳराजे
८. MS A/D omit

शान्त्यूर्ध्व ॐ मित्यत्रमः परमात्मं सरूपतयेति। अन्यदपि[१]–परमात्मं सरूपात्माङ् मकारस्सानुनासिकः। ॐमित्यत्र मकारो यः परे शान्तौ म एवहि।

परमात्मं सरूपम्। ॐशान्तिः इत्यारण्यशिक्षायाम्।

अथ वर्णानाम्॥५॥

इतः परं वर्णसꣳहिता वक्ष्यत इत्यधिकृत्य।

ऋकारर्कारेरषपूर्वो नकारो णकारꣳसमानपदे॥६॥

एवम्पूर्वो नो णमापद्यतेऽखण्डपदे।[२] 'ऋणवा' [तैसं. ६.३.१०] होतॄणाम् [तैसं. ४.३.१३] वर्णः [तैसं. ६.१.३] कृष्णः [तैसं. १.१.११]

व्यवेतोऽपि॥७॥

अन्येन व्यवेतोऽपि णत्वमाप्नोति। 'वृक्णम्' [तैसं. ५.१.१०] आरमणम् [तैसं. ६.५.११]

हिरण्मयम्॥८॥

स्पर्शपर इत्यस्यापवादः। 'हिरण्मयं दाम' [तैसं. २.४.१३]

पाणिगणपुण्यकण्वकाणगाणबाणवेणुगुणमणिप्रवादेषु पूर्वः॥९॥[३]

पाण्यादीनां प्रवादेषु पूर्वो णः प्रकृत्यैव वेदितव्यः। सुपाणिः [तैसं. ३.१.११] वृषपाणयः [तैसं. ४.६.६] हिरण्यपाणिम् [तैसं. १.४.२५] गणानां त्वां गणपतिम् [तैसं. २.३.१४] गणा मे [तैसं. ३.१.८] गणेन गणम् [तैसं. ५.४.७] पुण्यो भवति [तैसं. १.६.११] कण्वाः [तैसं. ४.३.१३] अकाणया [तैसं. ६.१.६] गाणपत्यात् [तैसं. ४.१.२] बाणवान् [तैसं. ४.५.१] वेणुर्वैणवी [तैसं. ५.१.१] वेणुना [तैसं. ५.२.५] यद्वेणोः [तैसं. ५.१.१] मणिना [तैसं. ७.३.१४] यथा गुणे [तैसं. ७.२.४] लिङ्गविभक्तिभेदसमासतद्धितादिभिर्निर्दिष्टाः प्रवादाः इति भाष्ये।

---

१. MS A/D omit माहेश्वर.....अन्यदपि

२. MS A/D समानपदे

३. MS C omits गणा मे।

पणिपणिं वीयमाणऊण्योः॥१०॥

अत्रापि प्रकृत्यैव णकारः। 'अग्ने देवपाणिभिः।' [तैसं. १.१.१३] पणिं गोषु। [तैसं. २.६.११] वीयमाणः। [तैसं. १.१.१३] ऊण्योः कविक्रतुम्। [तैसं. १.२.६]

टवर्गपरः॥११॥

[१]पूर्ववत्। कण्डूयेत [६.१.३]

चङ्कुणफणस्थूणौ हिणुयद्धिणोतिकौणेयोणिष्ठा-
उल्बणमुगणाश्रुतिश्चुपुणीका वाणिजायाणवश्चाट्णा-
रस्स्थाणुं तूणवेवीणायामश्लोणयापणेत वाणीः
कल्याणी कुणपं वाणः शतशोणाश्रुतिर्धाणिकामेणी॥१२॥

एष्वपि प्रकृत्यैव। निचङ्कुण [तैसं. १.४.४५] आपनीफणत् [तैसं. १.७.८] अयस्स्थूणौ [तैसं. १.८.१२] प्र हिणुयात् [तैसं. २.२.६] प्रहिणोति[२] [तैसं. २.२.६] वै कौणेयः [तैसं. २.३.८] येऽणिष्ठाः [तैसं. २.५.५] यज्ञ उल्बणम् [तैसं. ३.४.३] उगणा उत [तैसं. ४.१.१०] उगणाभ्यः [तैसं. ४.५.४] चुपुणीका[३] [तैसं. ४.४.५] वाणिजाय [तैसं. ४.५.२] अणवश्च मे [तैसं. ४.७.४][४] आट्णारः [तैसं. ५.६.५] यस्स्थाणुम् [तैसं. ७.३.१] तूणवे या वीणायाम् [तैसं. ६.१.४] अश्लोणया [तैसं. ६.१.६] इति पणेत [तैसं. ६.१.१०] इन्द्रं वाणीः [तैसं. १.६.१२] कल्याणी [तैसं. ७.१.६] अश्वकुणपम् [तैसं. ७.२.१०] वाणः शततन्तुः [तैसं. ७.५.९] शोणाय स्वाहा [तैसं. ७.३.१८] धाणिका [तैसं. ७.४.१९] वनस्पतीनामेणी[५] [तैसं. ५.५.१५]

अवग्रहो वृषण्शीर्षण्ब्रह्मण्क्षण्चर्मण्चर्षण्॥१३॥

एषु अवग्रहस्थो णः प्रकृत्यैव। वृषण्वान् [तैसं. २.१.११] शीर्षण्वान्

१. MS E adds प्रकृत्यैव
२. MS A/D हिणोति
३. MS D ....णिका
४. MS C/E अणवश्च मेणवः but read च मेणवः after आट्णारः।
५. MS E adds अम्बे वनस्पतीनामेणी
MSC reads only मेणी

[तैसं. ७.५.२५] ब्रह्मण्वन्तः [तैसं. ६.४.१०] अक्षण्वते [तैसं. ७.५.१२] चर्मण्वते [तैसं. ७.५.१२] चर्षणीधृतः [तैसं. ३.४.११] चर्षणी इत्यस्य ग्रहणं वैकृतनिराकरणार्थम्।

ऋण्णषण्णष्णाम्णराव्णग्राव्णचेति प्राकृताः॥१४॥

पाण्यादिचर्मणन्तेषु प्राकृतशब्दो मुख्यः। चतसृषु संहितासु णत्वभावात्। ऋण्णादिषु तु स्पर्शपर इति निषेधनिषेधार्थो। प्राकृतशब्दः इति भाष्ये।[१] 'असंतृण्णे' [तैसं. ६.२.११] 'स्वयमातृण्णाम्' [तैसं. ५.७.६] अभिषण्णः [तैसं. २.४.२] निषण्णा[२] [तैसं. २.४.२] पूष्णः [तैसं. १.३.१०] अर्यम्णे [तैसं. २.३.४] दधिक्रालाणः [तैसं. १.५.११] आग्राव्ण्णः [तैसं. ६.३.२]

न सुम्नोऽग्नि-युष्मानीतोन्तो लोपात्स्पर्शपरो व्यवायेषु शसचटतवर्गीयेषु॥१५॥

एषु नो णत्वं नापद्यतेघ्नः सुषुम्नः [तैसं. ३.४.७] इन्द्राग्निभ्याम्[३] [तैसं. ४.४.५] युष्मानीतः [तैसं. २.१.११] वृत्रघ्नः [तैसं. ४.७.१५] लोपात्परस्येदम्। 'रषः पूर्वो हवनीति प्राप्तिस्तस्यैव निषेधः सिंहावलोकनन्यायेनेति[४] भाष्ये। नखनिर्भिन्नम् [तैसं. १.८.९] अवरुन्धे [तैसं. २.४.११] स्पर्शपरस्येमे। स्पर्शशब्देन नित्यस्पर्श एव गृह्यते। अतः पूर्णेत्यादौ निषेधो न।[५] रशनाम् [तैसं. ६.३.६] रसेन [तैसं. १.४.४६] रोचना दिवि [तैसं. ७.४.२०] राजानौ [तैसं. २.६.२] प्रक्रीडिनः [तैसं. ४.३.१३] ताम् पृतनाम्[६] [तैसं. ३.५.३] 'जनप्रथनाय' [तैसं. ३.२.८] शादिव्यवहितानीमानि।

---

१. MS A/D omit इति भाष्ये।

२. MS A/D/E omit

३. MS A/D ग्नीभ्याम्

४. MS D reads something in the margin and rubs out. Then reads नित्यस्पर्शस्येव ग्रहणं अतः पूर्णेत्यादौ निषेधो न।

MS E adds after स्पर्शशब्देन–"द्वितीयचतुर्थयोरितिसूत्रे व्यञ्जनोत्तरयोरिति वाचो युक्त्यन्तरेण यत्र द्वित्वं तस्मात्परस्यैव ग्रहणम्। but rubs out.

५. MS A adds इति भाष्ये।

६. MS A/D omit ताम्

पृक्तस्वरात्परो ळो डं पौष्करसादेः पौष्करसादेः॥१६॥

पृक्तस्वरात्परो दुश्लिष्टलकारो[1] डकारमापद्यते समानपदे। मृडयन्तु [तैसं. ४.४.३] पृक्तस्वरादिति किम्? इलान्दम् [तैसं. ७.५.९] समानपद इति किम्? पितृलोकꣳसोमेन [तैसं. २.६.२]

॥ इति त्रयोदशोऽनुवाकः॥

---

१. MS A '' ळो दुश्लिष्ट डमापद्यते समानपदे।
MS E '' लो डमापद्यते समानपदे।
MS C also starts writing लो डम् etc. but rubs out and replaces in the margin with different hand.

॥अथ चतुर्दशोऽनुवाकः॥

स्वरपूर्वं व्यञ्जनं द्विवर्णं व्यञ्जनपरम्॥१॥

अच्पूर्वं व्यञ्जनपरं व्यञ्जनं द्वित्वमापद्यते। उरुप्प्रथस्व [तैसं. १.१.८] 'ह्रस्वपूर्वादनुस्वारयोगाच्छ्रींयत्र तावुभौ' इति माहेश्वरवचनात्।[१] ह्रस्वपूर्वानुस्वारयोगाद्योर्द्वित्वं स्यात्।[२] अन्यच्च 'ह्रस्वपूर्वादनुस्वारयोगाद्वीं चान्तगौ न ङौ' इत्यात्रेयवचनाध्रस्वपूर्वयोः पदान्तयोर्नङयोर्द्वित्वं स्यात्। अश्मन्न्। [तैसं. ४.६.७] प्रत्यङ् [तैसं. ७.५.९] पदान्तस्य णस्यापि द्वित्वं भवति। अन्तगा ङणना ह्रस्वाद्वित्वमिति माहेश्वरवचनात्। यथा-ब्रह्मण्वन्त इति ब्रह्मण्ण्वन्तः[३] [तैसं. ६.४.१०] चर्मण्ण् [तैसं. ६.१.९]

संयोगादिरियाद्वित्वमनुस्वारपरस्थितः। सꣳश्श्रवाह
अनुस्वारो द्विरुच्येत संयोगे परतस्स्थिते। सꣳꣳश्रवाह

लवकारपूर्वस्पर्शश्च पौष्करसादेः॥२॥

अस्य मते लपूर्वो वपूर्वो वा स्पर्शो द्विवर्णमापद्यते। लवौ स्वरपूर्वौ स्तश्चेत्। 'कल्प्पां जुहोति' [तैसं. ५.४.८] कल्प्पते [तैसं. ३.४.८] विभुदाव्न्ने [तैसं. ३.५.८]

स्पर्श एवैकेषामाचार्याणाम्॥३॥

एकेषां मते लवकारपूर्वस्पर्श एव द्वित्वमाप्नोति। अनेन नियमेन पौष्करसादिमते लवयोर्द्वित्वमस्तीति गम्यते। इदं सूत्रमिष्टं न तु पूर्वम्।

रेफात्परं च॥४॥

रात्परं व्यञ्जनं द्वित्वमापद्यते। 'अर्क्किणः' [तैसं. १.६.१२] 'ऊष्मा

---

१. MS A/D omit

२. MS A/D omit and read the last two tines. Then read ह्रस्व......प्रत्यङ् The rest portion is omitted.

३. MSE omits

स्वरपर' [तैप्रा. १४.१६] इति[१] निषेधज्ञापनाद्व्यञ्जनपर इति नियमो न। 'अर्क्कः' [तैसं. ७.५.९] अर्च्चन्ति [तैसं. १.६.१२]

द्वितीयचतुर्थयोस्तु व्यञ्जनोत्तरयोः पूर्वः॥५॥

स्वरपूर्वयोरेतयोर्व्यञ्जनोत्तरयोः पूर्वागमो भवति। द्वितीयस्य प्रथमः। चतुर्थस्य तृतीयः। 'विक्ख्याय' [तैसं. ४.१.२] साद्ध्या वै [तैसं. ६.३.४] तु शब्दो द्वित्वनिवर्तकः। अत्र 'उत्तर' इतिशब्दान्तरं 'व्यञ्जनपर' इति नियमं निवर्तयति। कुत्रचित् व्यञ्जनपरनिमित्तं विनाऽपि द्वित्वं पूर्वागमं च भवति इति भाष्ये। तथाहि–[२]

समानस्वरयोर्मध्ये लक्ष्याद्द्वित्वं हलः क्वचित्।
द्वितीयस्य चतुर्थस्य तथा पूर्वागमस्स्मृतः॥

इति व्यासः। अन्यदपि–

कुत्रचित्स्वरयोर्मध्ये द्वित्वं लक्ष्यानुसारतः।
पूर्वागमस्तथा तत्र ज्ञेयो वर्णविचक्षणैः॥

अत्ता हवीꣳषि [तैसं. २.६.१२] अन्नस्य [तैसं. २.१.३] प्रच्छत् छन्दः[३] [तैसं. ४.३.१२] अद्धि त्वम् [तैसं. २.६.१२] आगमस्येमे।

रेफात्पूर्वयोश्च नित्यम्॥६॥

रेफात्परं चेत्यस्यापवादः। रपूर्वयोद्वितीयचतुर्थयोर्नित्यं पूर्वागमस्स्यात्। 'ऊद्ध्र्वः[४] [तैसं. १.२.१४] 'अर्त्थेतः'[५] [तैसं. १.८.११] मूर्क्खाः[६] [तैसं. ६.६.४]

लकारपूर्वे च॥७॥

लपूर्वे चतुर्थे पूर्वागमः। प्रगल्ब्भोऽस्य [तैसं. २.५.५]

---

१. MS C omits इति

२. MS A/D omit तथाहि। read कुत्रचित्स्वर...विचक्षणैः। समाने स्वरयोर्भध्ये ....स्मृतः। इति व्यासः।

३. MS A/D omit छन्दः।

४. MS D reads ऊर्ध्वः

५. MS D अर्थेतः

६. MS D मूर्क्खाः

उपसर्ग पाथ एषोत्यातिधामपरमभूते पूर्वेषु छखिभुजेषु च॥८॥

एतत् पूर्वेषु छखिभुजेषु पूर्वागमः। 'आच्छृणत्ति [तैसं. ५.१.७] 'प्राक्खिदते' [तैसं. ४.५.९] 'परिब्भुज' [तैसं. ४.५.१] जेति किम्? 'विभु च' [तैसं. ४. ७.४] खीति किम्? 'निखातम्' [तैसं. ६.३.४] पाथः [तैसं. ४.६.८] 'एषच्छागः' [तैसं. ४.६.८] पाथ इति किम्? एष छन्दोभिः [तैसं. ७.५.१५] अतिच्छन्दसम् [तैसं. ५.३.८] अतिच्छन्दसाय [तैसं. ७.५.१४] धामच्छत् [तैसं. २.४.१०] परमच्छदः [तैसं. ४.६.२] भूतेच्छदाः [तैसं. ४.६.२]।

'पाथ एषोत्यातिभूते परमापोपसर्गत' इति माहेश्वरवचनात्।[१] 'छखिभुजा इयुः पूर्वं धामापात्युपसर्गतः' भूते च पाथ एषोति परमाद्यूर्ध्वतस्स्थिते[२] त्यात्रेय-वचनाच्चा[३]त्येतस्मात्परस्यापि। छन्दाःस्यपापच्छन्दाःसि।

अघोषादूष्मणः परः प्रथमोभिनिधानस्पर्शपरात्तस्य सस्थानः॥९॥

स्पर्शपरादघोषादूष्मणः परस्पर्शस्य सस्थानः प्रथमागमः स्यात् सोऽभिनिधान-संज्ञो भवति।[४] 'अशप्मम्' [तैसं. ४.६.१] ग्रीष्प्म [तैसं. २.१.२] कृष्ट्णः [तैसं. १.१.११] यः पाप्मना [तैसं. २.३.१३] सर्वविशेषणैः किम्? 'अपराह्णे रुक्मम्' [तैसं. ५.२.७] इष्वा [तैसं. ५.७.३] अत्र न। इदमेवेष्टं न तु परद्वयम्।

शात्तैत्तिरीयके न स्य ञो भवेत् काठके न चेत्। इति व्यासवचनादत्र[५] ञादेशः। प्राश्ञीयात् [तैसं. ३.४.३] काठके तु 'अश्नुते तं कामम्' इत्यादि।[६]

अघोषे प्लाक्षेः॥१०॥

अघोषस्पर्श इति विशेषः। 'निष्क्केवल्यम्' [तैसं. ४.४.२]

उत्तमपरात्तु प्लाक्षायणस्य॥११॥

उत्तमपरादघोषादूष्मणः परः प्रथमः स्यात्।[७] 'तीर्थे स्त्नाति' [तैसं. ६.१.

१. MS A/D omit
२. MS A/D omit भूते....स्थिते।
३. MS A/D omit च
४. MS E reads स्यात्
५. MS A/D omits वचनादत्र आदेशः।
६. MS A/D omit इत्यादि
७. MS A/D omit स्यात्। MS E ends here.

२] केचिदेवमूचुः। अघोषमूष्माणस्तु शब्दो निवारयति। तत्रेदमुदाहरणम्। 'अह्वाम्' [तैसं. २.४.१४]

प्रथमोष्मपरो द्वितीयम्॥१२॥

द्वितीयं भजते। 'विरप्फ्शिन्' [तैसं. १.१.९] 'प्रत्यङ्ख् सोमः' [तैसं. १.८.२१] 'तत्थ् सवितुः' [तैसं. १.५.६][१]

वाडवीकारस्यासस्थानपरः॥१३॥

असस्थान इति विशेषः। 'विरप्फ्शिन्' [तैसं. १.१.९] सस्थानत्वादत्र न। 'तत्सवितुः' [तैसं. १.५.६] इदमनिष्टम्।

अथ न॥१४॥

इत्यधिकृत्य।

अवसाने र-विसर्जनीय-जिह्वामूलीयोपध्मानीयाः॥१५॥

अवसाने वर्णः रादिचत्वारिश्च। द्वित्वं नापद्यन्ते। ऊर्क् [तैसं. ४.७.४] रेफात्परं चेति प्राप्तिः। नार्तिम् [तैसं. २.२.४] मनः क्षेमे [तैसं. ५.२.१] यः कामयेत [तैसं. २.१.२] यः पाप्मना [तैसं. २.३.१३] पूर्वसूत्रेणैषां प्राप्तिः।

ऊष्मा स्वरपरः॥१६॥

अच्पर ऊष्माव्द्वित्वं नापद्यते।[२] 'दर्शपूर्णमासौ'[३] [तैसं. २.२.५] 'वर्षाभ्यः [तैसं. ७.२.१०] बर्सम् [तैसं. २.५.७] बर्हिषा [तैसं. १.७.४]

प्रथमपरश्चप्लाक्षिप्लाक्षायणयोः॥१७॥

प्रथमपर ऊष्माव्द्वित्वं न भजते। 'सुश्चन्द्र' [तैसं. ४.४.४] अष्टौ [तैसं. ६.४.५] तस्मै[४] [तैसं. ६.३.३]

ऊष्माघोषो हारितस्य॥१८॥

अघोष ऊष्मा द्वित्वं नापद्यते। 'वैश्यः [तैसं. ७.१.१] पुष्यति [तैसं. २.१.९] तस्य [तैसं. १.१.१०] अघोषत्वेनात्र न। 'अह्वाम्' [तैसं. २.४.१४]

---

१. MS D ....चत्वारश्च।

२. MS A/D न।

३. MS D adds सर्व्वः

४. MS A/D तस्मात् [तैसं. ६.४.९]

रेफपरश्च हकारः॥१९॥

स्पष्टम्।[१] दुदुह्रे। अह्रयः [तैसं. १.५.६]

टवर्गश्च तवर्गपरः॥२०॥

तवर्गपरष्टवर्गो द्वित्वं नापद्यते।[२] 'वषट् ते' [तैसं. २.२.१२] 'विड् द्रविणम्' [तैसं. १.८.१३]

लतवर्गौ यवकारपरौ॥२१॥[३]

यर्वोत्तरौ लतवर्गौ द्वित्वं न। 'कल्याणी' [तैसं. ७.१.६] बैल्वः [तैसं. २.१.८] कन्या [तैसं. ३.१.११] सत्त्वा [तैसं. ७.५.१३]

परश्च॥२२॥

एताभ्यां[४] परवकारस्य द्वित्वं न। 'विभुदाव्ने' [तैसं. ३.५.८] इदं हारितपञ्च-कमनिष्टम्।

सवर्ण सवर्गीयपरः॥२३॥

एतत्परो द्वित्वं न भजते। 'अत्वक्काय' [तैसं. ७.५.१२] 'पिप्पका ते' [तैसं. ५.५.१९] अङ्कौ [तैसं. १.७.७] प्राञ्चम् [तैसं. ५.२.७] तन्ते [तैसं. ३.२.१०]

ङानुनासिकपूर्वस्तु ककारो मध्य आगमः।
गकारश्च तकारे च धकारे च यथाक्रमम्॥

इति आत्रेय[५]वचनाज्जातयोरागमयो[६] ककारगकारयोः पूर्वस्य द्वित्वं न।

---

१. MS A/D omit स्पष्टम्।

२. MS A/D omit आपद्यते।

३. MS A reads the porion for *sū*. 22 under 21 and vice versa as वकारस्य द्वित्वं न। विभुदाव्ने [तैसं. ३.५.८] इदं हारितपञ्चकमनिष्टम्। for (*Sū*. 21)

४. MS A as mentioned above reads यवोत्तरौ....स त्त्वा [See *Sū* 21]

५. MS A/D omit आत्रेय

६. MS A/D omit जातयो.....द्वित्त्वं न। read इदमपि उदाहरणम्।

'पाङ्क्तः' [तैसं. १.५.२] युङ्क्ध्वम् [तैसं. ३.४.८][१] इमौ ककारगकारागमौ पदान्तात्परौ न स्याताम्। 'प्रत्यङ् त्र्यहः' प्रत्यङ् धिष्णियान्[२]।

ङकारात्धपरे चैव ह्यनन्तात्तपरे तथा।
गकारश्च ककारश्चेदागमश्च यथाक्रमम्।।

इति व्यासवचनात्।[३]

नानुत्तमउत्तमपरः।।२४।।

उत्तमपरोऽनुत्तमोपरो[४] द्वित्वं आपद्यते। 'आट्ट्णारः' [तैसं. ५.६.५] पाप्मानम् [तैसं. १.४.४]

अथैकेषामाचार्याणाम्।।२५।।

अत्यधिकृत्य।

लकारो हशवकारपरः।।२६।।

एकेषां मते एवं परो लकारो द्वित्वं न भजते। 'मल्हाः' [तैसं. २.१.२] शतवल्शः [तैसं. १.१.२] हशपरे कार्यमिष्टमिति भाष्ये।[५] ऐकारादूर्ध्वो लवयोर्योग-स्तत्राप्यसंयुतेति माहेश्वरवचनादत्राप्य संयुतत्वम्। बैल्वः[६] [तैसं. २.१.८]

स्पर्शः स्पर्शपरः।।२७।।

स्पर्शपरो द्वित्वं न भजते। इदमनिष्टम्।

---

१. MS A/D omit इमौ....न स्याताम्। instead read इत्यात्रेयम्

२. MS A/D read these two example after ....यथाक्रमम्।

३. MS A/D add अत्र न।

४. MS D उत्तमपरोऽनुत्तमो

५. MS A/D भाष्यम्।

६. MS A/D omit ऐकारा....बैल्वः।
MS D writes in the main body of the text and rubs out दीर्घात्परश्च लवयोः संयोगो यत्र दृश्यते। असंयुक्तं भवेत्तत्र शास्त्रज्ञैरिति भाषितम्।

पदान्तश्च व्यञ्जनपरः प्राकृतः॥२८॥

एकेषां मते पदान्तः प्राकृतो नकारोन्तस्थादि व्यञ्जनपरो द्वित्वं नापद्यते[१] इति भाष्ये।[२] अत्र विशेषोऽस्ति[३]–

नकारान्तं पदं पूर्वं यवहेषु परेषु च।
नकारयवहा मध्ये तत्र वर्णमसंयुतम्॥ इत्यात्रेयः।[४]
ङनौ यत्र पदान्ते तु यवहेषु परेषु च।[५]
द्वित्वं नैवाभिगच्छेतां ङनौ व्यवृपरौ विनेति॥२९॥

जनान् यातयति [तैसं. ३.४.११] एतान् होमान् [तैसं. १.५.४] सहस्वान् वाजी [तैसं. ४.६.४][६] पराङ् वा वा, प्रत्यङ् होतारम्, यद्रियङ् वायुः[७] [तैसं. ५.५.७] अर्वाङ् यज्ञः [तैसं. ७.३.११][८]

रेफात्पूर्वो नकारो यः पदान्तो यत्र दृश्यते।
विशेषं तत्र जानीयाद्द्वित्वमित्यभिधीयते॥

'तान्न् रक्षध्वम्' [तैसं. १.२.७][९]

ह्रस्वपूर्वो नकारो यः पदान्तो वपरो यदि
विशेषं तत्र जानीयाद्द्वित्वमित्यभिधीयते॥

---

१. MS A/D न द्वित्वमापद्यते

२. MS A/D adds अन्यच्च 'नान्तो यादि परेषु च' इत्यात्रेयः। जनान् यातयति। एतान् होमान्। सहस्वान् वाजी।

३. MS A/D omit

४. MS A/D instead read रेफात् पूर्वं.....भिधीयते। तान् रक्षवध्म्।

५. MS A/D instead लकारस्यवकारस्य संयोगे स्वरितो यदि। विशेषं तत्र जानीयाद्द्वित्वमित्यभिधीयते। बिल्वः।

६. MS A/D cf note 4 above

७. MS A/D omit all these examples.

८. MS A/D omit

९. MS A/D see note 6 on p. 106.

वृत्रहन् वाजिनम्[१]

नकारान्तं पदं पूर्वं वकारादपरे यदि।
संयुतं तत्र जानीयाद्द्वित्वमित्यभिधीयते।।[२]
संयुक्तौ[३] नवकारौ च यकार: परतो यदि।
विशेषं तत्र जानीयाद्द्वित्वमित्यभिधीयते।

'धिष्णियान्व्याघारयति' [तैसं. ६.३.९] इति वचनानि[४] आत्रेयशिक्षायाम्।[५]

संयुक्तौ नहकारौ चेदृकार: परतो यदि।
संयुक्तं तत्र विज्ञेयं नोभयोर्व्यक्तिरिष्यते।[६] आसन्निषून्हृत्स्वस: [तैसं. ४.२.११]

अनृकारस्वरोर्ध्वेषु यवहेषु परेषु च।
नान्तगो संयुतं तत्र दीर्घाद्यो वोत्तरे यदि।

तथैवङोन्तगो यत्र हवयो: परभूतयो:। इति माहेश्वरशिक्षायाम्।[७]

उदात्तात्परोऽनुदात्त: स्वरितम्॥२९॥

प्रातिहत-पादवृत्त-तैरोव्यञ्जनविषयमेतत्। उच्चात्परो[८] नीच: स्वारं भजते। 'स इधान:' [तैसं. ४.४.४] अथाब्रवीत् [तैसं. ३.२.११] वस्व्यसि [तैसं.

---

१. MS A/D हृस्वपूर्वो......वृत्रहन्वाजिनम् reads afterwards. Here, reads the immediately succceding verse. नकारान्तं.....धीयते। and adds यस्मिन्वृत्रम्

२. MS A/D reads here हृस्वपूर्वो....। वाजिनम्।

३. MS A/D adds before
अवग्रहो नकारो य: पदान्तो यत्र दृश्यते।
विशेषं तत्र जानीयाद्द्वित्वमित्यभिधीयते।।

४. MS A/D omit वचनानि

५. MS A/D adds here ङनौ यत्र...ङनौ व्यवृपरौ विनेति। here read the four examples cited in note no. 9 of the last page and that of no. 1 of the present page.

६. MS A/D add इति

७. MS A/D omit अनृकार....माहेश्वरशिक्षायाम्।

८. MS A/D अस्मान्नीच:

१.२.५] प्रउगम् [तैसं. ४.४.२] वर्णविभागव्यवस्थायामनुदात्तत्वे सत्येव पुनस्तत्संहितायामेव तल्लक्षणस्वरितत्वम्। वस्व्यसीत्यादौ[१] विज्ञेयम्।

व्यञ्जनान्तर्हितोऽपि॥३०॥

स्पष्टम्। तदग्निराह[२]।

नोदात्तस्वरितपरः॥३१॥

उच्चस्वारपरो[३] नीचः स्वारं नापद्यते। तस्य ते [तैसं. ७.२.७] अथ क्व [तैसं. ३.१.२]

नाग्निवेश्यायनस्य॥३२॥

स्वारोच्चपरो[४] नीचः स्वारं नापद्यते इति न।[५]

सर्वो नेत्येके सर्वो नेत्येके॥३३॥

सप्तविधस्वरित एव नास्तीत्येके मन्यन्ते। तथाहि-वाजसनीये ब्राह्मणे द्वावेव स्वरौ उदात्तश्चानुदात्तश्च। सूत्रद्वयमनिष्टम्।

॥ इति चतुर्दशोऽनुवाकः॥

---

१. MS A/D प्रउगमित्यादौ

२. MS A/D तदग्ने [३.३.८]

३. MS A/D एतत्परो

४. MS A/D स्वारोदात्तपरो

५. MS A/D इत्यस्य मतम्

॥अथ पञ्चदशोऽनुवाकः॥

नकारस्य रेफोष्मयकारभावाल्लुप्ते च मलोपाच्च पूर्वस्वरोऽनुनासिकः॥१॥

नस्य रेफभावादूष्मभावाद्यकारभावाद्यकारे लुप्ते च मलोपाच्च पूर्वस्वरोऽनुनासिकस्स्यात्। 'अग्नीꣳरप्सुषदः' [तैसं. ५.६.१] कर्णाꣳश्च [तैसं. १.८.९] ताꣳस्ते, महाꣳइन्द्रः [तैसं. १.४.२०] सꣳशितम् [तैसं. ४.१.१०]

नैकेषाम्॥२॥

एकेषां मते पूर्वस्वरोऽनुनासिको न स्यात्।[१] इदमेवेष्टं न तु पूर्वम्।

ततस्त्वनुस्वारः॥३॥

अनुनासिकात्परोऽनुस्वारागमस्स्यात्। अनुस्वारलक्षणमाह[२]

आत्रेयः– अध्याये तैत्तिरीयाणामनुस्वारो यदा भवेत्।
तस्याद्यर्धोगकारस्स्यात्तच्छेषमनुनासिकम्।

अन्यदपि– अनुस्वारो यजुष्वेवमध्यायेपि यदा भवेत्।
तदा गकारसंयुक्तो न शान्तिः शासरूपरः॥ इति व्यासः। सꣳशितमित्यादि।[३]

स्त्रादिषु चैकपद ऊष्मपरः॥४॥

स्त्रादिष्वखण्डपदे ऊष्मपरोऽनुस्वारागमस्स्यात्। 'शोꣳसा' [तैसं. ३.२.९]

---

१. MS A/D भवति

२. MS A/D अनुस्वारस्वरूपमाह व्यासः and read अनुस्वारे इति omit example.

३. MS A/D omit अन्यदपि। read अध्याये.....अनुनासिकम्। इत्यात्रेयम्। add त्रीꣳरेकादशानित्यादि [तैसं. ३.२.११]

नान्तविकारात्पूर्वः॥५॥

पदान्तविकारात्पूर्वस्मिन् उक्तविधिर्न। 'बहिस्ते' [तैसं. ३.३.१०] 'हिपुजिगेति' प्राप्तिः [तैप्रा. १६.१३] अन्तविकारादिति किम्? 'मा हिꣳसीः' [तैसं. ४.२.१०]

अप्रग्रहाः समानाक्षराण्यनुनासिकान्येकेषाम्॥६॥

अप्रग्रहसंज्ञानि समानाक्षराण्यनुनासिकानि भवन्ति इत्येकेषां मतम्। कुलायिनीꣳ [तैसं. ४.३.४]

पदं च प्लुतꣳ शाङ्खायनकाण्डमायनयोः॥७॥

अनयोर्मते प्लुतं पदमनुनासिकं स्यात्।[१] त्वी३ [तैसं. २.४.१२] सूत्रद्वयमनिष्टम्।[२] कति[३] प्लुता इत्याशङ्क्याह–

पत्नीवाश्चेतव्याः कार्याश्चित्यारभ्याः पताउ च।
होतव्यां सत्यराजांश्च सृज्यां प्राश्यां च मीयताः।
कर्तव्या सहस्रामद्राक् सोमाः कामाश्च हा इति
ब्रह्मा त्वं द्विपदाहौषां स्थेया अग्ना इवत्यगान्।
हावुरत्नि छिनत्ती च जुहवानी न गच्छति।
एति लाजीन्छाचीन्सर्वे त्वन्तोदात्ताः प्लुता इमे।
पत्या इति गृहा इन्त्वी उत्ताना इत्यवेरपाः।
सोमपा असोमपा द्वौ अश्नुता उत्तिष्ठा[४] ये॥
सावित्रं नवेच्छाद्वौव्यमग्निहोत्रां न चेति च।
अवेत्योवभृथानाद्वौ रभ्याः पशूः शृतꣳहवीः॥
स्थेयोग्नीर्धस्विदासीदुपरिस्तुही च विन्दती
नकं त्रिपञ्चाशदूर्ध्वं चतुर्णां दशमाः प्लुता इति व्यासः।

अकारस्तु संहितायामपि॥८॥

---

१. MS A/D भवति

२. MS A/D इमेऽनिष्टे सूत्रे।

३. MS A/D read this passage 'कति...इति व्यासः' under the next *sūtra*.

४. MS A/D उत्तिष्ठया

संहितायामसंहितायां च प्लुतान्तोऽकारोऽनुनासिको भवति। सुश्लोकाँ४ [तैसं. १.८.१६] इ०[1]

सर्वमेकयमं पूर्वेषाः सर्वमेकयमं पूर्वेषाम्॥९॥

सर्ववर्णजातं एकउदात्तश्रुतिर्भवतीति यज्ञकर्मणां मतम्। पूर्वेषां केचिच्छाखिनां सर्वमेकश्रुतिर्भवतीत्यन्यमतम्। इदमनिष्टम्।

॥ इति पञ्चदशोऽनुवाकः॥

१. MS A/D read the passage quoted above.....कति....व्यासः।

॥अथ षोडशोऽनुवाकः॥

अथ सकारपराः॥१॥

सकारपरा एवेत्यधिकृत्य।

स्रशोहपाशपदादयस् स्वरपरे॥२॥

एते पदादयः सकारपरास्तस्मिन्सकारेऽच्परेऽनुस्वारागमं भजन्ते। 'विस्रꣳसयेत्' [तैसं. ६.२.९] 'शोꣳसा' [तैसं. ३.२.९] हꣳसः[1] [तैसं. १.८.१५] पाꣳसुरे [तैसं. १.२.१३] शꣳसति[2] [तैसं. ३.२.९]

विकृतेऽपि॥३॥

तस्मिन्स्वरे व्यञ्जनतामुपगतेऽपि उक्तविधिस्स्यात्। अपहंस्यग्ने [तैसं. ४.७.१३]

रापूर्वश्च॥४॥

रापूर्वः शकारः सपरोऽनुस्वारागमं भजते। नाराशꣳसीभ्यः [तैसं. ७.५.११] अपदाद्यर्थमिदम्।

शꣳस्ताऽनन्तोदाते॥५॥

उतशꣳस्ता। अन्तोदात्तत्वादत्र न। 'अश्वस्याविशस्ता' [तैसं. ४.६.९]

अशꣳसन्॥६॥

उक्तविधिस्स्यात्। व्यशꣳसन् [तैसं. ६.६.११]

न शसनं विशसनेन॥७॥

उक्तविधिर्न। स्रशोहेत्यस्यापवादः। 'शसनं वाजी' [तैसं. ४.६.७] सने। विशसनेन[3] [तैसं. ५.७.२३]

१. MS A/D add शुचिषत्

२. MS B/C/D शꣳसामि।

३. MS A/D read विशसनेन सर्पान् [तैसं. ५.७.२३]

मा पदादिरनुदात्तः॥८॥

पदादिर्नीचो[1] मोक्तं भजते। 'माꣳस्पचन्याः' [तैसं. ४.६.९]

पुमीपूर्वश्च नित्यम्॥९॥

'पु' 'मी' एवं पूर्वो मा उक्तं भजते। 'उत्पुमाꣳसꣳहरति'[2] [तैसं. ६.५.१०] मीमाꣳसन्ते [तैसं. ६.२.६] नित्यशब्दोऽनुदात्तनिवर्तकः।

सकायपरश्च॥१०॥

सकायपरो मा उक्तं भजते। 'अमाꣳसकाय' [तैसं. ७.५.१२]

नावग्रहपूर्वः॥११॥

मा पदादिरित्यस्यापवादः। 'पूर्णमासे वै' [तैसं. २.५.५] समासोऽत्र बहुव्रीहिः।

मासिमासुमासोमासमिति च॥१२॥

उक्तविधिर्न। 'मासीति' शाखान्तर इति भाष्यम्। 'मासूत्तिष्ठन्' [तैसं. ७.५.२] 'यावन्मासः', मासां पृष्ठानि[3] [तैसं. ७.५.९]

हि पु जिगा जिघा छꣳसिनेऽतꣳस यदा ताꣳसीत्
कनीया ज्याया द्राघीया श्रेया ह्रसीया
वसीया भूयाꣳसो जक्षिवा जघ्निवा जिगिवा
जीगिवा तस्थिवा दाश्वा दीदिवा पपिवा पीपिवा
विद्वा विविशिवा शुश्रुवासमृवा॥१३॥

उक्तविधिस्स्यात्।[4] 'मा हिꣳसीः' [तैसं. ४.२.१०] 'पुꣳस्वतीः' [तैसं. २.५.८] पुꣳसः [तैसं. ४.६.९] लोकमजिगाꣳसन् [तैसं. ५.५.५] त्वष्टारम् अजिघाꣳसन् [तैसं. ६.५.८] 'ब्राह्मणाच्छंसिने' [तैसं. १.८.१८] मुष्टिमतꣳसयत् [तैसं. ७.४.१९] 'अन्वाताꣳसीत्' [तैसं. ४.७.१३] कनीयाꣳसम् [तैसं. ५.३.

---

१. MS A/D पदादिर्मा नीचः उक्तं भजते।

२. MS A/D omit उत्।

३. MS A/D मासां प्रतिष्ठित्यै [तैसं. ७.५.१]

४. MS A/D भवति

११] त्रयो ज्यायाꣳसः[१] [तैसं. २.६.६] पक्षौ द्राघीयाꣳसौ [तैसं. ५.२.५] अथो रघीयाꣳसः [तैसं. ७.४.९] प्रश्रेयाꣳसम् [तैसं. २.४.१] अथ ह्रसीयाꣳसम्। [तैसं. ६.६.४] यथावसीयाꣳसम् [तैसं. ५.४.१०] भूयांसोऽन्येभ्यः [तैसं. ७.१.१] जक्षिवाꣳसः [तैसं. १.४.४४] जघ्निवाꣳसः[२] [तैसं. १.४.४४] जिगिवाꣳसः [तैसं. १.७.८] तस्थिवाꣳसः [तैसं. १.२.१४] दाश्वाꣳसम्[३] [तैसं. २.२.१२] दीदिवाꣳसम् [तैसं. २.५.१२] पपिवाꣳसम् [तैसं. १.४.४४] पीपिवाꣳसम् [तैसं. ३.१.११] विद्वाꣳसः [तैसं. २.५.११] प्रविविशिवाꣳसम् [तैसं. ४.७.१५] शुश्रुवाꣳसः [तैसं. २.५.९] ससृवाꣳसः [तैसं. १.७.८]

आकारेकारोकारास्सिषिपराः पदान्तयोः॥१४॥

सिष्योः[४] पदान्तयोः सतोरुक्तेभ्यः परोनुस्वारागमस्स्यात्। वयाꣳसि [तैसं. ५.७.२३] तमाꣳसि [तैसं. १.८.२२] हवीꣳषी [तैसं. ७.५.१४] ज्योतीꣳषि [तैसं. ५.४.१]

विकृतेऽपि॥१५॥

छन्दाꣳस्युप [तैसं. ५.३.८][६]

अनाकारो ह्रस्वꣳ साङ्कृत्यस्य[७]॥१६॥

अस्यमते पूवोक्तौ य्यौ ह्रस्वमापद्येते। तपूꣳपि [तैसं. १.२.१४] इदमनिष्टम्।

न पदे द्विस्वरे नित्यम्॥१७॥

पूर्वासां प्राप्तीनामपवादः।[८] 'स्तुतो यासि' [तैसं. १.८.५] 'पासि नुत्मनो[९] [तैसं. १.३.१४] प्रथमे मासि [तैसं. ७.५.३]

---

१. MS A/D omit त्रयो.....अथ ह्रसीयाꣳसम्।

२. MS A/D add वृत्रम्

३. MS A omit दाश्वाꣳसम्

४. MS A/D omit

५. MSS B/C/D/E/F omit हवीꣳषी & add तपूꣳषी

६. MS A/D add तपूꣳष्यग्ने [तैसं. १.२.१४]

७. MS C read सांकृस्य

८. MS A/D प्रासीनाम्

९. MS A/D omit त्मना

ऋजीषि जिगासि जिघास्यनासि यजासि ददासि दधासि वर्तयासि च॥१८॥

एषूक्तविधिर्न। तेनर्जीषि [तैसं. ३.२.२] अच्छा जिगासि [तैसं. ४.२.४] जिघासीति शाखान्तर इति भाष्ये।[१] त्वमजासि [तैसं. ७.४.१९] यजास्यग्ने [तैसं. ३.५.११] याभिर्ददासि [तैसं. ३.३.११][२] वर्तयासि नः [तैसं. ७.४.२०]

दꣳसनाभ्यो दꣳसोभिर्दꣳसं वृषदꣳशो दꣳशुका दꣳꣳष्ट्राभ्याꣳ परः॥१९॥

उक्तविधिस्स्यात्[३]। दꣳसनाभ्यो बृहत् [तैसं. ७.५.७] दꣳसोभिः सुजूः [तैसं. ५.६.४] पुरुदꣳसम् [तैसं. ४.२.४] वृषदꣳशस्ते [तैसं. ५.५.१२]

मꣳस्ये मꣳसतै यꣳसद्यꣳसन्वꣳसते वꣳसगः॥२०॥

एषूक्तविधिः।[४] अभिमꣳस्ये [तैसं. ३.१.९] शूर मꣳसतै [तैसं. ७.४.१५] यꣳसद्विश्वम् [तैसं. ४.६.१] शर्म यꣳसत् [तैसं. ४.६.६] वꣳसते रयिम् [तैसं. ४.६.१] न वꣳसगः [तैसं. २.६.११]

उन्न वꣳशम्॥२१॥

उत् न। एवं पूर्वो स्यादुक्तविधिः।[५] उद्वꣳशम् इव [तैसं. १.६.१२] प्राचीनवꣳशम् [तैसं. ६.१.१]

अक्रꣳस्तोत्क्रꣳस्यते रꣳस्यते भ्रꣳशते[६]॥२२॥

एषूक्तविधिः स्यात्। 'वाज्याक्रꣳस्त' [तैसं. ७.५.१९] उत्क्रꣳस्यते [तैसं. ७.१.१९] उपरꣳस्यते [तैसं. ७.१.१९] राष्ट्रं भ्रꣳशते [तैसं. ५.७.४]

रꣳह्यै च॥२३॥

पूष्णो रꣳह्यै [तैसं. १.३.१०]

---

१. MS A/D इति भाष्यम्
२. MS D adds उक्थं दधासि
३. MS A/D एषु पर एवानुस्वारागमः।
MS D adds सकार after एषु, and rubs out.
४. MS A/D भवति।
५. MS A/D भवत्यु
६. MS A/s read *Sū* 22 & *Sū* 23 together.

ऐकारउख्यस्य[१] नितान्तः॥२३॥

'रꣳह्या' इत्यत्रस्थैकारस्तीव्रतरप्रयत्नो भवतीत्यस्य मतम्। इदमनिष्टम्।

विरित्रिसंख्यासु॥२४॥

एभिर्यदि संख्योच्यते चेदुक्तविधिस्स्यात्। स्वितिशब्दं वर्जयित्वा।[२] 'विꣳशत्यै' [तैसं. ७.२.१७] चत्वारिꣳशते [तैसं. ७.२.१७] त्रिꣳशते [तैसं. ७.२.१७][३]

शिꣳशुमारशिशꣳषत्सꣳश्वा सꣳस्त्रा सꣳस्कृत्य सꣳसृष्ट सꣳस्कृतꣳ सꣳशितस्सꣳशिता किꣳशिल॥२५॥

सिन्धोः शिंशुमारः [तैसं. ५.५.११] उभयतः सꣳश्वायि [तैसं. २.६.८] संस्त्रावभागाः [तैसं. १.१.१३] एव संस्कृत्य [तैसं. ५.६.६] सꣳसृष्टजित् [तैसं. ४.६.४] नः संस्कृतम् [तैसं. १.४.४३] ब्रह्मसꣳशितः[४] [तैसं. ४.६.४] ब्रह्मसꣳशिता [तैसं. ४.६.४] किꣳशिल वन्य [तैसं. ५.५.९] परकिꣳशिल पदैकदेशः। किꣳशिलाय च [तैसं. ४.५.९]

सितृदृहकारपरः॥२६॥

सि, तृ, दृ, एवम्पूर्वो हकार[५] उक्तं स्यात्।[६] सिꣳहो वयः [तैसं. ४.३.५] तृꣳहन्ति [तैसं. १.५.७] दृꣳहस्व [तैसं. १.१.३]

मꣳहिष्ठस्य च॥२७॥

यविष्ठमꣳहिष्ठस्य [तैसं. ४.२.३]

आदिरꣳहतिरꣳहोऽꣳहोरꣳहोमुगत्यꣳहा अꣳहसोऽꣳहसाऽꣳशमꣳशुभिरꣳशभुवाऽꣳश्वꣳशू अꣳशवोऽ

---

१. MS D एकार....

२. MS A सुप्रत्ययं विना।
   MS D writes स्विति.....वर्ज। but rubs out & writes as सु...विना।

३. MS A/D add hereafter संख्येति किम्? 'विशे जनाय' [तैसं. २.५.१२] आस्ये किम्? 'तिष्वा रोचने' [तैसं. ४.२.४]

४. MS C omits ब्रह्मसꣳशितः [तैसं. ४.६.४]

५. MS A/D read हपर

६. MS A/D भवति

ंशुरंशुमंशूनंशुनाऽंशोरंशायोपांश्वंशौ॥२८॥

एषूक्तविधिस्स्यात्। 'परिद्वेषसो अंहति'[१] [तैसं. २.६.११] अंहोमुचम् [तैसं. १.६.१२] अंहोश्चिद्या [तैसं. १.४.२२] अंहोमुग्भ्याम् [तैसं. ७.५.२२] चात्यंहाः [तैसं. १.८.१३] मुञ्चन्त्वंहसः [तैसं. ४.७.१५] अंहसा वै [तैसं. २.४.२] अंशमा [तैसं. ७.१.६] षडभिः अंशुभिः[२] [तैसं. ६.४.५] त्वयांशभुवा [तैसं. ६.४.८] तेनांशुमत् [तैसं. ३.२.२] अन्कारदित्यनया।[३] लुम्पन्त्यनंशु [तैसं. ३.२.२] अंशू यौ, वा अंशवः[४] अंशुरंशुः [तैसं. १.२.११] आदित्या अंशुम् [तैसं. २.३.५] सोमोंशून्, अंशुना ते[५] [तैसं. १.२.६] वाऽंशोः [तैसं. ६.६.१०] स्वाहांशाय [तैसं. १.८.१३] उपांशुसवनो यत् [तैसं. २.३.५] उपांशौ सम् [तैसं. ६.४.६]

अवग्रहः उदात्तोऽंसेऽंसायांसाभ्यामंसाविति॥२९॥

आद्युदात्तेष्वेषूक्तविधिस्स्यात्। अंस उप [तैसं. ५.३.१] शित्यंसाय [तैसं. ७.३.१७] अंसाभ्या ं स्वाहा [तैसं. ७.३.१६] अंसावेव [तैसं. ५.३.१] आदेरुपलाब्धिरवग्रहात्।

नासावा नासावा॥३०॥

पूर्वस्यापवादः। 'ब्रूयादसावेहि' [तैसं. २.४.९]

॥इति षोडशोऽनुवाकः॥

---

१. MS C omits and adds ऊर्मिन।

२. MS A/D read अंशुभिः पवयति!

३. MS A/D अन्कारादिति वचनादिदमपि।

४. MS A/D अंशवः पशवः।

५. MS A/D omit ते।

॥अथ सप्तदशोऽनुवाकः॥

तीव्रतरमानुनासिक्यमनुस्वारोत्तमेष्विति शैत्यायनः॥१॥

एषु तीव्रतरमानुनासिक्यं भवतीत्यस्य मते।[१] 'अग्नीꣳरप्सुषदः' [तैसं. ५.६.१] 'यं काममित्यादि [तैसं. ७.१.१]

समꣳसर्वत्रेति कौहलीपुत्रः॥२॥

सर्वत्रानुनासिक्यवर्णेषु[२] तीव्रतरत्वं सममित्ययं मन्यते। सꣳरराणः [तैसं. ४.६.१] न्यङ्ङ्गिः [तैसं. ५.५.३] उपहूतां४ [तैसं. २.६.७] इ०

अनुस्वारेऽष्विति भारद्वाजः॥३॥

सूक्ष्मतममानुनासिक्यम् अनुस्वार इत्यस्य मतम्। त्वꣳहसः [तैसं. ४.६.६][३]

नकारस्य रेफोष्मयकारभावालुप्ते च मलोपाच्चोत्तरमुत्तरं तीव्रतरमिति स्थविरः कौण्डिन्यः॥४॥

सूक्ष्मतमम्। त्रीꣳरेकादशान् [तैसं. ३.२.११] समम्-शुक्लाꣳश्च [तैसं. २.३.१] तीव्रम्-महाꣳइन्द्रः [तैसं. १.४.२०] तीव्रतरम्-सꣳशितम् [तैसं. ४.१.१०]

व्यञ्जनकालश्च स्वरस्यात्राधिकः॥५॥

सानुनासिकस्वरस्य ह्रस्वार्धकालोधिकस्स्यादिति कौण्डिन्यो मन्यते। 'युञ्जाथाꣳ रासभम्' [तैसं. ४.१.२]

---

१. MS A/D मतम्।
२. MS A/D वर्णे
३. MS A/D त्वꣳसः।

स्वारविक्रमयोर्दृढप्रयत्नतरः पौष्करसादेः॥६॥

स्वरिते विक्रमे अनुदात्ते च[१] दृढप्रयत्नतरस्स्यात्। 'योऽस्य स्वोऽग्निः।' [तैसं. ५.७.९] आदिना स्वर्यतेपि च।[२]

ह्रस्वो दीर्घश्च मध्येनान्त्ये न चेद्द्वित्वउत्तरे।

द्विमात्रिके चावसाने दीर्घोन्त्य स्वरितो भवेदिति माहेश्वरवचनात्।

स्वर्यते चादितो ह्रस्वो दीर्घोमध्यात्तथैव च।

संयुतोर्ध्वे तु दीर्घेश्चदन्त्यस्वारो भवेत्तदेति व्यासवचनाच्च।

ह्रस्वस्वरितश्चेत्तस्यादिस्वर्यते। दीर्घस्तु मध्य स्वर्यते।

संयोगोर्ध्वे सति दीर्घस्यान्तभाग स्वरितो भवति।

उदाहरणानि—स इधानः [तैसं. ४.४.४] आप्यायध्वम् [तैसं. १.१.१] वा आह्रियमाणायाम् [तैसं. १.७.७] यत्संज्ञपयन्ति [तैसं. ६.३.११] षष्ठेऽहन्नहन्षष्ठे [तैसं. ७.२.८] द्वित्व उत्तर इति नियमात् 'स शीर्ष्णाम् [तैसं. ५.१.८] इत्यादौ न।

प्रयत्नविशेषात्सर्ववर्णानामिति शैत्यायनः॥७॥

सर्ववर्णानां प्रयोगस्योचितस्य प्रयत्नविशेषात्प्रयत्नतरो भवतीत्यस्य मतम्। एत्सूत्रसप्तकमनिष्टम्।

नातिव्यक्तं न चाव्यक्तमेवं वर्णानुदिङ्गयेत्।
पयःपूर्णमिवामत्रः हरन्धीरो यथामतिरित्यात्रेयः आत्रेयः॥८॥

मतिमनतिक्रम्य यथामतिः धीर एवमुच्चारयेत्।

॥इति सप्तदशोऽनुवाकः॥

---

१. MS A/D omit अनुदात्ते च।

२. MS A/D omit आदिना.....मित्यादौ न।

॥अथ अष्टादशोनुवाकः॥

ओकारं तु प्रणवं एकेऽर्धतृतीयमात्रं ब्रुवते॥१॥

प्रणवे ओकारम् अर्धाधिकद्विमात्रं ब्रुवते। 'ॐ इषे त्वा' [तैसं. १.१.१]।[१] प्रणवस्वरूपं तूक्तं माहेश्वरशिक्षायाम्–

ब्रह्माविष्णुरुद्रोमस्त्रिव्यूहोहं समहत्यपि।
स शक्तौ लीयते सैवों परो नादो महेश्वरः।
अउमनादाः क्रमेण ज्ञेयाश्च प्रणवे स तु।
आदावुच्चश्चतुर्मात्रोऽन्ते च मध्ये त्रिमात्रिकः।
स्त्रवत्यादावनुक्तेन्ते रङ्गोन्ते नादसंज्ञकः।

अन्यदपि–

वेदस्योपक्रमे विद्वान् अवसानेऽप्यतन्द्रितः
उच्चरेत् प्रणवं ब्रह्म रक्षायै छन्दसां स्फुटम्।
आदावनुक्ते स्त्रवति परस्ताच्च विशीर्यते।
यजुः प्रणव उच्चस्स्यात्स्वारास्स्युरों तदादि षट्॥

इति व्यासः। वेदोपक्रमे प्रणवोच्चारणमवश्यं कुर्यादेतत्साधिका श्रुतिरपि।

ओमिति ब्राह्मणः प्रवक्ष्यं नाहेति।[२]
यो वेदादौ स्वरः प्रोक्त इति च।

---

१. MS A/D omit प्रणवस्वरूपं तूक्तं....नादसंज्ञकः। Instead reads वेदोपक्रमे प्रणवोच्चारणे....नाहेति।

२. MS A/D add thereafter कालनिर्णयेप्येवम्।
स्वाध्यायारम्भशेषस्य प्रणवस्य स्वरस्य च।
अध्यायस्यानुवाकस्यादन्ते सार्धतृतीयता॥
सन्ध्यक्षराणां वेदे च प्रणवं चान्तरात्तथा।
अध्यायस्य मुखे चान्ते भूत्वा विद्वानतन्द्रितः॥

(Contd...)

उदात्तानुदात्तस्वरितानां कस्मिंश्चिदिति शैत्यायनः॥२॥

एतेषां[१] मध्ये कस्मिंश्चित्स्वरः प्रणवे प्रयोक्तव्यः इत्यस्य मतम्।

धृतः[२] प्रचयः कौण्डिण्यस्य[३]॥३॥

धृतप्रचयः[४] प्रचयपर्यायः। मध्यमेन स वाक्प्रयोगः। उच्चनीचसमाहार-विलक्षणेन प्रत्ययेन प्रणव उच्चार्य इति कौण्डिण्यमतम्।

स्वरितः प्लाक्षिप्लाक्षायणयोः॥४॥

अनयोः पक्षे स्वरितो स्यात्।[५] एतत्सूत्रचतुष्टयमनिष्टम्।

उदात्तो वाल्मीकेः॥५॥

अस्य मते उदात्तो स्यात्।[६]

यथाप्रयोगं वा सर्वेषां यथाप्रयोगं वा सर्वेषाम्॥६॥

उदात्तप्रयोगं वाऽस्येति[७] सर्वऋषीणां मतम् इति माहिषेयपक्षः। वररुचिपक्षस्तु अध्येता येन स्वरेण आरम्भो यत्र कुर्यात्तदेव स्वरः प्रणवस्य। नेदमिष्टम्।

॥ इति अष्टादशोऽनुवाकः॥

(Contd...)

संरक्षणाय वेदानामोङ्कारं तूच्चरेत्सदा।
स्रवत्यादावनुक्ते च तस्यान्ते तु विशीर्यते।
आद्यन्तप्रणवौ तस्य स्यातामङ्गानि वै ततः॥ इति व्यासः।
प्रणवं सम्पुटं कृत्वा गायत्रीं वेदमुच्चरेत्।
अउकारमकाराश्च ज्ञेयाः सन्ति सदात्र तु।
तस्मात्सर्वं चतुर्मात्र ऊमिति प्रणवः स्मृतः।
यजुः प्रणव उच्चस्स्यात् स्वारास्स्युरोंतदादि षट्।
प्रारम्भकश्चतुर्मात्रो वेदस्थ स्यात्तदर्धकः॥
अध्ययनानुवाकान्त्यः कर्माधश्चत्रिमात्रिक इति।
वेदोपक्रमे विद्वानवसानेप्यतन्द्रितः।
उच्चरेत्प्रणवं ब्रह्म रक्षायै छन्दसां स्फुटम्।

१. MS A/D एषां
२. MS C दृढः MS D दृतः
३. MS A कौण्डिन्यस्य
४. MS C दृढः MS A दृतः
५. MS A/D भवति
६. MS A/D भवति
७. MS A/D कुर्यादिति

॥अथ एकोनविंशत्यनुवाकः॥

स्वरितयोर्मध्ये यत्र नीच ॱ स्यादुदात्तयोर्वाऽन्यतरतो वोदात्तस्वरितयोः स विक्रमः॥१॥

यत्र स्थले स्वारयोर्मध्ये उच्चयोर्मध्ये स्वारोच्चयोर्मध्ये वा यो नीचः स विक्रमसंज्ञस्स्यात्। 'योऽस्य स्वोऽग्निः' [तैसं. ५.७.९] वोढवे [तैसं. १.६.२] धन्वनागाः [तैसं. ४.६.६] 'तस्य क्व' [तैसं. २.६.५]

प्रचयपूर्वश्च कौण्डिण्य[१]स्य॥२॥

प्रचयपूर्व इति विशेषः। 'पर्यवदतां या' [तैसं. १.७.२] उपरिष्टाल्लक्ष्मा याज्या [तैसं. २.६.२] नेदम् इष्टम्।[२]

द्वियम एके द्वियमपरे ता अणुमात्राः॥३॥

यमः स्वरितः इत्यर्थः। द्वौ यमौ यत्र वर्तेते स द्वियमः। द्वियमपरो यस्मात्स द्वियमपरः।[३] तयोः सतोः याः स्वरितप्रकृतयः ताः सर्वाः अन्ततोऽणुमात्रा निहता भवन्ति। ते १न्योन्यम् [तैसं. ६.१.५] सा१पोरभ्य म्रियत [तैसं. ६.१.१] इदमनिष्टम्।

तस्यामेव प्रकृतौ॥४॥

द्वियमस्थले पूर्वस्यामेव स्वरितप्रकृतौ अणुमात्रिकोऽपि निहतत्वं भवति। त्रियमस्थले तु पूर्वयोरेव अणुमात्रतया निहतत्वम्। अन्यदपि।[४]–स्थितः प्रणवोत्तरे

---

१. MS A/D न्यस्य

२. MS A/D इदमनिष्टम्

३. MS C द्वियमः

४. MS A/D omit......अन्यदपि।...
...स्वारस्य चान्त्वर्णेयोणुर्नीचः स्यात्प्रणवोत्तरे।

इति व्यासवचनात्[१] स्वरिते परे पूर्वस्वरितस्यान्त्योणुर्नीचः स्यात्।[२] 'तेऽन्योन्यम्' [तैसं. ६.१.५] सो१पोऽभ्यं म्रियत [तैसं. ६.१.१]

उच्चोर्ध्वे यददीव्यादित्रिकं नकं च नेति च।

यच्चकम्पौ स्थितैङ्रूपो स्वाराः कम्पाश्च सांहिताः इति व्यासः।[३] तेन यो१स्मत् 'हा१वुहा' इ०

न पूर्वशास्त्रे न पूर्वशास्त्रे॥५॥

प्रथमसूत्रे योक्ता विक्रमसंज्ञा सा कम्पविधौ न।

॥ इति एकोनविंशत्यनुवाकः॥

---

१. MS A/D omits व्यास

२. MS A/D writes उच्चोर्ध्वे....सांहिताः प्रणवं स्वरित इत्यर्थः इति व्यासः। before examples

३. MS A/D omit

॥अथ विंशत्यनुवाकः॥

इवर्णोकारयोर्यवकारभावे क्षैप्रउदात्तयोः॥१॥

उच्चयो[१]र्वोर्यवभावे सति य स्वारो विहितः स क्षैप्रसंज्ञस्स्यात्। व्येव [तैसं. ५.३.११] स्वंस्माँ[२] [तैसं. ४.७.१५]

स यकारवकारं त्वक्षरं यत्र स्वर्यते स्थिते
पदेऽनुदात्तपूर्वेऽपूर्वे वा नित्य इत्येव जानीयात्॥२॥

पदकाले अनुदात्तपूर्वे वा पूर्वाभावे वा स यः स वश्च स्वरितो नित्यसंज्ञस्स्यात्। 'वायव्यम्' [तैसं. १.८.७] बिल्वः [तैसं. २.१.८] सर्वत्रेति पदादिष्वित्यर्थः।[३]

[४]अपि चेन्नानापदस्थमुदात्तमथ चेत् साꣳहितेन[५] स्वर्यते स प्रातिहतः[६]॥३॥

पूर्वपदस्योदात्तादुत्तरपदस्थपरो नीचः साꣳहितेन विधिना स्वर्यते स प्रातिहतसंज्ञस्स्यात्। इषे त्वा [तैसं. १.१.१][७]

तस्मादकारलोपोऽभिनिहितः॥४॥

नानापदस्थोदात्तात्परभूतनीचस्याकारस्य लोपे सति यः स्वारः[८] सोऽभि-निहितसंज्ञस्स्यात्। तेऽब्रुवन् [तैसं. २.५.१] सोऽब्रवीत्[९] [तैसं. २.१.२]

---

१. MS A/D उच्चयोर्ध्वो
२. MS B/C स्वस्मै [४.७.१५]
३. MS A/D पदजटास्वित्यर्थः
४. MS A adds अपिशब्दः अनुदात्तमात्राकर्षक इति भाष्ये।
५. MS A adds विधिना
६. MS A/D add संज्ञस्स्यात्
७. MS A/D add तं ते [तैसं. ३.२.१०]
८. MS A/D स्वरितः
९. MS A/D exchange the order.

ऊभावे प्रश्लिष्टः॥५॥

ऊभावे स्वरितः प्रश्लिष्टसंज्ञस्स्यात्। 'सून्नीयम्' [तैसं. ६.२.४]

पदविवृत्यां पादवृत्तः॥६॥

पदयोविवृत्तिः तस्यां यः स्वर्यते स पादवृत्तसंज्ञः स्यात्। 'स इधानः' [तैसं. ४.४.४] ता अस्मात् [तैसं. २.१.२]

उदात्तपूर्वः तैरोव्यञ्जनः॥७॥

उदात्तपूर्व इत्युक्ते[१] सति पुनरत्र तत्कथनादेकपदस्थोदात्तविशेषो गृह्यत इति भाष्यम्। एकपदस्थोदात्तपूर्वो यः स्वारः[२] स तैरोव्यञ्जनस्स्यात्। इन्द्रः [तैसं. ७.१.५] प्रउगम् [तैसं. ४.४.२][३]

इति स्वारनामधेयानि॥८॥

एतानि स्वारनामानि। नीचोच्चस्वारप्रचयानां स्थानान्याह व्यासः–

कनिष्ठिकानामिकामध्या[४]तर्जनीषूत्तमे करे।
नीचस्वारधृतोदात्तानङ्गुष्ठाग्रेण निर्दिशेत्।
स्वरानाद्यन्तमध्यासु तद्रेखासु च तान्क्रमात्।
स्वारमुच्चमिवोर्ध्वे[५] च ह्यनामिकान्परान्त्ययोः॥

अनामिकाया मध्यान्तरेखयोरित्यर्थः।

स्वारकम्पे स्वरावेतावनामिकान्तिपाद्ययोः। अनामिकाया अन्त्याद्यरेखयोरित्यर्थः।

पृथक्तदिष्टरेखा स्यादङ्गुलीयोत्तरस्य हि।
विरामे व्यञ्जनस्यैव पृथक्स्थानं न विद्यते॥

---

१. MS A/D उदात्तपूर्वोधिकारे सति

२. MS A/D स्वरितः

३. MS D writes the following verses in the main body of the text and rubs out :
अवसानेन्त्यवर्णाश्च नादा इति बुधैः स्मृताः।
नादानुस्वारयोः पूर्वः स्वारभागुच्चवत्स्थितः।
स्वर्यतेऽस्मात्परावेव नादानुस्वारकावपि। इति व्यासः

४. MS A/D .....मध्यात्

५. MS A/D .....ऊर्ध्वं

सुहस्तस्वरविन्यासात् निर्मलाध्ययनं भवेत्।
तत्पूतो ब्राह्मणो यस्तु ब्रह्मणा सह मोदते।[१]

क्षैप्रनित्ययोर्दृढतरः॥९॥

एतयोर्दृढतरः प्रयत्नस्स्यात्।

अभिनिहते च॥१०॥

एतस्मिन्दृढप्रयत्नस्स्यात्। न तु दृढतर[२] इति पृथक्सूत्रारम्भात्प्रतीयत इति भाष्यम्।[३]

प्रश्लिष्टप्रातिहतयोर्मृदुतरः॥११॥

एतयोर्मृदुतरः प्रयत्नस्स्यात्।

तैरोव्यजनपादवृत्तयोरल्पतरोल्पतरः॥१२॥

एतयोरल्पतरः प्रयत्नः स्यात्। यथा दीपवेणुपत्रशिखयोरल्पस्यान्तरमस्ति तथैवात्रापीति भाष्यम्।

॥ इति विंशत्यनुवाकः॥

---

१. MS A/D add इति व्यासः

२. MS D writes दृढतर but rubs out तर.

३. MS A भाष्ये

॥अथैकविंशत्यनुवाकः॥

व्यञ्जनं स्वराङ्गम्॥१॥

व्यञ्जनं स्वराङ्गं स्यात्।

दुर्बलस्य यथा राष्ट्रं हरते बलवान् नृपः।
दुर्बलं व्यञ्जनं तद्वद्धरते बलवान्त्स्वरः। इति न्यायात्।
उदात्तश्चानुदात्तश्चस्वरितश्च स्वरास्त्रयः।
ह्रस्वदीर्घप्लुता इति कालतो नियमा अचीति विशेषत्वात्।

'स्वरास्तु ब्राह्मणा[१] ज्ञेया' इत्यादिवचनात्स्वर एव अङ्गी। स्वरः एकमात्रः। अर्धमात्रम् व्यञ्जनम्। तयोः सन्धौ कृते सति विशेषकालः प्रसक्तः तत्प्रतिषेधार्थं व्यञ्जनं स्वराङ्गमित्युक्तम्। अतः स्वरसंसृष्टव्यञ्जनस्य स्वरकाल एव कालः। क्षीरोदकसम्पर्के क्षीरस्यैवोपलब्धिरिति वदति भाष्यम्। अङ्गसंज्ञायाः प्रयोजनमाह व्यासः–स्वराणां पूर्वतश्चैव ह्युदात्तादिस्वरास्स्मृताः। व्यञ्जनानां तदाप्त्यर्थमङ्गताद्य[२] विधीयते[३]॥[४]

तत्परस्वरम्॥२॥

तदङ्गभूतव्यञ्जनं परस्वरं भजते। 'इमानेव' [तैसं. ५.५.५] कर्मधारयः समासः।

---

१. MS C ...णो

२. MS A/D ....अङ्गताय

३. MS C ....वीधीयते

४. MS A/D add स्वर्यते चादितो ह्रस्वो दीर्घोमध्यात्तथैव च।
संयुतोर्ध्वे तु दीर्घश्चेदन्त्यस्वारो भवेत्तदा॥ इति व्यासः
निरिष्येत् लोकास्त्र्यलिखिताः वा आह्रियमाणायाम्

अवसितं पूर्वस्य॥३॥

अवसानस्थं व्यञ्जनं पूर्वाङ्गं स्यात्॥[१] ऊर्क् [तैसं. १.२.२] हविः [तैसं. १.२.४] नादानुस्वारयोः पूर्वस्वारभागुच्चवत्स्थितः। स्वर्यतेऽस्मात्परावेव नादानुस्वारकावपि॥ यथा–मित्रः। जनान्।[२] इति व्यासवचनान्नादानुस्वारभिन्नानां[३] अङ्गत्वेन स्वरितस्वरो न स्यात्।[४] नादसंज्ञामाह व्यासः–अवसानेऽन्त्यवर्णाश्च नादा इति बुधै स्मृताः।[५] अन्यदपि–"परायुक्तं च योगाद्यनुस्वारो रश्चरूत्ररेवोर्ध्वो यदि"[६] इति माहेश्वरवचनात्। ऋकारपरे सति रेफस्य पूर्वाङ्गत्वम्। एकारादेरूर्ध्वो रेफश्चेत्पूर्वाङ्गः पराङ्गो भवति। यामेवात्रिर्ऋत्धिम्। ऋषेर्ऋ। तन्नैऋतम्।[७]

संयोगादि॥४॥

संयोगादिव्यञ्जनं पूर्वस्याङ्गं स्यात्। अप्स्वन्तः[८] [तैसं. १.४.८५]

परेण चासंहितम्॥५॥[९]

परस्वरेणायुक्तं व्यञ्जनं पूर्वाङ्गं स्यात्। संयोगादित्यस्य अपवादः। तत्सवितुः [तैसं. १.५.६] 'अर्वासीत्यत्र तु परेण चासंहितं नान्तस्थापरमसवर्णमित्युभयो प्राप्तिः। तत्रैव संयोगादित्यस्य चारितार्थ्यम्।

अनुस्वारः॥६॥

पूर्वस्याङ्गं स्यात्। अꣳशुः [तैसं. १.२.६]

---

१. MS A/D पदान्तवर्तिव्यञ्जनं पूर्वस्याङ्गं स्यात्।

२. MS A/D omit these two examples
MS C writes these examples in the margin.

३. MS A/D व्यञ्जनानाम्

४. MS A/D add तस्मात्

५. MS A/D add ऋकारपरभूते च रेफः पूर्वाङ्गतां भजेत्।
ए च स्वारात्परो रेफो ह्रस्वस्वरात् परस्थितः।
अनुस्वारात्परो रेफस्स्वरितः प्रचयोच्चगा।

६. MS A/D omit अन्यदपि...............ऋर्षत्रर्ऋ।

७. MS A/D add ऋर्षेत्रऋषेः। निर्ऋतिम्। क्रतुꣳक्रतुपते।

८. MS A cites 'तत्सवितुः which the other two mss cite under *sū* 5.

९. MS A does not read this *sūtra* and the portion परस्वरेण....अपवादः

स्वरभक्तिश्च॥७॥

पूर्वस्याङ्गं स्यात्। योगविभागात्स्वरभक्तेः क्वचित्पूर्वाङ्गत्वं स्यात्। तथा हि–[१]

स्वरभक्तिः परा स्वारात्प्रचयत्वमवाप्नुयात्। स्वारे दीर्घे तु नान्त्याया धूर्षदं च स्वतन्त्रतेति[२] माहेश्वरवचनात् उदाहरणानि–यद्दर्शपूर्णमासौ कोऽर्हति सहस्रम् [तैसं. २.१.५] अन्त्या स्वरिता चेत्तस्यास्तु पूर्वाङ्गत्वमेव। दोषावस्तर् [तैसं. १.२.१४] हविष्मतीः [तैसं. १.३.१२] महार्हाः।[३] प्रपहाः।[३]

नान्तस्थापरमसवर्णम्॥८॥

अन्तस्थापरं व्यञ्जनं तस्याः अन्तस्थायाः असवर्णं पराङ्गं भवति। अध्यवसाय [तैसं. ६.१.५] यदश्रु अश्लोणया [तैसं. ६.१.६] इषे त्वा [तैसं. ४.३.७] असवर्ण इति किम्?[४] परिचाय्यम् [तैसं. ५.४.११]

नासिक्याः॥९॥

नासिक्याः परं भजन्ते। 'रुक्मम्' [तैसं. ५.२.७]

स्पर्शश्चोष्मपर ऊष्मा चेत्परस्य॥१०॥

ऊष्मपरस्पर्शः परस्वरं भजते असावूष्माप्रतीक[५]श्चेत्। षट्थ् सम्पद्यन्ते [तैसं. ५.४.३] वषट्थ् स्वाहा [तैसं. ७.३.१२] ऊष्मपरश्चेदिति[६] किम्? अक्ष्णया [तैसं. ५.२.७]

स्वरितात्सꣳहितायामनुदात्तानां प्रचय उदात्तश्रुतिः॥११॥

स्वारात्परेषां नीचानां नीचयोर्नीचस्य वा सꣳहितायाम् उच्चवच्छ्रुतिस्स्यात्

---

१. MS D adds स्वाराध्रस्वात्परां भक्तिं प्रचयत्वं नयेद्बुधः।
ऋतस्य धूर्षदं चेति स्वतन्त्रा भक्तिरुच्यते॥

२. MS A/D स्वतन्त्रा धूर्षदं भजेत्।

३. These words probably are not from the TS.

४. MS A/D असवर्णत्वादत्र न।

५. MS A/D ....परश्चेत्

६. MS A/D ऊष्मपराङ्गश्चेदिति किम्?
MS D reads अनूष्मपरत्वादत्र न and rubs out.

स प्रचयसंज्ञस्स्यात्। 'अग्ने दुध्र गह्य' [तैसं. ५.५.९] 'कि॒शिल' [तैसं. ५.५.९][१]

नोदात्तस्वरितपरः॥१२॥

उच्चस्वारपरो[२] वा नीचः प्रचयो न। 'तदाहुः'[३] [तैसं. ७.१.४] तया देवतया [तैसं. ४.२.९][४]

स्पर्शादनुत्तमादुत्तमपरादानुपूर्व्यान्नासिक्याः॥१३॥

उत्तमपरादनुत्तमात्स्पर्शाद्यथाक्रमं नासिक्या आगमास्स्युः। प्रथमस्पर्शात्प्रथमनासिक्यः। द्वितीयाद्द्वितीयः। एवमन्येऽपि।[५] 'सँवन्त्सराय [तैसं. २.२.६] पलिक्क्नीम्,' अग्ग्निम् [तैसं. १.१.७] घ्घ्नन्ति वै [तैसं. १.७.२] उपज्ज्मन्[६], आट्ट्णारः [तैसं. ५.६.५] दध्ध्मसि अस्तभ्भ्नात् [तैसं. १.२.८] इत्यादि।

तान्यमानित्येके॥१४॥

यमानित्येके ब्रुवते।

हकारान्नणमपरान्नासिक्यम्॥१५॥

नणमपरं हकारमारुह्य नासिक्यं भवति। सानुनासिको हकारस्स्यादित्यर्थः।[७] अह्ने [तैसं. ४.४.१] पराह्ने [तैसं. २.१.२] ब्रह्म वै [तैसं. ३.५.७] अत्र विशेषमाह शिक्षाकारः–

हकारमौरसं विद्यादन्तस्थासु परासु च।

संनह्यति[८] [तैसं. १.६.९] जिह्वाग्रेण [तैसं. ५.७.११]

---

१. MS A/D omit

२. MS A/D उच्चस्वारे

३. MS A/D change the order of the examples

४. MS B/C/E/F तयादेवाः

५. MS A/D एवमन्यत्रापि

६. MS A उपज्ज्मिन्

७. MS A/D change order of the examples as अह्ने, ब्रह्म वै, अपराह्ने

८. MS A/D omit संनह्यति

'उत्तमेषु परेष्वेव नासिक्यत्वमिहाधिकम्।' अह्नम् [तैसं. २.४.१४] ब्रह्म वै [तैसं. ३.५.७] अपराह्णे [तैसं. २.१.२] 'नासाभ्यामुत्सृजेत्वायुत्यन्तहम-सङ्गमे। नासाभ्यामत्यन्तं वायुं नोत्सृजेत्।[1] ब्रह्य वै [तैसं. ३.५.७] न वदेदुरसात्यन्तमन्तस्थाभिश्च सङ्गमे। संनह्यति[2] [तैसं. १.६.९] बृहस्पतिः[3] [तैसं. १.२.२] अत्र तु कण्ठस्थानम्।[4]

रेफोष्मसंयोगे स्वरभक्तिः॥१६॥

रेफोष्मणो संयोगे रेफस्वरभक्तिस्स्यात्।[5] स्वरभक्तेस्स्वरूपं तूक्तं माहेश्वर-शिक्षायाम्–

स्वरोर्ध्वोष्मोर्ध्वश्च रोल स्वरभक्तिमवाप्नुयात्।
स्वरभक्तेस्स्वरूपं तु अर्धपादद्वयात्मकम्॥
पूर्वार्धं संवृतो होर्ध्वे न्योर्ध्वेषु विवृतोत्तरे।
क्रमेण पादश्चत्वारः होर्ध्वो लः कर्विणीचरः।
करेणु हरिणी रः शसोर्ध्वोलः शोध्वे हारितः।
रः षोर्ध्वः सा हंसपदाप्येवं भक्तिश्च पञ्चधा।

अन्यदपि[6]–

ऋकारस्य स्वरूपं तु तद्बुध्वा बोद्धुं हि शक्यते।
स्वरभक्तिरतो विद्यादृकारमिह विस्तरात्॥
ऋकारस्य स्वरूपं हि शिलष्टपादचतुष्टयम्।
पादेषु तेषु विज्ञेयावादावन्तौ स्वरात्मकौ।
अणूरेफस्य मध्ये च विज्ञेयौ व्यञ्जनात्मकौ।
रेफस्य चादिभूतं हि पादं पूर्वेण योजयेत्॥

---

१. MS A/D omit this line

२. MS A/D नह्यति

३. MS A/D omit

४. MS A/D omit

५. MS A/D Instead read एवं संयोगे सति रेफस्य समानस्वरऋकारस्यावयव-स्स्यात्। मात्रिक ऋकारस्याद्यणुस्वर भागः मध्ये रेफो द्वयणुभागः। अन्तोऽणुभागः। अत्र रेफेऽर्धमात्रे भज्यमाने सति तावणुसहितौ पूर्वोत्तरौ भागौ प्रत्येकं स्वरभक्त्याख्यां भजते।

६. MS A/D omit upto अन्दपि

स्वरात्मकेन पादेन ह्युत्तरेणोत्तरं तथा।
स्वरपादान्वितौ भागौ स्वरभक्तिरितीरिताविति।।[१]

सा क्व पूर्वा क्व परेत्याह[२] व्यासः–

ह[३] परे तु हलन्ता स्यात् स्वरभक्तिश्च संवृता।
अजन्ता शषहोर्ध्वे च विवृता समुदीरिता।

अन्यदपि–

शषसेषु स्वरोदया हकारे व्यञ्जनोदया।
शषसेषु च विवृता हकारे संवृता विदुरिति।।[४]

तासां नामान्याह–

"करेणुरहयोर्विद्यात्कर्विणी लहकारयोः।
हरिणी रशसानां च हरितालशकारयोः।
यातु हंसपदा नाम सा तु रेफषकारयोः।
एवं पञ्चविधां भक्तिमुच्चरेत्स्वर्गकामुकः।

लस्य तु रेफवत्सर्वम्"[५] उदाहरणानि–दर्शपूर्णमासौ [तैसं. २.२.५] वर्षाह्वाम् [तैसं. २.४.१०] बर्सम् [तैसं. २.५.७] तर्हि [तैसं. १.७.७]

---

१. MS A/D omit इति & adds
शिलष्टा नीचहकारेण युक्ता न पृथगुच्यते।
ह्रस्वात्स्वारात्परान्त्यायात् तत्रैवा यं न चान्यथा। धीतिभिर्हितः

३. MS A/D omits ह परे तु हलन्ता स्यात्.....अन्यदपि

४. MS A/D Hereafter adds ह परे तु हलन्ता....समुदीरिता इति व्यासः।

५. MS A/D adds hereafter प्रमाणं त्वाह–ऊष्मोत्तरस्य रेफस्य स्वरभक्तिर्बुधैः स्मृता। लकारस्य तदूर्ध्वे च स्वरभक्तित्वमुच्यते। इत्यात्रेयः।
also adds स्वरोर्ध्वोष्मणि रेफस्य लस्यापि स्वरभक्तिता। इति व्यासः।

न क्रमे प्रथमपरे प्रथमपरे॥१७॥

क्रमो नाम[१] द्वित्वम्। पूर्वस्यापवादः। दाश्शर्यम् [तैसं. ३.२.२] अदश्शर्म [तैसं. ३.२.५][२]

ह्रस्वस्वारात्परायाश्चेन्नीचे भक्तिर्नहपरे।[३] धीतिभिर्हितः [तैसं. ४.२.७]। काश्चित्स्वतन्त्रा स्वरभक्तयस्ता आह या या काण्डविधायोर्ध्वमृषिभ्यो ह्यृषयो ह्यृषिः। इत्यास्त्रशीमकापूर्वमृषं चेति स्वतन्त्रता।[४] अरुणाः काण्डर्षयः' एतत् अधिविधाय ऋषिरवोचत अग्निर्देवता ब्रह्म इत्यार्षम्। 'सहस्रशीर्षं देवम्' 'यदह्ना' 'पापमकार्षम्' इत्यारण्यशिक्षायाम्।

॥ इत्येकविंशत्यनुवाकः॥

---

१. MS C ना
२. MS A/D add अ न। न क्रमे प्रथमपरे इति नियमात्।
३. MS A/D omit ह्रस्वस्वारात्प......परे।......हितः।
४. MS A/D add इन्द्रियाय ऋषिभ्यः []

॥अथ द्वाविंशत्यनुवाकः॥

शब्दः प्रकृतिः सर्ववर्णानाम्॥१॥

स्वरव्यञ्जनात्मको राशिर्वर्ण इत्यर्थः तेषां रवः कारणं स्यात्।

तस्य रूपान्यत्वे वर्णान्यत्वम्॥२॥

स्थानभेदाद्ध्वनेः[1] रूपान्यत्वे वर्णान्यत्वं स्यात्। अ इ[2] वित्यादि।

तत्र शब्दद्रव्याण्युदाहरिष्यामः॥३॥

तेषां संघातप्रयोगे शास्त्रे यानि साधनानि सन्ति तानि व्याख्यास्यामः।

वर्णकारौ निर्देशकौ॥४॥

एतौ वाचकौ स्याताम्।

चापीत्यन्वादेशकौ॥५॥

एतावन्वादेशकौ स्याताम्।

त्वथैवेति विनिवर्तकाधिकारकावधारकाः॥६॥

क्रमेणैते उक्तार्थिनः।[3]

वेति वैभाषिकः॥७॥

अयं वैकल्पितस्स्यात्।[4]

नेति प्रतिषेधकः॥८॥

अयं निषेधकः।

---

१. MS C स्नानभेदा

२. MS C अ इ उ वित्यादि

३. MS A/D एते उक्तार्थिनः क्रमेण स्युः।

४. MS C/D .....वैकल्पिकस्य।

आयामो दारुण्यमणुता खस्येत्युच्चैः कराणि शब्दस्य॥९॥

उच्चैरुदात्त इत्युक्तं तदर्थमारभ्यते, गात्राणां दैर्ध्यं, स्वरस्य कठिणता गलविवरणस्य संवृतता एतानि साधनान्युदात्तशब्दं कुर्वन्तीत्यर्थः।

अन्ववसर्गो मार्दवमुरुता खस्येति नीचैः कराणि॥१०॥

अन्ववसर्गो गात्राणां विनतता, स्वरस्य स्निग्धता, कष्ठस्य स्थूलता एतानि साधनानि नीचशब्दस्य।

मन्द्रमध्यमताराणि स्थानानि भवन्ति॥११॥

मन्द्रं प्रथमम् मध्यमं द्वितीयम्। तारं तृतीयम्। एषां प्रयोजनमग्रे वक्ष्यते।

तत्रैकविंशतिर्यमाः॥१२॥

तत्र पूर्वोक्तेषु स्थानेषु एकविंशतिर्यमाः स्वराः स्युः। तेषामप्यग्रे प्रयोजनम्।

ऋग्विरामः पदविरामो
विवृत्तिविरामस्समानपदविवृत्तिविरामस्त्रिमात्रो
द्विमात्र एकमात्रोऽर्धमात्र इत्यानुपूर्व्येण॥१३॥

ऋग्विरामादयस्त्रिमात्रादिकालाः क्रमेण स्युः।[1] क्रमेण उदाहरणानि—सहमादयध्यै३। सातये[2] हुवे वाम्३ [तैसं. १.१.१४] ऋग्विरामोऽयम्। 'इषे। त्वा।[3] [तैसं. १.१.१] पदविरामोऽयम्। स इधानः [तैसं. ४.४.४]* अन्त्योऽयम्। अथ[4] मात्राकालमाह शिक्षाकारः—

चाषोक्त एकमात्रस्याद्वायसेन द्विमात्रकः।
मयूरेण त्रिमात्रश्च जानीयात्काललक्षणम्॥१॥
कालेतिसूक्ष्मकोऽणुस्यान्मात्रार्धं व्यक्तिमात्रके।[5]
अङ्गुलिस्पर्शनं यावान्तावान्कालस्तु मात्रिकः॥२॥
हलुत्तरं हल वै तदणुमात्रं प्रकीर्तितम्।

१. MS A/D omit क्रमेण उदाहरणानि.....सहमादयध्यै३।
२. MS A/D add वाजस्य
३. MS D इषे२। त्वा२।
४. MS A/D omit अथ
५. MS A/D ...मात्रकम्।

* त१एनम् [तैसं. २.३.११]। विवृत्तिविरामोऽयम्। प्र३।उगम् [तैसं. ४.४.२]

विश्वप्स्निया [तैसं. १.५.३]

विरामो वर्णयोर्मध्ये ह्यणुकालोस्त्यसंयुते।

यो वै पवमानानाम् [तैसं. ३.२.१]

हलो भक्ति विसर्गोन्तो ह्रस्वान्नो यवहोत्तरः।
स्पर्शोर्ध्वौ[१] वोर्ध्वमात्रस्तेऽवसानेऽलस्त्रिपादता।

एते वर्णा अर्धमात्रकालास्स्युः। पदान्तो नकारः। अवसानेऽलस्त्रिपादमात्रः। क्रमेणोदाहरणानि–वाक् [तैसं. १.३.९] यत् [तैसं. १.२.१] बर्सम् [तैसं. २.५.७] शतवल्शम् [तैसं. १.१.२] यः कामये,[२] मनःक्षेमे [तैसं. ५.२.१]

अब्रुवन्यः ओमन्वती [तैसं. २.६.९] उशन्नग्ने [तैसं. ४.३.१३] विभुदाव्ने [तैसं. ३.५.८] अस्तु बाल् [तैसं. ३.३.१०]

विसर्गोन्तेऽर्धमात्रस्याद्विरामः क्षपरेऽपि च। 'मनःक्षेमे'
संयुतोर्ध्वे च पूर्वत्र द्विरोष्ठयेप्यौवयोस्तथा।

संयोगे परे विरामोऽर्धमात्रः। तद्रुद्रस्य। द्विरोष्ठ्ये औकारवकारयोः पूर्वोर्धमात्रो विरामः। तनुवौ [तैसं. ५.७.३] बभूवुः [ऋ. ७.८८.५] रुरुरौद्रः

पिपीलिका दीर्घसमे च मध्यमा।
सवर्णता पाकवती पदैक्ये।
दृष्टा च वत्सानुसृतिस्त्वसाम्ये।
त्वथो[३]चिमुख्यास्तु[४] विरामकालाः।।

दीर्घयोः समः तत्र या व्यक्तिः सा पिपीलिका। तत्राणुमात्रः। 'ते एनम्' 'वा आह्रियमाणायाम्'।

सवर्णा व्यक्तिः। सा मध्यमा। तत्रार्धमात्रः। 'य आत्मानम्' बाहू उपस्तुत्यम् [तैसं. ३.१.५] समानपदे व्यक्तिः सा पाकवती। तत्र पादोनमात्रः। प्रउगम् [तैसं. ४.४.२][५]

१. MS A/D ....र्धो
२. MS A/D omit this example
३. MS A/D त्वधो
४. MS A/D ....मुस्या
५. MS A/D omit प्रउगम्। read पुर एता उक्थउक्थे

अवशिष्टा वत्सानुसृतिः। तत्र मात्रिकः। लोके इन्द्रः। त एनम्।

आभ्यो विरामा अण्वादयस्स्युः। अत एव क्रमादुक्तम्। इति तद्व्याख्याकारेण उक्तम्।

स्वरोदये त्वनुस्वारो भवेदध्यणुमात्रिकः।
विरामश्च तयोर्मध्ये वैशेषिकाच्च दीर्घयोः।

स्वरोर्ध्वोनुस्वारः सपादमात्रः। स्वाꣳअहम् अनुस्वारपर स्वारयोर्मध्ये[१] विरामः सपादमात्रः। दीर्घयोर्मध्ये या व्यक्तिः सा वैशेषिका। देवाꣳ आज्यपाꣳ आवह। देवाꣳ ईडेन्यान् [तैसं. २.५.९]

प्रणवान्ते पवर्गोर्ध्वे अवग्रहान्त एव च।
वाक्यान्ते तु विरामश्च सार्धमात्रः प्रकीर्तितः।

पवर्गोर्ध्वे प्रणवान्ते अवग्रहान्ते वाक्यान्ते च विरामः सार्धमात्रः।[२]

ॐ१ पाकयज्ञमिति पाकऽयज्ञम् [तैसं. १.७.१] द्वाभ्याम् [तैसं. १.७.४] द्विप्रतिष्ठो हि।

पदप्रणवयोर्नित्यं विरामस्याद्विमात्रिकः।
पदावसाने अपवर्गपरप्रणवावसाने च द्विमात्रो विरामः।

ॐ युञ्जानः प्रथमम् [तैसं. ४.१.१]

ऊष्मरेफपरश्चैव ह्यनुस्वारो द्विमात्रकः।
संयुतोत्तर इत्येष एकमात्रः प्रकीर्तितः।।

सꣳशितम् [तैसं. ४.१.१०] सꣳश्रवां [तैसं. १.७.२]

स्यातां सोर्ध्वखषोर्ध्वे[३] च ङ्नौ ह्रस्वाद्विमात्रिकौ। षपरो नित्यखषोर्ध्वे[४]
हकारे हल्परे तथा।

सन्तसदृङ्क्समानैः[५] प्रत्यङ्खक्षडहः[६] षष्ठे हन्नहन्थ्यष्ठे[७] आत्मन्ह्याङ्गानि[८]

---

१. MS A/D स्वरयो
२. MS A/D omit पवर्गोर्ध्वे....सार्धमात्रः।
३. MS A/D थोर्ध्वे
४. MS C थोर्ध्वे
५. MS A/D सन्स
६. MS A/D प्रत्यङ्क्षडहः
७. MS A/D षष्ठेहन्नहन्त्षष्ठे
८. MS A/D आत्मन्ह्यङ्गानि

असंयुतश्च नो दीर्घान्मात्रिको यवहोत्तरे।
ह्रस्वान्नादो द्विमात्रस्स्यादन्यत्राप्येकमात्रिकः।

तान्यज्ञः, एतान्वै, एतान्होमान्, ह्रस्वात्परो द्विमात्रः। प्रत्यङासीनः, सन्नतम् अन्यत्रैकमात्रः। पराङ् [तैसं. १.५.९] तान् [तैसं. १.२.७] ताम् [तैसं. १.१. ९]

अजेकद्वित्रिमात्रोस्त्रिकिको द्विश्चैकगोद्विगः।[१]
त्रिमात्रता[२] विरामस्यादृगन्तेधात एव च।।३।।

अङ्गे त्वं नो अन्तम३ अत त्राता शिवो भव वरुथ्यः३[४] [तैसं. १.५.६]

होता यक्षदग्नीन्त्यन्ते देवं बर्हिश्च पञ्चमे।
सहाम्भसि पितृप्रश्ने ऋक्सामि धनेषु चेत्।
सङ्गथे वामस्य३वे तु यज३।[५] देवीर्द्वारः
वह्निधनेषु त्रिमात्रिको नासार्धमात्रिकः इत्यर्थः।
काण्डप्रश्नानुवाकान्ते दशाष्टौ पञ्चमात्रिकाः।
ग्रन्थानां परिपूर्णे तान्त्रिगुणकाल उच्यते।

जनदुस्त्रियासु [तैसं. १.८.२२] ॐ आप उन्दन्तु [तैसं. १.२.१] पशून्पाहि [तैसं. १.१.२]।।५।। यज्ञस्य घोषत् [तैसं. १.१.२] सवा न[६] इन्दुः, जातवेदसे [तैसं. २.२.३] समुद्रो बन्धुः [तैसं. ७.५.२५] ब्रह्मसन्धत्तम् इति व्यासशिक्षायाम्।

अन्यशिक्षायामपि–

आदिवर्णे चतुर्थे च सप्तमे दशमे तथा।
द्वादशेषु स्वरेष्वेवं मात्राकालः प्रकीर्तितः।
पञ्चमश्चाष्टमश्चैव द्वितीयैकादशस्य च।

---

१. MS A/D द्विगाः
२. MS A/D ...गो
३. MS A/D अन्तमः।
४. MS A/D वरुध्यः।
५. MS A/D यज।
६. MS A/D सुवा ज....

एकारादि चतुर्णां च द्विमात्राकाल ईरितः।
नवमस्य तृतीयस्य षष्ठस्य प्लुतता भवेत्।
व्यञ्जनं त्वर्धमात्रं स्यादवसाने समीर्यते॥

'तत्' [तैसं. १.१.१४]

त्रिपादत्वं लकारस्य पञ्चमानां तु केवलात्।
दीर्घात्प्लुताच्च कालो हि मात्रिकः परिकीर्तितः॥

बाल् [तैसं. ३.३.१०] तान् [तैसं. १.२.७] ताम् [तैसं. १.१.९]

पञ्चमानां द्विमात्रत्वं ह्रस्वस्योपरि तिष्ठताम्।

प्रत्यङ् [तैसं. १.५.३]

विवृतौ पदयोर्मध्ये एकमात्रः प्रकीर्तितः।

अथो ओषधीषु।

पदमध्येऽर्धमात्रस्याद्विवृत्ताविति निश्चितः।

प्रउगम् [तैसं. ४.४.२]

आदिह्रस्वो वत्सानुसृतिरन्ते वत्सानुसारिणी।
पाकवत्युभयोर्ह्रस्वात् दीर्घौ चोभौ पिपीलिका।[१]

'त एनम्'। ता उप। स ईधानः [तैसं. ४.२.२] स ईम्

अवसाने द्विमात्रत्वं पदानामिति निश्चयः।

'इषे त्वा' [तैसं. १.१.१]

अनुस्वारस्य मात्रत्वं संयोगे परतस्स्थिते।

सꣳश्रवाः [तैसं. १.७.२]

अनुस्वारो द्विमात्रस्याद्रेफोष्मसु परेषु च।
संयोगे परभूते स्यान्मात्रिकस्तु द्विरूपवत्॥
मात्राद्विमात्रानुस्वारो द्विमात्रान्मात्र एव तु।
मात्रिकादपि संयोगो मात्रिकस्तु द्विरूपवत्॥[२]

---

१. MS A/D पाकवती पादमात्रा पिपीलिका

२. MS A/D omit this verse.

सꣳशितम् [तैसं. ४.७.१०] ताꣳहस्ते। सꣳश्रवाः [तैसं. ४.७.२]

ओष्ठ्ययोर्स्वरयोर्मध्ये संयोगादिर्यदि स्थितः।
विसर्गात् क्षपरादूर्ध्वमुभयत्रार्धमात्रिकः।।
तकारादूर्ध्वो विसर्गादूर्ध्व इत्यर्थः।

उत्पूतशुष्मम् [तैसं. १.६.१] मनः क्षेमे [तैसं. ५.२.१]

इलमध्ये तु कालस्य मात्रार्धं परिकीर्तितम्।
इलयोर्मध्ये मात्रार्धम्–इलान्दम् [तैसं. ७.५.९]
अर्धमात्राभवेद्व्यक्तिवाक्यान्तेध्यर्धमात्रकम्।

उभयोर्यथासंख्येन–बर्हिषा [तैसं. १.६.७] द्वाभ्याम् [तैसं. १.७.४][१]

अवग्रहावसाने तु मात्राकालः प्रकीर्तितः।
ऋगर्धयोस्त्रिमात्रत्वमवसाने प्रकीर्त्यते।
ऋगर्धयोरवसाने त्रिमात्रत्वम्। 'पतिः पृथिव्या अयम्३।[२]

नासिक्यो व्यक्तिमध्यस्थो सपादो[३] मात्रिको भवेत्। व्यक्तिमध्यस्थो नासिक्यः सपादमात्रः–यद्ध्रां ४[४] इत्यपतत् तां ३ इमि।

व्यक्तेरस्याश्चतत्कालो भवेदिति विनिर्णयः।
अस्या व्यक्ते सपादमात्र कालः।
समाप्तावनुवाकस्य मात्राणां पञ्चकं स्मृतम्।

पशून् पाहि [तैसं. १.१.२]

अष्टौ दशेति विज्ञेयं प्रश्ने काण्डे यथाक्रमम्।

कल्पयाति [तैसं. १.१.१४] जनदुस्त्रियासु [तैसं. १.८.२२]

तन्त्राणां च समाप्तौ तु त्र्यहः काल इष्यते।[५]

---

१. MS A/D add.....समदामुपस्थे

२. MS A/D omit the above example and write अग्निर्मूर्धा....., अपाꣳरेवति।।३।।

३. MS A/D .....सपदो

४. MS A/D यद्ध्रां३....

५. MS A/D इतिष्यते

अन्यच्च–

ऋकारपूर्वः प्रथमो हल्परस्त्वेकमात्रिकः।
ऋकारात्प्रथमस्यापि[1] द्वित्वं न स्यात्कथंचन।।१।।

ऋक्त्वम् तत्कृत्वा

वाक्यप्रतीकयजुषाम् पदे[2]ऽध्यर्धमात्रता।
ब्रह्म सन्धत्तं तन्मे जिन्वतम्१।।[3]
त्वं नो अग्ने स त्वन्नो अग्ने१।[4]
संकुसुको विकुसुकः, शिवो मेऽस्तु सदाशिवोम्१।।
पदान्ते च तथा[5] कम्पा अन्ततो निहताणुकाः।
शेषस्योदात्तता वा स्यात्स्वारता च व्यवस्थया।।

चकारो द्विमात्राकर्षकः।[6] अन्तिमाणुव्यतिरिक्तशेषस्य[7] व्यवस्थया उदात्तता च स्वारता[8] वा स्यात्। तेन यो[9]२ स्मत् सो[10]२ पो[11]भ्यं म्रियत। इति कालनिर्णये।[11] अन्यदपि–

चाषोक्त एकमात्रस्स्यात् काकोक्तश्चद्विमात्रिकः।
मयूरोक्तस्त्रिमात्रस्स्याज्जानीयात्काललक्षणम्।।
ह्रस्वश्च मात्रिको ज्ञेयो द्विमात्रो दीर्घ एव च।
त्रिमात्रिकः प्लुतो रङ्गो त्रिचतुर्मात्रिकौ च तौ।।

दीर्घरङ्गः त्रिमात्रिकः। स्वाँ३अहम्।

१. MS A/D ऋकारप्रथम
२. MS C यजुषामपदे
३. MS A/D omit १।।
४. MS A/D omit १।।
५. MS C यथा
६. MS A/D add an example 'आप शुन्धन्तु'
७. MS A/D add स्य (व्यतिरिक्तस्य)
८. MS A/D सारता
९. MS A/D यो३स्मत्
१०. MS A/D सो३पो३भ्यं
११. MS A/D omit from अन्यदपि to माहेश्वरशिक्षायाम्।

प्लुतरङ्गश्चतुर्मात्रिकः। सुश्लोकाँ४ इत्यादि।

विरामोर्धमात्रश्चैकपदव्यक्तौ च मात्रिकः।
व्यक्तौ च वाक्यप्रतीकयजुष्वध्यर्धमात्रिकः॥
द्विमात्रिकः पदेष्वृग्वदृगर्त्धेषु त्रिमात्रिकः।
पञ्चमात्रोऽनुवाकेष्टौ प्रश्ने काण्डे दशेति च।
ग्रन्थानां च समाप्तौ तु त्रिगुणः काल इष्यते।
ङर्नौद्विमात्रिकौ स्यातां ह्रस्वात्सोर्ध्व खथोत्तरौ।
षोर्ध्वानित्यखथोर्ध्वेनः स्म व्यञ्जनोर्ध्व होत्तरे।
ह्रस्वाद्विमात्रानुस्वारो द्विमात्रान्मात्रिको भवेत्।
योगोद्विरूपवध्रस्वान्मात्रिकश्चेत्स्वरोत्तरे।
सपादश्च विरामोऽत्र दीर्घमध्येधिको भवेत्।
अन्तोकारो विरामे च दीर्घवत्सार्धमात्रिकः।

तेन मे तप१॥ तेन मे ज्वल१॥ प्रजा असृजत१॥ यद्बलन्तं यच्च दीर्घं योगपूर्वं गुरूणि च। ज्ञेयान्येतानि सर्वाणि गुरूणि विद्याच्छेषान्यतोन्यानि लघूनि च। इति माहेश्वरशिक्षायाम्।

अस्मिन्नुदाहरणे सर्वाणि लघूनि जानीध्वम्। गणस्वरूपमाह व्यासः–[१]

तान्त्रिस्त्रिरक्षराश्चैव गणा इति बुधैः स्मृता।
त्रिलोनस्वस्त्रिगुर्मोभूरादौकेंदूयभौ शुभम्।

द्यौस्तोन्ते सोऽनिलस्तापं मध्येग्नीनौ रजौ क्रमादिति।[२] क्रमेणोदाहरणानि[३]– भवति [तैसं. १.५.२] न[४] गणः। आकाशदेवता। देवत्रा [तैसं. १.३.१०] मगणः। पृथ्वीदेवता। वरेण्यम् [तैसं. १.४.७५] यगणः।

---

१. MS A/D add युक्तोर्ध्वं व्यञ्जनान्तं च दीर्घं गुर्वीतरल्लघु।

२. MS C omits इति

३. MS A/D add त्रीणि लघूनि यस्य स नगणः सुवर्देवता।
त्रीणि गुरुणि यस्य सः मगणः भूमिदेवता।
आदौ लघु यगणः उदकदेवता। आदौ गरु भगणः इन्दुर्देवता।
अन्ते लघु तगणः द्यौर्देवता। अन्ते गुरु सगणः वायुर्देवता
मध्य लघुरगणः अग्निदेवता। मध्ये गुरु जगणः सूर्यदेवता।

४. MS A/D omit from नगणः–यगणः।

जलदेवता।[1] धावति। [तैसं. २.२.४] भगणः। चन्द्रदेवता। ऋध्नोति [तैसं. १.५.७] तगणः। आकाशदेवता। यदुभौ। सगणः। वायुदेवता। प्रथमम् [तैसं. १.३.१४] रगणः। अग्निदेवता। करोति [तैसं. १.५.२] जगणः। सूर्यो देवता।

यद्व्यञ्जनान्तं यदु चापि दीर्घम्।
संयोगपूर्वं च तथाऽनुनासिकम्।
एतानि सर्वाणि गुरूणि विद्यात्।
शेषाण्यतोऽन्यानि ततो लघूनि॥१४॥

व्यञ्जनान्तम्–पुत्रम् [तैसं. १.३.११] दीर्घम्। पिता[2] [तैसं. १.२.४] संयोगात्पूर्वम्–अश्मा [तैसं. ४.६.३] सानुनासिकम्। विंशत्यै [तैसं. ७.२. १२] एतानि गुरूणि। एभ्यः शेषाणि लघूनि तान्यग्रे विवृणोति।

अव्यञ्जनान्तं यद्ध्रस्वमसंयोगपरं च यत्।
अननुस्वारसंयुक्तमेतल्लघु निबोधत॥१५॥

मदुदयनाः [तैसं. ६.१.५] अस्मिन्नुदाहरणे सर्वाणि लघूनि जानीध्वम्।[3]

॥इति द्वाविंशत्यनुवाकः॥

---

१. MS A/D omit जलदेवता.....सूर्योदेवता। and add new examples भवति शार्यते, वरेण्यः, धावति, अन्नेषु, सविता, युञ्जते, करोति, स्थापितव्या शुभावर्णा गणाश्चेतयादिवचनात्।

२. MS A/D omit पिता

३. MS A/D adds after जानीध्वम्। जातिविचारमाह शिक्षाकारः।
वर्गाणां प्रथमा वर्णा स्वराश्च ब्रह्मजातयः।
द्वितीयाश्च तृतीयाश्च चतुर्था क्षत्रजातयः।
अन्तस्थाश्चोत्तमाश्चैव वैश्याः खलु समीरिताः।
अनुस्वारो विसर्गश्च प्रचयः शूद्र ईरिताः॥
यज्जातिस्खलनं तेषां तज्जातिहननं भवेत्।
अन्यदपि– ब्रह्मजातिर्भवेदुच्चः क्षत्रजातिश्च नीचकः।
वैश्यजातिर्भवेत्स्वारः शूद्रस्तु प्रचयस्तया।
स्वराश्च प्रथमाश्चैव द्वितीया ब्रह्मजातयः।
तृतीयाश्च चतुर्थाश्च क्षत्रजातय ईरिताः।
उत्तमाश्चैवमन्तथा वैश्या हि परिकीर्तिताः।
शूद्रास्स्युः शषसाहश्च ह्यनुस्वारो विसर्गकः।
यदन्यज्जातिरुच्येत तद्विनाशकरो भवेत।
यज्जात्युच्चारणं तेषां तज्जातिपरिरक्षणमिति व्यासः।

॥अथ त्रयोविंशत्यनुवाकः॥

अथ वर्णविशेषोत्पत्तिः॥१॥

विशेषोत्पत्तिरुच्यते इत्यधिकृत्य।

अनुप्रदानात्संसर्गात्स्थानात्करणविन्ययात्।
जायते वर्णवैशेष्यं परिमाणाच्च पञ्चमादिति॥२॥

अनुप्रदानादिभिः पञ्चभिः करणैः वर्णवैशेष्यं जायते। अनुप्रदानं[1] मूल-कारणम्। संसर्गः कण्ठस्थानम्। स्थानं वर्णस्थानम्। करणं व्यापारः। परिमाणम्[2] मात्राकालः। एतत्सर्वं वर्णानां बोद्धव्यम्।

वर्णपृक्तश्शब्दो वाच उत्पत्तिः॥३॥

पृक्तो मिश्रः। वर्णमिश्रशब्दो वचनस्योत्पत्तिकारणं स्यात्।

सप्तवाचस्स्थानानि भवन्ति॥४॥

स्पष्टम्। तान्युत्तरसूत्रे वक्ष्यन्ते।

उपांशुध्वाननिमदोपलब्धिमन्मन्द्रमध्यमताराणि॥५॥

उपांशु इति प्रथमं वाचस्स्थानम्। एवमन्यान्यपि नामतः सप्तैतानि जानीयात्। तेषां लक्षणान्यग्रे वक्ष्यन्ते।

करणवदशब्दममनःप्रयोगमुपा॑शु॥६॥

करणवदिति तूष्णीभावनिवृत्त्यर्थम्। नास्ति शब्दो यस्मिन् इति[3] अशब्दम्। नास्ति मनःप्रयोगो यस्मिन् ईदृशमुपांशु। उच्चादीनां तत्राबोधः।

---

१. MS A/D omit अनुप्रदानम्।

२. MS A/D omit परिमाणम्

३. MS A/D omit इति

अक्षरव्यञ्जनानामनुपलब्धिर्ध्वानः॥७॥

अचां हलां चानुपलब्धिर्ध्वानः। उपांशुलक्षणेऽनुपलब्धौ सत्यां पुनर्वचनं किञ्चिदव्यक्तशब्दोपलब्धिविधानार्थमिति भाष्यम्।

उपलब्धिर्निमदः॥८॥

अचां हलां च किञ्चिद् व्यक्तोपलब्धिर्निमदः स्यात्[१]॥८॥

सशब्दमुपब्दिमत्॥९॥

अज्झलां च[२] सशब्दउपब्दिमन्नाम चतुर्थस्थानम्।

उरसि मन्द्रः कण्ठे मध्यमः शिरसि तारम्॥१०॥११॥१२॥

उरसि स्थाने प्रयोग[३] उपलभ्यते तन्मन्द्रं पञ्चमस्थानम्। मन्द्रमिति प्रातः-सवनम्। कण्ठे स्थाने उपलब्ध्यते तन्मध्यमं षष्ठं स्थानम्। शिरसि स्थाने उपलब्ध्यते तत्तारं सप्तमस्थानम्। तृतीयसवनमित्यर्थः।

मन्द्रादिषु त्रिषु स्थानेषु सप्त सप्तयमाः॥१३॥

एषु त्रिषु स्थानेषु एकैकस्मिंत्सप्त सप्त यमाः भवन्ति। यमाः स्वराः उदात्तादय इति यावत् 'के यमा' इत्याशङ्क्योत्तरसूत्रेणाह।

क्रुष्टप्रथम[४]द्वितीयतृतीयचतुर्थमन्द्रातिस्वार्याः॥१४॥

सप्तैते यमसंज्ञकाः।

तेषां दीप्तिजोपलब्धि॥१५॥

तेषां सप्तयमानाम् उत्तरोत्तरा दीप्तिजा पूर्वपूर्वोपलब्धिस् स्यात्। अतिस्वार्यदीप्तिजा मन्द्रोपलब्धिः। मन्द्राश्चतुर्थः। चतुर्थात् तृतीय इ०

द्वितीयप्रथमक्रुष्टास्त्रय आह्वारकस्वराः॥१६॥

एते त्रय आह्वारकस्वरास्स्युः एषां तैरेव प्रयोगो ज्ञातव्यः। आह्वरकाणां स्वरा इत्यर्थः।

---

१. MS A/D omit स्यात्

२. MS A/D read अझ्झलां च सशब्दम्

३. MS omits प्रयोग

४. MS C reads प्रथ omits म

मन्द्रादयो द्वितीयान्ताश्चत्वारस्तैत्तिरीयकाः॥१७॥

मन्द्रचतुर्थतृतीयद्वितीयास्तैत्तिरीयकास्स्युः॥

द्वितीयान्मन्द्रस्तैत्तिरीयाणां तृतीयचतुर्थावनन्तरम्
तच्चतुर्यममित्याचक्षते॥१८॥१९॥२०॥

तैत्तिरीयाणां द्वितीयान्मन्द्रो जायतेऽनन्तरं तृतीयचतुर्थौ स्याताम्। एतद्वितीया-दिस्वरमण्डलं चतुर्यममित्याचक्षते। द्वितीय उच्चः। मन्द्रो नीचः। तृतीयचतुर्थौ स्वारप्रचयौ।

तस्मिन्द्वियमाऽन्तरा वृत्तिः॥२१॥

स्वरितप्रचययोर्मध्ये वृत्तिरनुदात्ते भवतीत्यर्थः। 'सनः पर्षदति'[१] पर्यवदताया[२] [तैसं. १.७.२] केचिदन्यथा कथयन्ति। चतुर्यमस्वरमण्डले द्वयोर्यमयोरन्तरा[३]-वृत्तिस्स्यात्।[४] मध्ये वर्तमानावित्यर्थः।

तथा हि–अनुदात्तो हृदि ज्ञेयो मूर्ध्न्युदात्त उदाहृतः।
स्वरितः कर्णमूलीयः सर्वास्य प्रचयः स्मृतः॥[५]

कौहलेप्याह–

उदात्तमाख्याति वृषोऽङ्गुलीनां प्रदेशिनीमूलनिविष्टमूर्धा।
उपान्तमध्ये स्वरित धृतं च कनिष्ठिकायामनुदात्तमेव।

अन्यदपि–

कनिष्ठिकानामिकामध्यात्तर्जनीषूत्तमे करे।
नीचस्वारधृतोदात्तानङ्गुष्ठाग्रेण निर्दिशेत्॥

तामुपदेक्ष्यामः॥२२॥

तस्य चतुर्यमस्य भेदभिन्नावृत्तिर्नाम। 'ताम्' उच्यते।[६]

---

१. MS A/D omit अति

२. MS A/D पर्यवदताया

३. MS A/D द्वियमान्तरावृत्तिः

४. MS A/D add स्वरद्वयस्य

५. MS A/D add अस्यार्थः–उच्चनीचयोर्मध्ये स्वारप्रचयोरन्तरावृत्तिर्भवति।

६. MS A/D उच्यन्ते

तच्चतुर्यममित्युक्तम्॥२३॥

ते मन्द्रादयो यमसंज्ञकास्स्युः। मतान्तरनिवृत्त्यर्थम् इदं सूत्रं पुनः कथितम्। 'उदात्तश्चानुदात्तश्च स्वरितश्च स्वरास्त्रय' इत्यादिनियमप्रतिषेधार्थं चेति।

क्रमविक्रमसम्पन्नामद्रुतामविलम्बिताम्।
नीचोच्चस्वारसम्पन्नां वदेद्धृतवतीः समाम्।
वदे[२]द्धृतवतीः समामिति॥२४॥

द्वित्वविक्रमसम्पन्नाम् अत्वरिताम् अमन्दां नीचोच्चस्वरितप्रचयसहितां वृत्तिं वदेत्।[३]

॥ इति त्रयोविंशत्यनुवाकः॥

१. MS A/D reads some irrelevant passage same as quoted in 22.15 in the main body of the text.

२. MS C also reads the following irrelevant passage. The same passage is quoted by Ms A under *sūtra* 22.13.

गणस्वरूपमाह व्यासः।

युक्तोर्ध्वं व्यञ्जनान्तं च दीर्घं गुर्वीतरल्लघु।
तत्त्रित्रिरक्षराश्चैव गणा इति बुधैः स्मृताः।
त्रिलोनस्वस्त्रिगुर्मोभूरादौकेन्दु यभो शुभम्।
द्यौस्तोनते सोनिलस्तापं मध्येग्नीनौ रजौ क्रमादिति।
त्रीणि लघूनि यस्य सः नगणः सुवर्देवता।
त्रीणि गुरूणि यस्य सः मगणः भूमिदेवता।
आदौ लघु यगणः उदकदेवता।
आदौ गुरु भगणः इन्दुदेवता।
अन्ते लघु तगणः द्यौर्देवता अन्ते गुरु सगणः वायुर्देवता
मध्ये लघु रगण अग्निर्देवता मध्ये गुरु जगणः सूर्यदेवता।

॥अथ चतुर्विंशत्यनुवाकः॥

अथ चतस्रस्संहिताः॥१॥

चतस्रः संहिता उच्यन्त इत्याधिकृत्य।

पदसꣳहिताऽक्षरसंहिता वर्णसꣳहिताऽङ्गसंहिता चेति॥२॥

आनवमादेकादशद्वादशत्रयोदशस्यादौ सूत्रचतुष्टयं च पदसꣳहिता। दशमोऽक्षरसंहिता। त्रयोदशचतुर्दशषोडशश्चवर्णसꣳहिता। व्यञ्जनं स्वराङ्गमित्यङ्गसंहिता। एतास्वन्यत्रविहितं निषिद्धं च कार्यं सर्वसंहितासु कुर्यात् इति भाष्यम्।[१]

नानापदसंधानसंयोगः पदसꣳहितेत्यभिधीयते॥३॥

'अग्ने दुध्र गह्य' [तैसं. ५.५.९]। सन्धानं संयोगाधिक्यम्।[२]

यथा स्वमक्षरसꣳहितादीनामपि एवम्॥४॥

स्वमतिक्रम्य वर्तत इति यथा स्वम् क्रियाविशेषणमेवैतत्। एवमक्षरसꣳहितादीनामपि यथा स्वं स्वरूपं निरूपणीयम्। केवलस्वरयोः संधिःअक्षरसंहिता। एकपदे स्वरव्यञ्जनसंयोगो वर्णसंहिता।[३] एकपदे केवलव्यञ्जनसंयोगोऽङ्गसंहिता।[४] क्रमेणोदाहरणानि। अथाऽब्रवीत् [तैसं. ३.२.११] अधिषवणम् [तैसं. १.१.५] अक्ष्णया [तैसं. ५.२.७] अन्या तु प्रकृतिसंहिता प्रागुक्ता एव।[५]

गुरुत्वं लघुता साम्यं ह्रस्वदीर्घप्लुतानि च।
लोपागमविकाराश्च प्रकृतिर्विक्रमः क्रमः।

---

१. MS A/D omit इति भाष्यम्। and add अत्रार्षग्रहणादिको विशेषो नास्ति।

२. MS A/D reverse the order of these two sentences.

३. MS A अङ्गसंहिता।

४. MS A omits this sentence.

५. MS A/D अन्यत्र पदसंहितेत्यवान्तरभेदो विज्ञेयः।

स्वरितोदात्तनीचत्वं श्वासो नादोऽङ्गमेव च।
एतत्सर्वं तु विज्ञेयं छन्दोभाषामधीयता॥५॥

गुरुत्वादष्टादशविधं एतत्सर्वं विज्ञेयं वेदरूपां वाचमधीयता। अथवा 'छन्दोभाषां' वेदलक्षणमित्यर्थः। एतत्साधिका श्रुतिरपि–शीक्षां व्याख्यास्यामः। वर्णः स्वरः। मात्रा बलम्। साम सन्तानः इत्युक्तः शीक्षाध्यायः इति। अस्यार्थः[१]– शिक्ष्यन्ते स्वरवर्णादयो यत्रासौ शिक्षा, तां कथयिाष्याम:। अकारादि वर्णः। उदात्तादि स्वरः, ह्रस्वदीर्घादिका मात्रा। स्पृष्टत्वादि प्रयत्नो बलम्। यस्य यः कालः उचितः तेनैवोच्चारणं साम्यम्। पूर्वोत्तरवर्णयोः संहिता संतानः। इति शिक्षारूपोऽध्याय उक्तः। गुरुत्वाद्युदाहरणानि। 'वषट्थ्स्वाहा' [तैसं. ७.३. १२] 'भवति [तैसं. १.५.१] वायावेव [तैसं. ६.३.७] ही३इति [तैसं. ७.१. ६] ईमन्द्रासु [तैसं. ४.१.८] त्रपुश्च मे [तैसं. ४.७.५] समिन्द्रणः [तैसं. १. ४.४४] अग्ने दुध्र गह्य[२] [तैसं. ५.५.९] प्रपा असि [तैसं. २.५.१२] वोढवे [तैसं. १.६.२] तत्त्वा न्यञ्चम् [तैसं. ५.५.३] चिनुयात्[३] [तैसं. ५.५.३] गां वाव तौ तत् [तैसं. १.७.२] अवदतां या [तैसं. १.७.२] तत् [तैसं. ७.१. १४] भागधे [तैसं. २.५.६] तं मत्स्यः प्राः [तैसं. २.६.६] विज्ञेयमिति नित्यविधिरिति भाष्ये।

पदक्रमविशेषज्ञो वर्णक्रमविचक्षणः।
स्वरमात्राविभागज्ञो गच्छेदाचार्यसꣳसदम्।[४]
वैशंपायनो ब्रवीदिति वैशंपायनो ब्रवीदिति।[५]

वैशम्पायनोऽब्रवीत्। पदानां क्रमः तस्य विशेषः तं जानाति यः, वर्णानां क्रमे निपुणो यः, स्वरमात्राविभागं जानाति यः, एवं विधः पुरुषः ब्रह्मलोकं गच्छेत् गच्छति। वेदत्यागे दोषमाह श्रुतिः[६]–

१. MS A/D omit from अस्यार्थः–शिक्षारूपोऽध्याय उक्तः।
२. MS A/D omit
३. MS A/D omit
४. MS A/D add before after repeating the last two words.
५. MS A/D does not repeat and does not add in the main body of the text.
MS D writes in the margin indicating it as the part of the main body.
६. MS A/D तथा च श्रुतिः।

'यस्ति[१]त्याज्यं सखिविदं सखायं न तस्य वाच्यपि भागो अस्ति, यदीँ शृणोत्यलकँ शृणोति न हि प्रवेद सुकृतस्य पन्थाम्' इति। तस्मात्स्वाध्यायो-ऽध्येतव्यः यं यं क्रतुमधीते तेन तेनास्येष्टं भवत्यग्नेर्वायोरादित्यस्य सायुज्यं गच्छति।'[२] यस्स्वाध्यायं[३] त्यजति स शुभं नाप्नोति यस्तु अध्ययनं करोति स सर्वमाप्नोति अग्निवाय्वादित्यानां सायुज्यं गच्छति इति।[४]

किञ्च यावतीर्वैर्देवतास्ताः सर्वा वेदविदि ब्राह्मणे वसन्ति। इत्यस्य भाष्ये तु–अग्निर्अवमो देवतानां विष्णुः परमः इत्युक्तत्वादग्निप्रभृतयो विष्णुपर्यन्ता यावन्त्यो देवताः सन्ति ताः सर्वाः पाठतोऽर्थतश्च वेदविदि ब्राह्मणे वसन्ति। एकैकस्मिन् मन्त्रे एकैको देवः प्रतिपाद्यतेते च मन्त्राः सर्वेऽध्येतुर्वाचि विदितुर्मनसि च वर्तन्ते अतो वेदविदां ब्राह्मणानां सर्वदेवात्मकत्वात्प्रतिदिनं नमस्कुर्यात् तदीयम् अशुभं विद्यमानमपि न कीर्तयेत् इति माधवेनोक्तम्। अन्यदपि स्वाध्यायप्रवचने एवेति नाको मौद्गल्यः। तद्धितं तद्धितपः।[५] इति[६] द्विरुक्तिः। तद्[७] भाष्ये

---

१. MS A — यस्ति सखि विदँ सखायम्....

२. MS A/D — add अस्य व्याख्यायामपि....

MS D — adds after....अपि–अर्थज्ञो वानर्थज्ञ इति तु माधवेन किमपि निर्णीतम्। किंतु यस्त्वा........but rubs out.

३. MS A/D — य तस्त्वाध्यायं.....

४. MS A/D — add–किञ्च ये अर्वाङुत वा पुराणे वेदं विद्वाँसमिति अभिवदन्ति आदित्यमेव ते परिवदन्ति सर्वे अग्निं द्वितीयं तृतीयं च हँसमितीति। अर्वाञ्चम् इदानींतनमनुष्यम् अध्येतृरूपम् उत वा पुराणे अथा पुरातनं व्यासवसिष्ठादिरूपं वेदं विद्वाँसं पाठादर्थाच्च वेदतत्त्वा भिज्ञं महात्मानं ये मूर्खाः अभितो वदन्ति तत्र तत्र निन्दति ते मूर्खाः। सर्वे आदित्यमेव निन्दन्ति ततो द्वितीयमग्निं निन्दन्ति ततस्तृतीयं हंसगमनशीलं वायुं निदन्ति अस्य वेदविदोऽग्निवाप्वादित्य सायुज्ययोग्यत्वात्। एतन्निन्दैव तेषां निन्दा इत्यनेन मन्त्रेण अत्र्या-दिरूपत्वलक्षणं वेदविन्माहात्म्यं दर्शितमिति।

५. MS C — तद्धितपेस्तपः।

MS D — तद्धितस्तद्धितपः।

६. MS A/D — अत्रापि

७. MS A/D — अस्य भाष्येऽपि

तु–स्वाध्यायाधीनं ह्यर्थज्ञानं अर्थज्ञानायत्तं च परः श्रेयः।[1] प्रवचनं च तदविस्मरणार्थं धर्मवृद्ध्यर्थं च। स्वाध्यायेन च विशुद्धसत्त्वस्य विद्योत्पत्तिरवकल्प्यते। स्वाध्याय-प्रवचनाभ्यां न प्रमदितव्यम्। ते हि नियमेन कर्तव्ये इत्यर्थः, इति शङ्करभगवता उक्तम्। स्वाध्यायः अध्ययनं प्रवचनमध्यापनं ब्रह्मयज्ञो वा, इति तेनैवोक्तम्। तथा च हिरण्यकेशीये कल्पे–तपः स्वाध्याय इति हि ब्राह्मणमिति। तथा च मार्कण्डेयपुराणे–

संहितावान्स्वर्गगामी पदवांश्च महर्गतिः।
क्रमीजनतपः सत्यगामी वैकुण्ठभाग्जटी।।१।।

मनुः–योऽनधीत्य द्विजो वेदानन्यत्र कुरुते श्रमम्।
स जीवन्नेव शूद्रत्वम् आशु गच्छति सान्वयः।

शिवगीतायाम्[2]–

यो वेदाध्ययनं यज्ञं दानानि विविधानि च।
मदर्पणधिया कुर्यात्स मे भक्तः स मे प्रियः।।

भगवद्गीतायाम्–

वेदैः साङ्गपदक्रमोपनिषदैरिति।

याज्ञवल्क्यः–

यज्ञानां तपसां चैव शुभानां चैव कर्मणाम्।
वेद एव द्विजातीनां निःश्रेयसकरः परः।
यं यं क्रतुमधीयेत तस्य तस्याप्नुयात्फलमिति।।३।।

गारुडपुराणे–

आहुः समस्तविद्यानां वेदविद्यामनुत्तमाम्।
अतस्तद्दातुरस्त्येव लाभः स्वर्गापवर्गयोः।।[3]

---

१. MS A — परश्रेयः।

२. MS A/D — omit शिवगीतायाम्–प्रियः।.....निषदैरिति। adds this portion after गारुडपुराणे।

३. MS B/C — अतस्तद्दानशीलश्च सर्वदानफलं लभेत्।

विद्यानां परमा विद्या ब्रह्मविद्या समीरिता।
अतस्तद्दानशीलश्च सर्वदानफलं लभेत्।[१]

देवीपुराणे–

वेद एव द्विजातीनां साधनं यशसः फलम्।
अतोऽस्याध्ययनाभ्यासात्परं ब्रह्माधिगच्छति।।

संस्काररत्नमालायां स्मृतिसारसमुच्चये[२]–

वेदो यस्य शरीरस्थो न स पापेन लिप्यते।
वेदात्मा स तु विज्ञेयः शरीरैः किं प्रयोजनम्।।
वेदाक्षराणि यावन्ति पठितानि द्विजातिभिः।
तावन्ति हरिनामानि कीर्तितानि न संशयः।।
यस्य वेदश्च वेदी च विच्छिद्येते त्रिपूरुषम्।
स वै दुर्ब्राह्मणो नाम[३] सर्वकर्मबहिष्कृतः।।
नित्यं नैमित्तिकं काम्यं यच्चान्यत्कर्म वैदिकम्।
अनधीतस्य विप्रस्य सर्वं भवति निष्फलम्[४]।।
अनधीतो द्विजो यस्तु शास्त्राणि तु बहून्यपि।
शृणोत्याब्रह्मणो नाशं नरकं स प्रपद्यते।[५]
नाधीतवेदो यो विप्र आचारेभ्यः प्रवर्तते।
नाचारफलमाप्नोति यथा शूद्रस्तथैव सः।
अनधीतस्य विप्रस्य पुत्रो वाऽध्ययनान्वितः।
शूद्रपुत्रः स विज्ञेयो न वेदफलमश्नुते।

---

१. MS C omits this verse.

२. MS A/D omit the passage from स्मृतिसारसमुच्चय and that of हेमाद्रि and add it later on. The beginning is स्मृतिसारसमुच्चये. हेमाद्रौ कौर्मे–वेदाक्षराणि.............न संशय इति

३. MS C omits नाम

४. MS A/D निष्फलं भवेत्।

५. MS A/D प्रतिपद्यते

---

* After the first verse वेदोयस्य.....प्रयोजनम् reads हेमाद्रौ कौर्मे।

अनभ्यासाच्च वेदानां आचारस्य च लङ्घनात्।
आलस्यादन्नदोषाच्च मृत्युर्विप्रं जिघांसति।

बृहन्नारदीये–

अनधीत्य तु यो वेदान् शास्त्राणि पठयते द्विजः।
शूद्रतुल्यः स विज्ञेयो नरकायोपपद्यत इति।

वाराहे–

स्व शाखां प्रथमं[१] यस्तु पठित्वान्यां पठेद्यदि।
प्रत्यक्षरं तु लभते गायत्र्यादिद्विद्द्गुणं फलमिति।

भागवते कापिलगीतायाम्–

ततो वर्णाश्च चत्वारस्तेषां ब्राह्मण उत्तमः।
ब्राह्मणेष्वपि वेदज्ञो ह्यर्थज्ञोऽभ्यधिकस्ततः।
अर्थज्ञात्संशय्यश्छेत्ता[२] ततः श्रेयान्स्वकर्मकृत्।
मुक्तसङ्गस्ततो भूयान दोग्धा धर्ममहात्मन इति।

ब्रह्मपुराणे[३]–

न तत्कल्पसहस्रेण गदितुं शक्यते फलम्।
यद्वेददानादाप्नोति स्वल्पादपि महामते।।

विष्णुधर्मोत्तरे–

वेददानादवाप्नोति सर्वयज्ञफलं नरः।
उपवेदप्रदानेन गन्धर्वैः सह मोदते।

भविष्यपुराणे–

अपुत्रो लभते पुत्रमधनो धनवान्भवेत्।
सदाध्ययनयुक्तस्तु परब्रह्मणि लीयते।

---

१. MS A/D प्रथमो

२. MS A/D संय

३. MS A/D read this passage from ब्रह्मपुराण after that of the देवीपुराणम्।

महाभारते–

यो ब्रूयाच्चापि शिष्येभ्यो धर्म्यां ब्राह्मीं सरस्वतीम्।
पृथिवी-गो-प्रदानाभ्यामतुल्य[१]फलमश्नुते।[२]

व्यासशिक्षायाम्–

सुव्यक्तः सुस्वरो धैर्यं तच्चित्तं च चतुर्गुणाः।
एतद्युक्तः पठेद्वेदं स वेदफलमश्नुते।
संहितां च पदं चापि क्रमं चापि जटां पठन्।
लक्षणज्ञस्तदाप्नोति ब्रह्मलोकं च शाश्वतम्।
यो जटामात्रविद् ब्रह्मा संधिज्ञो विष्णुरुच्यते।
ईश्वरः स्वरसंधिज्ञ इत्येवर्षिभिरीरितः।
एवं विदित्वा यो विप्रः समाहितमनाः शुचिः।[३]
जटां नित्यमधीयानो सोऽक्षय्यं फलमश्नुते।

यजुर्वेदस्वरूपमाह व्यासः–

यजुर्वेदः पिङ्गलाक्षः कृशमध्यो बृहद्गलः।
बृहत्कपोलः कृष्णांघ्रिस्ताम्रः[४] काश्यपगोत्रजः।
लक्षणेन विना विद्या निर्मलापि न शोभते।
अप्राणस्य च देहस्य भूषणैरप्यलंकृतः।[५]

मुक्ताभरणसंयुक्ता पूर्णचन्द्रनिभानना।
दिव्यमाल्याम्बरधरा नीलेन्दीवरलोचना।

---

१. MS D — अतुल्यम्

२. MS D — add after this verse second & third verse quoted below and omits व्यासशिक्षायाम्–the first verse.

३. MS D/A — add इत्यारव्यशिक्षायाम्।

४. MS A/D — नाम्नः

५. MS A/D — add लैङ्गे– सर्वेषां शृणु यज्ञानां ब्रह्मयज्ञः परः स्मृतः।
ब्रह्मयज्ञरतो मर्त्यो ब्रह्मलोके महीयते।।१।।
ब्रह्मयज्ञेन तुष्यन्ति सर्वे देवाः सवासवाः।
ब्रह्मा च भगवान्विष्णुः शङ्करो नीललोहितः।
वेदाश्च पितरस्सर्वे नात्र कार्या विचारणेति।।

आलोकोद्भासिवदना ताम्बूलग्रासिशोभिता।
शिवालिङ्गनसञ्जातपुलकोद्भासिविग्रहा।
सच्चिदानन्दरूपाढ्या जगन्माता शिवाम्बिका।
अङ्कस्थयानयायुक्तात्प्रसादाच्च महेश्वरात्।
गद्रे इत्युपनाम्ना च रामचन्द्रस्य सूनुना।
महादेवेन विदुषा रचिता धीमतां मुदे।
व्याख्येयं प्रातिशाख्यस्य भाष्यशिक्षानुसारिणी।
अत्र न्यूनाधिकं किञ्चिज्जातं मन्दधिया क्वचित्।
तत्सर्वं शोधनीयं तु सर्वलक्षणस्पर्शिभिः।[१]

इति[२] गद्रे इत्युपनामक वेदार्थज्ञ-रामचन्द्रात्मज-महादेव विरचितायां लक्षण-चन्द्रिकायां प्रातिशाख्यव्याख्यायां द्वितीयोध्यायः।।२।।

।। इति प्रातिशाख्यव्याख्यासमाप्ता।।

---

१. MS A/D ....दर्शिभिः।

२. MS A Col. इति श्रीगद्रे इत्युपनामक-रामचन्द्रात्मजमहादेवविरचितायां लक्षणचन्द्रिकायां द्वितीयो ध्यायः।

MS A adds a line

MS C श्री उमामहेश्वरार्पणमस्तु।। शके १७११ ईश्वरनामसंवत्सरे चैत्र शुक्ल ८ गुरुवासरे इदं पुस्तकं दात्ये इत्युपनामक-जनार्दन भट्टात्मज-महादेवेन-लिखितम्। गद्रे इत्युपनामक वेदार्थज्ञ महादेवभट्टस्येदं पुस्तकम्।।

Select Bibliography

1. Aithal, Parameshvara (1991) reprint (1993) *Vedalakṣaṇa: Vedic Ancillary Literature, A Descriptive Bibliography,* M. Banarsidass, N. Delhi.
2. Allen, W.S. (1953) *Phonetics in Ancient India,* London Oriental Series, Vol. 1, London : Oxford University Press.
3. Bare, James (1980) *Phonetics and Phonology in Panini, The System of Features Implicit in the Astadhyayi,* Natural Language Studies, No. 21, Ann Arbor : Dept. of Linguistics, the University of Michigan.
4. Cardona, Georg (1983) *Linguistic Analysis and Some Indian Traditions,* Pt. Shripad Shastri Deodhar Memorial Lectures, BORI, Pune.
5. Chatterji, K.C. (1948) reprint (1964) *Technical Terms and Technique of Sanskrit Grammar,* University of Calcutta, Calcutta.
6. Deshpande, Madhav (1994) प्राचीन भारतीय ध्वनिशास्त्र in वाचस्पत्यम् *Pt. Vamanshastri Bhagvat Felicitation Vol.* Edited by Saroja Bhate and Madhav Deshpande, pp. 57-69.
7. Deshpande, Madhav, (ed. & tr) (1997) *Śaunakīyā Caturā-dhyāyikā,* Dept. of Sanskrit and Indian Studies, Harvard University.
8. Devashali, G.V. (1978) *Vedavikṛtilakṣaṇasaṅgrahaḥ,* BORI, Pune.
9. Ghosh, Manmohan (1938) reprint (1986) *Paṇinīyaśikṣā,* critically edited in all its five recensions with Introduction, translation and notes, University of Calcutta, reprint Indian Books Centre, Delhi.

10. Indra (1973) "प्रातिशाख्यों में प्रयुक्त पारिभाषिक शब्दों का आलोचनात्मक अध्ययन" VVRI, Hoshiyarpur.

11. Jha, V.N. (1992) *A Linguistic Analysis of the Rgveda Padapatha,* Sri Satguru Publications, Delhi.

12. Keith, A.B. (ed &tr) (1909) *Aitareya Āraṇyaka* (with parts of the *Śāṅkhāyana Āraṇyaka*).

13. Kulkarni, N.R. (1995) *A Grammatical Analysis of the Taittirīya Padapāṭha,* Sri Satguru Publications, Delhi.

14. Mahulkar, D.D. (1981) *The Prātiśākhya Tradition and Modern Linguistics,* M.S. University Baroda, Baroda.

15. Mimansaka, Yudhishir(ed) (2024 Samvat) शिक्षासूत्राणि-आपिशलि-पाणिनिचन्द्रगोमिविरचितानि, Ajmer.

16. Pattabhiramashastri (ed) (1976) *The Vyāsaśikṣā*, the Kashi Sanskrit Series 225, Chaukhamba Sanskrit Samsthan, Varanasi.

17. Phatak, Madhukar (1972) पाणिनीयशिक्षाया: शिक्षान्तरै: सह समीक्षा Benaras.

18. Rangacharya, K. & Shamasastri, R. (1906) *Taittirīya Prātiśākhya with the Commentaries Tribhaṣyaratna & Vaidikābharana,* Govt. Oriental Library Series, Bibliotheca Sanskrita, No. 33, Mysore.

19. Shastri, Mehadeva R. & Rangacharya K. (1894) reprint (1898) *Taittirīya Saṁhitā with the Commentary of Bhaṭṭa-bhāskara,* Govt. Oriental Library Series, Bibliotheca Sanskrita No. $. Vols. I-XIII Madras.

20. Sharfe, H. (1977) *History of Grammatical Literature,* Wiesbaden.

21. Sharma, Venkatarama, V. (1930) *Taittirīya Pratishakhya with the Commentary Badakramasadana by Mahiṣeya*, Madras Uṇiversity Sanskrit Series I, University of Madras.

22. Sonatakke, N.S. & Dharmadhikari, T.N. (ed) (1970, 1972, 1990, 1999) *Taittirīya Saṁhitā,* Vol. 1, 2, & 3, Vaidik Samshodhan Mandal, Pune.

23. Suryakanta (ed) (1939) reprint (1971) *Ṛktanta ascribed to Śākatāyana,* Lahore, reprint Meherchand Lachhmandas.

24. Varma, Siddheshvar (1929) *The Phonetic Observations of Indian Grammarians,* London.

25. Varma, Virenderakumar (1972) *Ṛgvedaprātiśākhyam with the Commentary of Uvata,* Banaras Hindu University Sanskrit Series V, Banaras.

26. Vyas, Yugalkishor (183) *Śikṣāsaṅgrahaḥ* Banaras Sanskrit Series, Banaras.

27. Whitney, W.D. (1868) *Taittirīya Prātiśākhya with the Commentary Trihaṣyaratna,* New Haven.

APPENDIX I

Sūtra Index

अ

अभ्यावर्तिन्नपूपमपिदधाम्यद्यान्वदितिशर्माग्नेर्जिह्वामग्नयः
पप्रयोऽस्माकमस्मेधत्तांशमाश्वाश्रुतिरश्यामामाऽर्यमन्नस्मत्पाशानस्मिन्यज्ञे
ऽस्ताऽव्यथमानाऽभिद्रोहमधाय्यदोऽयोदुग्धा अरिष्टा अरथा
अर्चन्त्यन्तरस्यामत्रस्थान्नायाङ्गिरस्वदकरम् १२.७

अमी चक्षुषी कार्ष्णी देवता फल्गुनी मुष्टी धी नाभी वपाश्रपणी
अहनी जन्मनी सुम्निनी सामनी वैष्णवी ऐक्षवी दर्वी द्यावापृथिवी ४.१२

अरतिमस्य यज्ञस्य अतिद्रुतो अतियन्त्यनृणो विष्यन्ननमीवोऽन्नेष्वर्चिर-
जीतानज्यानिमह्रिया अम्बाल्यर्वन्तमस्त्व कृणोदङ्गिरोऽप्सु यो
अस्कभायदच्युतोऽश्वसनिरस्थभिरशिश्रेदङ्गेऽघ्निय ११.१७

अरमृकारपरे १०.८

अवग्रह-आशी-र्धूस्सुवरिति रेफं परस्सकारष्षकारम् ५.१०

अवग्रह इत्येकम् ५.१८

अवग्रहः ६.९

अवग्रहः उदात्तोऽꣳसेऽꣳसायाꣳसाभ्यामꣳसाविति १६.३०

अवग्रहो वृषण्छीर्षण्ब्रह्मण्णक्षण्चर्मण्चर्षण् १३.१३

अवर्णे नाप्युपसंहृतमोष्ठहनू नातिव्यस्तम् २.१२

अवर्णपूर्वस्तु लुप्यते ९.९

अवर्णव्यञ्जनशकुनिपत्न्यृतुमृत्युमलिम्लुबृहस्पतिपूर्वः ६.७

अवर्णव्यवेतोऽपि ७.५

अवसानेरविसर्जनीयजिह्वामूलीयोपध्मानीयाः १४.१५

अवसितं पूर्वस्य २१.३

अवा सचस्वा नुदा मृडा वर्धा शिक्षा रक्षाऽद्या भवा भजा यत्रा चरा
पिबा ना धामा धारया धर्षा धा वर्धया बोधाऽत्रा तत्रा
मुञ्चाऽश्वस्या पृणस्वा हिष्ठा त्वंतरा जनिष्वा युक्ष्वाच्छा ३.८

अविकृत एकेषाम् ५.३९

अव्यञ्जनान्तं यद्ध्रस्वमसंयोगपरं च यत्।
अननुस्वारसंयुक्तमेतल्लघु निबोधतैतल्लघु निबोधत २२.१५

अशꣳसन् १६.६

असदामासिञ्चꣳश्च ६.३

अवग्रह: उदात्तोऽᳲसेऽᳲसायाᳲसाभ्यामᳲसाविति १६.३०

अशᳲसन् १६.६

असदामासिञ्चᳲश्च ६.३

ष

स

ह

APPENDIX II

The Lakṣaṇacandrikā and Tribhāṣyaratna

The Lakṣaṇacandrikā quotes extensively from the Tribhāṣyaratna. The following are the places where it refers to the said text as "*Bhāṣya*".

१. एफस्तु रस्य १.१९

लचं–तु शब्द कारोत्तर त्वमकार व्यवेतत्वं च निर्वर्तयतीति भाष्ये।

त्रिर–रस्य तु एफशब्द आख्या भवति। यथा–'रेफोष्मपरः [तैसं. १३. २] इति रेफस्य व्यञ्जनत्वाविशेषात् प्राप्तं कारोत्तरत्वम्, अकारव्यवेतत्वं तदुभयं तु शब्दो निवारयति।

२. आदिरस्योदात्तसमः शेषोनुदात्तसमः इत्याचार्याः १.४६

लचं–द्वौ समौ इत्याचार्या ब्रुवते। यथा 'वरिवः' [तैसं. ३.३.११] तस्यादिरित्यारभ्यास्मिन्विकल्पजाले सूत्रमेतदेवेष्टम्, न तूपरितनमिति भाष्यम्।

त्रिर–...........यथा 'सखिभ्यो वरिवः' [तैसं. ३.३.११]। तस्यादिः [तैप्रा १.४१] इत्यारभ्याभिहितेऽस्मिन् विकल्पजाले सूत्रमेतदेवेष्टम्। "प्रश्लिष्ट प्रातिहतयोर्मृदुतरः" [तैप्रा २०.११] "तैरो व्यञ्जनपादवृत्तयोः" [तै प्रां २०.१२] इति लक्षणानुकूल्यात्। न तूपरितनमपि सूत्रमिष्टम्, एतल्लक्षण- प्रातिकूल्यात्।

३. उपबन्धस्तु देशाय नित्यम् १.५९

लचं–कण्ठोक्ति विनाऽन्यनिषेधः उपबन्धे न भवति इति नित्यशब्दार्थः इति भाष्ये।

त्रिर..........कण्ठोक्तिरुपबन्धप्राप्तिमेव निवर्तयति। नित्यशब्दस्तु प्राप्त्यन्तरमपि परिहरति।..........

४. यथोक्तं पुनरुक्तं त्रिपदप्रभृति त्रिपदभृति १.६१

लचं–..........ऋक्षु ब्राह्मणवाक्येषु त्रिपदमात्राद्वा कार्यं भवतीति वररुचिमाहिषेयात्रेयैरुक्तम्। तथैव भाष्ये।

त्रिर–..........ब्राह्मणवाक्येषु तु त्रिपदमात्राद्वा कार्यं भवति। ब्राह्मणवाक्येषु पूर्वस्थलस्यैवोक्तः। यथा–'इमामगृभ्णन्' [तैसं. ४.१.२] इत्यत्र "मर्यश्रीस्स्पृहयद्वर्णो अग्निः" [तैसं. ४.१.२, ५.१.३] इत्येतद् वाक्यम् "उत्क्राम" [तैसं. ५.१.३] इत्यात्रापि तथैव भवति।

५. औष्ठौ तूपसंहततरौ २.१४

लचं..........स व्यञ्जनस्योक्तविधिर्न इति 'तु' शब्दार्थ इति भाष्ये।

त्रिर......तु शब्दः ओष्ठयोः पूर्वोक्तविधिं निवारयतीति वररुचिरुवाच। माहिषेयस्तु बभाषे–"बन्धोः" [तैसं. २.५.८] इत्यादिकमोकारं सव्यञ्जनं व्यस्ततो निवारयतीति।

६. एकेषामनुस्वारस्वरभक्त्योश्च २.१९

लचं–स्वरभक्तेर्ऋकारतुल्यत्वमिति वररुचिमतम्। तच्चिन्त्यम् इति भाष्ये।

त्रिर–............स्वरभक्तेः ऋकारतुल्यत्वम् इति वररुचिमतम्। तच्चिन्त्यम्।

७. अनादेशे प्रण्यस्ता जिह्वा २.२०

लचं–अकारे उच्चार्यमाणे अनुपदेशविषय इति भाष्यम्।

त्रिर–.....एकारस्य जिह्वामध्यान्तनिष्पाद्यत्वमस्तीति तदवयवस्याप्यकारस्य तथात्वमस्तीति अकारत्वसाम्यात् अन्यत्रापि 'अथ' इत्यादौ तथात्वं प्रसज्येत। तच्चानिष्टम्।

८. एकारे च २.२३

लचं–एकारे कार्ये पूर्वविधिर्भवति। सव्यञ्जनस्यैकारस्य विधिरयमिति भाष्ये।

त्रिर–'ईषत्प्रकृष्टौ' (तैप्रा. २.१५) इत्यादिसूत्रत्रयेण एकारस्य स्थानकरणे निर्दिष्टे। इह तु अन्ये तस्यैव निर्दिश्येते। तदेकस्मिन् उभयथा कर्तुं न शक्यते, विरोधात्। तस्मादत्र योगविभागः कर्तव्यः। अव्यञ्जने तल्लक्षणं सव्यञ्जने त्वेतदिति। कुतोऽयं नियमः? उच्यते–एकारेऽतिसामान्योक्तौ सत्यां

प्रथममव्यञ्जनस्यैव ग्रहणं मुख्यम्। तथा सति प्रथमं प्रतीते तस्मिन् प्रथमं लक्षणं युज्यते। सव्यञ्जने तु पारिशेष्यादेतदिति विज्ञेयम्।

९. उकारस्तूत्तरस्य २.२१

लचं–औकारस्य शेषः अध्यर्धउकारो भवति। इकारनिषेधकस्तु शब्द इति भाष्ये।

त्रिर–'उत्तरस्य' औकारस्येत्यर्थः। अध्यर्धः 'उकारः' औकारस्य शेषः भवति। यथाऽनयोरुभयोरप्यादिरकार एव तद्वदिकार एव शेषः प्रसक्तः। तन्निषेधति तुशब्दः।

१०. अथ आदौ उत्तरे विभागे ह्रस्वं व्यञ्जनपरः ३.१

लचं–पदादौ दीर्घस्य पूर्वपदेन विभागः। पदान्ते दीर्घस्य उत्तरपदेन विभागः। विभागपदस्यायमर्थः इति भाष्यकारेणोक्तम्।

त्रिर–विभागशब्दस्यायमर्थः–पदादौ दीर्घस्य पूर्वपदेन विभागः।

११. पूर्वजप्रभृत्यायम् ४.२३

लचं–'पूर्वश्चासौ जे च पूर्वजे' इति विग्रहो भाष्यकारेणोक्तः।

त्रिर–..........पूर्वजे इति पदमत्र कार्यभाक्त्वेन नोच्यते, येन पौनरुक्त्यं भवेत्, किन्तु पूर्वश्चासौ जेशब्दश्च पूर्वजे।

१२. आकार एकारपूर्वस्तु बहुस्वरस्य ते थे ४.४०

लचं–व्रीडादिनिमित्तसापेक्षतानिवर्तकस्तु शब्द इति भाष्ये।

त्रिर–वीड् (तैप्रा. ४-३८) आदिनिमित्तसापेक्षतानिवर्तकः तुशब्दः इति वररुचिपक्षः।

१३. अनवर्णपूर्वस्तु रेफपरो लुप्यते ८.१६

लचं–'न धिपूर्वे' इति सूत्रं त्रिशेषत्वेन स्थानशब्दस्य सिद्धयर्थमेव इति निर्णयो भाष्ये कृतः।

त्रिर–स्थानशब्दस्य (श्च?) कथं सिध्येत्? ग्रहणादिसामर्थ्याभावात्। तस्मात्तदर्थं वा तत् सूत्रं सार्थकमिति सन्तोष्टव्यम्।

१४. ऊष्मपरोऽघोषपरो लुप्यते काण्डमायनस्य ९.१

लचं–'शुक्लास्स्युस्यु'। एवं विकल्पाश्रयणे सति लक्षणान्तर्गतं 'येषु लुप्यते तानि पदानि वक्ष्याम' इति वचनं सरलं भवतीति भाष्ये।

त्रिर–......एवञ्च विकल्पाश्रयणे सति लक्षणान्तरगतं "येषु पादेषु लुप्यते तानि पदानि प्रवक्ष्यामः" इति वचनं सरलं भवति।

१५. स्वरितानुदात्तसन्निपाते स्वरितम् ९.१२

लचं–स्वरितशब्देनात्र नित्यस्वरित एव गृह्यत इति भाष्यम्।

त्रिर–.......इह स्वरितस्याविशेषणग्रहणे नित्यस्वरित एव गृह्यते। तस्य सव्यञ्जनानामक्षराणां च पदावयवम् उत्पत्तिकाल एव सम्भवात्।

१६. धातारातिरुप.....महापृष्ठे ११.३

लचं–....अस्यानुवाकस्य शेषभूता या ऋक् सापि स्वीकृतेति भाष्ये।

त्रिर.........अस्यानुवाकस्य शेषभूता या ऋक् अन्यत्र स्थिता साऽपि स्वीकर्तव्येति।

१७. गाहमाने–जायमाने.......क्रतो पूर्वः १२.८

लचं–अन्वतप्यन्तेत्यस्याकारस्य लोपनिमित्तमेवेति भाष्यम्।

त्रिर–'यानग्नयोऽन्वतप्यन्त' [तैसं. ४.२.६]। उकारस्य वकारविक्रियायां व्यञ्जनपरो नकार इति 'यवनह' [तैप्रा. १२.४] निषेधाभावादलोपे प्राप्ते तदपवादोऽयम्।

१८. पाणि–गण–पुण्य–कण्व.......१३.९

लचं–.......लिङ्ग–विभक्ति–भेद–समास–तद्धितादिभिः निर्दिष्टः प्रवादा इति भाष्ये।

त्रिर–पाणीत्यादिशब्दानां प्रवादेषु पूर्वः प्रथमो णकारः प्रकृत्यैव वेदितव्यः। प्रकर्षेण वादः प्रवादः लिङ्गविभक्तिभेदसमास–तद्धितादिभिर्निर्देश इत्यर्थः।

१९. ऋण्णषण्ण...........चेति प्राकृताः १३.१४

लचं–ऋण्णादिषु तु स्पर्शपर इति निषेधनिषेधार्थं प्राकृतशब्दः इति भाष्ये।

त्रिर–प्राकृतशब्दोऽयं पाण्यादिष्वेव चर्षण्पर्यन्तेषु मुख्यः।
............ऋण्णेत्यादिषु तु न मुख्यः। किन्तु प्राप्त्यभावेऽपि णत्वप्रापणार्थः।
तथाहि–ऋण्णादौ पूर्वणकारस्थ स्पर्शपरत्वान्निषेधः,........।

२०. द्वितीयचतुर्थयोस्तु व्यञ्जनोत्तरयोः पूर्वः १४.५

लचं–कुत्रचित् व्यञ्जनपरनिमित्तं विनाऽपि द्वित्वं पूर्वागमं च भवति इति भाष्ये।

त्रिर–............अन्यथापि कुत्रचित् कार्यद्वयदर्शनात्। 'अत्ता हवींषि' इत्यादौ द्वित्वम्। प्रच्छछन्दः इत्यादौ पूर्वागमः।

२१. लकारो हशवकारपरः १४.२६

लचं–.........हशपरे कार्यमिष्टमिति भाष्ये।

त्रिर–.........अत्र हशपरे कार्यमिष्टं न तु वकारपरे।

२२. पदान्तश्च व्यञ्जनपरः प्राकृतः १४.१८

लचं–एकेषां मते पदान्तः प्राकृतो नकारोऽन्तस्यादिव्यञ्जनपरो द्वित्त्वं नापद्यत इति भाष्ये।

त्रिर–....एकेषां मते पदान्तः प्राकृतो.....द्वित्वं नापद्यते।

२३. मासिमासुमासोमासामिति च १६.१२

लचं–मासीति शाखान्तर इति भाष्यम्।

त्रिर–केचिदत्र 'प्रथमे मासि पृष्ठानि' [तैसं. ७.५.३] इत्युदाहरन्ति। तदसाधु। 'न पदे द्विस्वरे नित्यम्' [तैप्रा. १६.१७] इत्यनेनैव निषेधसिद्धेः। तस्मादन्यशाखायां बहुस्वरमुदाहरणम् अवधारणीयम्।

२४. ऋजीषि-जिगासि.........वर्तयासि च १६.१९

लचं–तेनर्जीषि, अच्छा जिगासि, जिघासीति शाखान्तर इति भाष्ये।

त्रिर–तेनर्जीषि सर्वाणि, अच्छा जिगासि, प्रथमे जिघासि इति शाखान्तरे।

२५. उदात्तपूर्वः तैरोव्यञ्जनः २०.७

लचं–उदात्तपूर्व इत्युक्ते सति पुनरत्र तत्कथनादेकपदस्योदात्तविशेषो गृह्यते इति भाष्यम्। एकपदस्योदात्तपूर्वो यः स्वारः स तैरोव्यञ्जनस्स्यात्।

त्रिर–उदात्तपूर्वाधिकारे सति पुनरत्र तत्कथनादेकपदस्थउदात्तविशेषोऽवगम्यते। तस्मादेकपदस्थोदात्तपूर्वो यः स्वरितः स तैरोव्यञ्जनो वेदितव्यः।

२६. अभिनिहते च २०.१०

लचं–न तु दृढतर इति पृथक्सूत्रारम्भात्प्रतीयत इति भाष्यम्।

त्रिर–नतु दृढतर इति पृथक्सूत्रारम्भात् प्रतीयते।

२७. तैरोव्यञ्जनपादवृत्तयोरल्पतरोल्पतरः २०.१२

लचं–यथा दीपवेणुपत्रशिखयोरल्पस्यान्तरमस्ति तथैव अत्रापि इति भाष्यम्।

त्रिर–........यद्यप्यल्पतरमृदुतरदृढभावास्तत्रोक्ताः तथाऽपि 'दीपवद्वेणुपत्रवत्' इति शिक्षाऽनुरोधात् कोमलशिरस्कत्वं सर्वत्र विज्ञेयम्।

२८. व्यञ्जनं स्वराङ्गम् २१.१

लचं–क्षीरोदकसम्पर्के क्षीरस्यैवोपलब्धिरिति वदति भाष्यम्।

त्रिर–यथा क्षीरोदकसम्पर्के क्षीरस्यैवोपलब्धिर्नोदकस्य तथा स्वरव्यञ्जनसम्पर्के स्वरस्यैवोपलब्धेर्वैशिष्टयम्।

२९. पदसंहिताऽक्षरसंहिता वर्णसंहिताऽङ्गसंहिता चेति। २४.१

लचं–एतास्वन्यत्रविहितं निषिद्धं च कार्यं सर्वसंहितासु कुर्यादिति भाष्यम्।

त्रिर–एतेषु अन्यत्र च विहितं निषिद्धं च कार्यं सर्वसंहितासु कुर्यात्। यत्रार्षग्रहणादिको विशेषो नास्ति।